The-
ology
&
Life

THEOLOGY AND LIFE SERIES

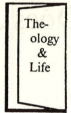

Theology & Life

Volume 33

The Liturgy
That Does Justice

by

James L. Empereur, S.J.
and Christopher G. Kiesling, O.P.

A Michael Glazier Book
THE LITURGICAL PRESS
Collegeville, Minnesota

A Michael Glazier Book
published by
THE LITURGICAL PRESS

Typography by Brenda Belizzone, Mary Brown, Laura Burke, Cyndi Cohee.

1	2	3	4	5	6	7

Library of Congress Cataloging-in-Publication Data

Empereur, James L.
   The liturgy that does justice / by James L. Empereur and
Christopher G. Kiesling.
       p.   cm. — (Theology and life series ; v. 33)
   "A Michael Glazier book."
   ISBN 0-8146-5643-9
   1. Catholic Church—Liturgy. 2. Liturgics. 3. Christianity and
justice. 4. Sociology, Christian (Catholic) 5. Catholic Church-
Doctrines. I. Kiesling, Christopher. II. Title. III. Series.
BX1970.E47   1990
246'.02—dc20   87-82344
                                                 CIP

Table of Contents

❧

TO

CHRISTOPHER GERARD KIESLING, O.P.

1925 - 1986

THE LITURGIST WHO DID JUSTICE

Authors' Note

It is not easy to define liturgy. The word is used equivocally today. The classical definition means a function undertaken on behalf of the people such as some public service. One of the meanings of liturgy in the New Testament is that of divine worship. Early in the history of the church the word was restricted to meaning the Mass. This is still the meaning in the churches of the East. There is no agreement among the Christian churches today on the meaning of liturgy. For some it refers to the outward forms of worship as they are governed by positive law. This is the juridical definition of liturgy. Here liturgy equals what is prescribed in the official liturgical books of a denomination. The modern liturgical movement has broadened the notion of liturgy to mean all worship offered to God by the church. According to this approach liturgy means the "public worship of the Mystical Body of Christ," a view embraced and promoted by the encyclical, *Mediator Dei* (1947). Under the umbrella of this more comprehensive definition are found the more specific ones with their varying emphases on the centrality of the priesthood of Christ, or the reactualization of the redemptive actions of Christ, or the sanctifying power of God in the church's worship.

We have opted for the more comprehensive definition of liturgy as the worship offered to God by the church. While acknowledging the need that liturgy be regulated by ecclesiastical authority, we reject a purely juridical notion of the liturgy. Liturgy is more than what can be found in the approved books of ritual. We do not endorse a definition of liturgy which would consider the private recitation of the breviary as liturgical but would not allow the notion of liturgy to include a group of Christians engaged in the communal praying of the rosary. This does not mean that all worship by Christians is liturgy. Private prayer is true worship. But liturgy is the church as such at worship. This takes place when the church becomes a visible reality, when the church sums itself up in the assembly at prayer. It is the kind of worship that stresses the communal over the individual and which is characterized by Christological and trinitarian dimensions. Liturgy may reach its highest form of expression in the eucharist, but it cannot be restricted to that one liturgical service.

We use the word, liturgy, in this book in a somewhat equivocal manner since it is impossible to do otherwise today. Our use is almost always broader than the eucharist and is never limited to the juridical reality. It is not the same as private prayer. Our usual use of the term, liturgy, will refer to the rites of the church in the approved ordering. But our overarching definition of liturgy is more inclusive. Thus, we see no need to make use of the category, *paraliturgical.* We consider worship often so designated, e.g., the stations of the cross, to be true liturgy. Such services may not have the same kind of approval as do the rites of baptism and marriage. But to the extent that they are instances of the church coming to an event of offering itself to God in assembly, they are authentic acts of liturgy. In this sense, liturgy means for us, the symbolic articulation of the Christian community's relationship with its God in communal ritual activity.

A difficult and confusing area in theological writing today is the matter of inclusive language. This is especially true when composing a book on liturgy and social justice. To the best of our abilities we have tried to model the proper use of gender-inclusive language throughout the book. But this has been done according to our own best insights and careful judgment. As anyone sensitive to the use of language in theology and liturgy knows, there are still areas of ambiguity and unresolved issues. We have had to make our own decisions here. Many will not agree. We can only hope that our struggle with this important issue of social justice will not offend. We believe it to be more important to raise consciousness in this area than to resolve the questions of inclusivity. Others will reach other concrete conclusions regarding inclusive language.

Some decisions were made. The biblical texts are taken from the *New American Bible.* Although our book is ecumenical in its concerns, there is a certain Roman Catholic emphasis. We believe the readers will respect and expect this since the authors are both Roman Catholic. Quotations from the official rituals as well as from primary and secondary sources are for the most part left with their gender bias, if such be the case. If the biblical material and the quotations were for public proclamation, clearly, a different decision would be required. But this book is for study purposes and the reader should be able to make the necessary adjustments. For instance, the chapter on the lectionary is written for a church which is not yet fully sensitive in this area. We cannot be oblivious to the fact that many congregations still pray to God with the words, "Father," and "Lord." We have tried to address this fact by often supplying "Mother" in conjunction with "Father." We do not do this in every case, but only enough times to make the point. "Lord" is more difficult because it is not always clear if the referent is God or Christ. For some, "Lord" is clearly sexist and should never be used. Others have not made a final determination in this matter. We have chosen to live with some of the ambiguity here.

Both of us have tried to be careful to be inclusive in the writing of the text itself. This is easy when referring to human beings. But we have no consistent principle which governs our use of gender language when referring to God. Sometimes, we use both masculine and feminine references together; sometimes, we use masculine references in some sentences and feminine references in other sentences. Sometimes we refer to God more abstractly. Sometimes we use circumlocutions. We hope here to model a variety of ways of dealing with issues without opting for one solution as the final one.

Many people have contributed to this book indirectly. A special note of gratitude is due to those members of the North American Academy of Liturgy who participated in the study group on liturgy and social justice. They helped to shape the thought of the authors of this book. We wish to acknowledge the following permissions: to Simon and Schuster for a lengthy quotation from Michael Harrington's *The Vast Majority: A Journey to the World's Poor;* to *Worship* for revisions in the article, "Liturgy and Consumerism," by Christopher Kiesling, which appeared in volume 52 (July 1978); and to *New Catholic World* for some of the material in an article, "Social Justice and the Eucharist," by Christopher Kiesling which appeared in the July/August 1981 issue. A special note of thanks to Patrick F. Norris, O.P., for his research into the sociological and economic data for this book. We are grateful to Shane Martin, S.J., who was most helpful in the final editing of the manuscript.

✻

Special Note From
James L. Empereur, S.J.

Christopher Gerard Kiesling, O.P., died September 2, 1986. Chris had very much wanted to see this book in some published form before he died. It is a personal sadness for me that it was not possible. It is to Chris that I owe a great deal of my sensitivity to the relationship of social justice to the church's worship. This Jesuit was often called to justice by this Dominican. For many years Chris chaired the study group on liturgy and social justice at the meetings of the North American Academy of Liturgy of which I was a member. I am indebted to Chris Kiesling for some of my deepest theological convictions. All liturgists should see his life and his interest in justice issues as a challenge. Chris was able to transcend the narrow perspective that sometimes characterizes the professional liturgist. He was able to do this because he was such an exemplary member of the Order of Preachers. In one of his many letters to me, Chris was reflecting on how easy it is to find excuses to avoid doing difficult things, in this case, to finish our book. He wrote: "It is so easy to find an excuse not to start. I hope I can see this as a penitential aspect that I need to incorporate into my life as a Dominican dedicated to a ministry of the word, to be engaged in when convenient and inconvenient, in season and out of season." With esteem, gratitude, and love I dedicate *The Liturgy That Does Justice* to Christopher Kiesling, O.P.

Epiphany, 1990

1

The Challenge

On our TV screens we have seen glimpses of miserable starving children in famine-struck Ethiopia or other parts of the world. But, as Arthur Simon says in *Bread for the World,* "famine is merely the tip of the iceberg. Beneath that tip is the far more pervasive and stubborn problem of chronic malnutrition."[1] According to the UN Food and Agriculture Organization, at least 450 million people in developing countries are malnourished.[2] But people have a *right* to adequate food, shelter, and clothing.[3] Nevertheless, according to the World Bank, in 1980, 750 million persons were without the basics of life; they were living in "absolute poverty." This number constitutes one-third of the population of developing countries. Half of this number was children.[4] Those bloated stomachs and protruding eyes appear on our TV screens because peoples in developing countries are powerless. They do not have control over their resources, production, and products. They are manipulated by the rich nations of the world and by the rich classes within their own borders.[5]

---

[1]Arthur Simon, *Bread for the World,* rev. ed. (New York: Paulist Press; Grand Rapids: Wm. B. Eerdmans, 1984), p. 8.

[2]Ibid., p. 7.

[3]James B.McGinnis, *Bread and Justice: Toward a New International Economic Order* (New York: Paulist Press, 1979), pp. 10-11, 22-25.

[4]Simon, *Bread for the World,* p. 7.

[5]McGinnis, *Bread and Justice,* pp. 27-35, 44-49; Michael Harrington, *The Vast Majority: A Journey to the World's Poor* (New York: Simon and Schuster, 1977), pp. 129-51.

But hunger, poverty, and powerlessness are not restricted to the developing countries in Africa or Latin America. They are found right here in the United States. In 1962 Michael Harrington shocked the conscience of the United States with his book, *The Other America: Poverty in the United States*.[6] He revealed the appalling poverty that lay hidden behind the facade of abundance in the "affluent society" described by the well-known economist John Kenneth Galbraith in his book by that name.[7] Again in 1984 and 1985 the U.S. bishops in the drafts of their pastoral letter on the U.S. economy have noted the poverty which continues to infect a considerable portion of the population of the weathiest nation on earth and threatens middle-class citizens.[8]

Denial of the rights to food, clothing, and shelter is not the only injustice widespread in our society and around the world. Amnesty International reported in 1984 that from January to December 1983 there were at least 5,073 prisoners of conscience in the world (that is, persons held in captivity solely for their beliefs, not because of any violence on their part); and torture was practiced in sixty-six countries.[9] The Center for Disease Control in Atlanta reported that 1.3 million abortions were performed in 1981 in our country alone.[10] Women are discriminated against in the job market because of their sex.[11] Education in inner-city schools is inferior, perpetuating the inability of the poor

[6](New York: Macmillan, 1962).

[7]*The Affluent Society* (Boston: Houghton Mifflin, 1958).

[8]*Catholic Social Teaching and the U. S. Economy*, nos. 8, 187-204, in *Origins* 14 (1984): 342, 362-64; second draft, nos. 20, 169-83, in *Origins* 15 (1985): 260, 274-75.

[9]*Amnesty International Report 1984* (London: Amnesty International Publications, 1984), p. 382.

[10]Center for Disease Control, *Morbidity and Mortality Weekly Report*, 6 July 1984. Other groups of institutes provide higher figures for years since 1981, so that the figure for 1985 is more likely around 1.5 million.

[11]U. S. Commission on Civil Rights, "Disadvantaged Women and Their Children," (Washington, D. C., 1983); Jill Craig, "U.S. Women: Hardship or Hope?" *Network* 11 (July-August 1983): 11-18; Margaret Casey, "Feminization of Poverty," *Network* 13 (May -June 1985): 10.

to better their condition.[12] The list of injustices could go on—not simply scattered unjust deeds here and there, but unjust patterns in the organization and conduct of life nationally and internationally.

A Challenge to Christian Worshipers

In 1977 Michael Harrington wrote in his book *The Vast Majority*:

> Though I left the Catholic Church long ago, I have always had an affection for Christ—which is to say the Christ of the *Catholic Worker*, of the Sermon on the Mount, of compassion and gentle love. But now I want to curse him. Who is he to set up his anguish as a model of meditation for the centuries? He was crucified only once, that is all. If you assume that he was God, which I do not, then you can say that he must have felt a terrible psychological loss as they nailed his divinity to the cross. But only one time; only for a matter of hours. Just one excruciating struggle up the hill with the means of his death on his back; just one crown of thorns. A terrible, but just one. In Calcutta, I think, people are crucified by the thousands every day, and then those who have not died are crucified again and again. If he were half the God he claims to be, he would leave his heaven and come here to do penance in the presence of a suffering so much greater than his own, a suffering that he, as God, obscenely permits. But he does not exist. There is no easy transcendental answer to this agony. There is only our fallible, failing, necessary fight. And if we were to win it, the happiness of numberless generations would not pay these people back for a single day of their suffering.[13]

---

[12]Gene I. Maeroff, "Despite Head Start, 'Achievement Gap' Persists for Poor," *New York Times*, 11 June 1985, p. 19; Charles M.Payne, *Getting What We Asked For* (Westport, Conn.: Greenwood Press, 1984), pp. 7-42; Charles Viet Willie, *The Sociology of Urban Education* (Lexington, Mass.: D. C. Heath Co., 1978), pp. 1-52.

[13](New York: Simon and Schuster, 1977), p. 95.

Harrington's cutting words challenge Christians who gather weekly to worship Jesus Christ as Lord and Savior. Those words forcefully call Christian worshipers to make God-in-Christ's-reality, presence, compassion, and healing of humanity visible and tangible through their efforts to establish social justice in neighborhood, city, nation, and world community—and, yes, in parish, diocese, presbytery, district, synod, and universal church. Every age needs its theodicy, its justification for the existence of God and for God's ways. In our day the "faith that does justice"[14] is the necessary apologetic.

So we Christians who gather to worship must see to it that our liturgy expresses and fosters a faith that does justice. How liturgy may do that can be dealt with at three levels.[15] First is the level of actual celebration in a specific place at a definite time. Only those involved in such particularized instances of worship can shape it to express and inspire effectively a faith that does justice. A second level for dealing with liturgy which entails doing justice is that of the liturgical rites of churches. These rites are generally formulated by official groups in the various churches, or at least require approval by church officals before use as a church's own worship. A third level of dealing with liturgy's connection with social justice is that of our understanding of liturgical rites. We ourselves can begin now to discern more fully and more clearly the message calling us to do justice that is already in the existing liturgical texts and rituals.

Current liturgical rites can surely be improved in their expression and power to evoke faith that does justice. But liturgical reforms take a long time. It has to go through the gauntlet of official groups and official approval at level two. We cannot afford to wait. We must look carefully at the churches' liturgies which we now celebrate, casting upon

---

[14]See John C. Haughey, ed., *The Faith That Does Justice* (New York: Paulist Press, 1977), especially the essay by Avery Dulles, "The Meaning of Faith Considered in Relationship to Justice," pp. 10-46.

[15]Christopher Kiesling, "Liturgy and Social Justice," *Worship* 51 (1971): 359-60.

them the light of prolonged thought until we perceive in them the call to social justice latent there. Then, when we celebrate actual liturgies at level one, we will experience them differently; they will say things to us that we did not hear before. We can celebrate them, or supplement them, in ways that highlight their subtle social message. Such scrutiny at the third level can also help church liturgical commissions and officials at the second level see what improvements need to be made.

This book works at the third level and aims at promoting understanding of the liturgy's connection with social justice or sometimes social injustice!

A Separation to be Overcome

In an address delivered in Boston in June, 1983, at a Consultation on Future Liturgical Renewal, Monsignor John J. Egan of the Archdiocese of Chicago called attention to the split between the movements for liturgical reform and social justice.[16] He noted the different situations earlier in this century in the United States. Dom Virgil Michel of St. John's Abbey in Collegeville, Minnesota, not only pioneered a liturgical movement in this country beginning in the 1920's, but was also concerned about social life in the nation.[17] The Liturgical Conference, which emerged in Chicago in 1943, for many years drew the interest and participation of men and women who were concerned both about liturgical reform and about the quality of life in society and in the church. In some of the themes of the annual National Liturgical Weeks sponsored by the Liturgical Conference, we see a double focus on liturgical renewal and social life: Sacrifice and Society (1943), The Family in Christ (1946), Liturgy and Social Order (1955),

---

[16]"Liturgy and Justice: An Unfinished Agenda," *Origins* 13 (1983): 245-53. For the split in Protestantism, see James F. White, *Sacraments as God's Self Giving* (Nashville: Abingdon Press, 1983), pp. 93-94.

[17]Paul Marx, *Virgil Michel and the Liturgical Movement* (Collegeville: Liturgical Press, 1957), pp. 106-75, 298-347.

Education and the Liturgy (1957), *Worship in the City of Man* (*sic*) (1966).

A coupling of liturgical renewal and social justice concerns is found in the eighteenth century in John Wesley's compiling a pocket-sized dictionary explaining difficult words because he was "earnest in his belief that literacy must be part of the salvation of the laboring class."[18] Social reform was linked to liturgical renewal in the Puseyite movement in the Anglican Church of England in the nineteenth century.[19] Another instance of combined social and liturgical reform occurred in England in the earlier part of this century with experiments in "house churches" in parish life and neighborhood renewal.[20] The late John A. T. Robinson of *Honest to God* fame wrote inspiringly of the liturgy in relation to social action in his book *Liturgy Coming to Life*, which was based on actual experience.[21]

Why the separation today? Monsignor Egan, in the address mentioned above, attributes it to the specialization of our age. So much knowledge is required and so much concentration demanded to achieve even modest changes in worship or social order that a person can scarcely engage in both. Another possible reason for the separation is people's personalities. Some people are oriented to vigorous action and they take naturally to fighting for social justice. Other persons are more contemplative or artistic and are attracted to liturgical renewal. A certain vindictiveness may also be at work among us. Social justice activists write off liturgists and liturgy because the liturgists seem unconcerned that their liturgy may be reinforcing an unjust status quo. Liturgists are turned off by the social actionists and their objectives because the social actionists appear to have no interest in, or respect for, the canons of authentic liturgy.

---

[18]Margaret Lane, *Samuel Johnson and His World* (New York: Harper and Row, 1975), p. 108.

[19]R.W. Franklin, "Pusey and Worship in Industrial Society," *Worship* 57 (1983): 386-42.

[20]E.W. Southcott, *The Parish Comes Alive* (London: A.R. Mowbray, 1956).

[21](Philadelphia: Westminister Press, 1964.)

But a concerted effort to overcome the split must be made. Liturgical renewal and reform are impossible in isolation from efforts to restructure the social order, as we shall see in chapter eleven. The social justice ministry without renewed worship, on the other hand, lacks roots and cannot achieve its goal, as we shall point out in chapter twelve.

The Nature of Social Justice

Our concern is liturgy and *social* justice. The expression "social justice" has precise meaning which increases the challenge facing Christian worshipers today. The term is not simply a fashionable word for good deeds, loving action, or ethical conduct which one would expect to flow from liturgical participation. Nor is it simply the "in way" of referring to the fact that Christian worship and life have a social dimension.

Four kinds of justice are distinguishable. (1) There is one-to-one justice, called *Commutative justice* (*Commutatio* in Latin means "exchange"). When I respect my neighbor's reputation and property, or do an honest day's work for my wages, I practice this sort of justice. (2) *Distributive justice* is practiced by those who distribute the common wealth of the community, and by those who cooperate with that distribution. The government official who gives plush jobs in return for a "kickback" violates distributive justice, and so do those who give the bribes and take the jobs. (3) We practice *General justice* when our individual conduct promotes the common good, when, for example, I do not drive a car while I am intoxicated and liable to an accident which will foul traffic and injure or even kill people. The term *legal justice* can embrace the above forms of justice insofar as their norms become imbodied in civil and criminal law. (4) The precise meaning of *social justice* has shifted in the course of recent decades, but today the term generally refers to the structures, patterns of organization, or institutions of society, the manners in which they function, and the corresponding judgments and attitudes in the minds of people.[22] As such, social justice very much sets

[22]For examples of these social structures, see Joseph Gremillion, *The Gospel of*

the norms for other kinds of justice—what constitutes a fair price in a one-to-one exchange; whether a gift of money is bribe or simply a way of doing business; whether one's possession of a gun violates general justice.[23]

Determined by societal patterns of organization, social justice or injustice escapes individual control. I alone cannot change the economic organization of world trade and thereby conquer once and for all the hunger, malnutrition, and death which plague East Africa. I alone cannot reverse the feminization of poverty in the United States. In fact, once institutionalization of any practice occurs in a society, it is extremely difficult for even large groups of people to change the practice.[24] It is easier to level a mountain range for a highway than to remove racism from the U. S. way of life. Even if old laws can be changed or new ones put in place, they can be dodged, or loopholes found, by unconverted hearts. So social justice both in the objective sense of a just organization of society and its practices, and also in the subjective sense of individuals' wanting and doing what makes a justly functioning society, is very difficult to achieve.

When, therefore, we seek liturgy which fosters social justice, we are confronted with an immense challenge—celebrating liturgy which changes not only the hearts of worshipers but, through them, the way the world—and the church—are organized and function.

A Judeo-Christian Perspective

Social justice in a Judeo-Christian perspective, we must always keep in mind, is not a cold, dry, impersonal, legal

---

Peace and Justice (Maryknoll, N.Y.: Orbis Books, 1976), pp. 15-21, 47-55; Harrington, *Vast Majority*, pp. 130-51; McGinnis, *Bread and Justice*. pp. 6-74, 100-113, and, for an especially graphic expression of structural oppression, 246-53.

[23]For more ample treatment of the various kinds of justice, see Christopher Kiesling, "Social Justice in Christian Life according to Thomas Aquinas," *Spirituality Today* 31 (1979): 231 45.

[24]For the intractability of social structures, see Peter L. Berger and Thomas Luckmann, *The Social Construction of Reality* (Garden City, N. Y.: Doubleday, Anchor Book, 1967; original 1966). For a more popular presentation, see Peter L. Berger, *Invitation to Sociology* (Garden City, N.Y.: Doubleday, Anchor Books, 1963).

equality between people. The blindfolded woman balancing scales is not an adequate symbol of social justice for Christian or Jewish faith. Social justice is born of love of God and of neighbor as self; it has the warmth, compassion, forgiveness, tenderness of love about it. It is highly personal. Social justice is, really, a factor in our love of neighbor, for justice gives structure to love, as Paul Tillich would say,[25] so that our love is not mere good feeling. Only love, moreover, embracing mercy and forgiveness, assures the authenticity, integrity, and fullness of social justice, as Pope John Paul II argues in his encyclical *Dives in misericordia* (Rich in mercy).[26]

This integral sense of justice approximates the notion of justice in the Bible. The Hebrew Scriptures contain the words *mispat* (translated sometimes as "judgment" —in the sense of establishing someone in the right, sometimes as "justice" or sometimes as "just"), *sedek* (translated sometimes as "righteousness" or "justice"), and *sedekah* ("righteous" or "just"). These words express concrete actions or qualities of actions or persons which meet a standard legally or in some other context, such as the religious sphere. They can signify conduct in accord with the Law, or they can refer to God's saving work, as the New Testament equivalents tend to do. They can also signify rights, in the sense of claims, or laws. They do not refer much to things, or to equality. So the biblical notion of justice has an expanse to it of which our popular notion of justice is only a part, unless it is thought of together with love, mercy, forgiveness, and other qualities.[27]

[25] *Love, Power, and Justice* (New York: Oxford University Press, 1954), p. 71. For continuity in Catholic thought between present emphasis on justice and previous stress on love, see Stanley F. Parmisano, "Social Justice: The Broader Perspective," *Spirituality Today* 37 (1985): 13-26.

[26] 30 November 1980, nos. 145-58, in Claudia Carlen, comp., *The Papal Encyclicals* (Wilmington, N. C. : McGrath publishing Co., 1981) 5:293-94.

[27] For a more complete treatment of the biblical notion of justice, see John L. McKenzie, *Dictionary of the Bible* (Milwaukee: Bruce, 1965), s.v. "Judgment" and "Righteous, Righteousness"; Xavier Leon Dufour, ed., *Dictionary of Biblical Theology* (New York: Desclee, 1967), s.v. "Justice": Jose Miranda, *Marx and the Bible* (Maryknoll, N.Y.: Orbis Books, 1974), pp. 109-99; John R. Donahue, "Biblical Perspectives on Justice," in John C. Haughey, ed., *The Faith That Does Justice* (New York: Paulist Press, 1977), pp. 68-112.

This Judeo-Christian understanding of social justice prevents the pursuit of justice for all from becoming simply materialistic. People need decent housing, so the buildings in an area are leveled by bulldozers and functional high-rise apartments are built. In the process, a neighborhood is destroyed—a whole network of interpersonal relationships which are more necessary for human life than freshly plastered walls. Justice is not done to these people, even though they now have "decent" housing.

The wholesome notion of social justice prevents the establishment of justice for the oppressed from becoming simply an exchange of places between those "on top" and those "on the bottom." Pope John Paul II strongly reminds us that the experience of the past and our own time testifies that the struggle for justice alone can beget spite, hatred, and cruelty, and, in the name of justice, enemies are killed, freedom limited, and fundamental human rights denied.[28]

The full Judeo-Christian ideal of social justice has a depth, a richness, and a personal quality to it that goes beyond legislation and laws, for it participates in the very justice of God.[29] The social justice which we seek requires, ultimately, spiritual discernment, a "reading of the signs of the times" in the light of the gospel. Something more than economic and sociological data are needed in planning the just society. A vision of the whole human person and of the human person's destiny is at least equally important. A respect and love for each person and his or her unique identity are required. A sense of the beautiful must also be incorporated into the effort. Liturgy is not the exclusive source of this vision, love, respect, and sense of beauty, but it is a significant one. It can, therefore, be an important contributor to the struggle for social justice. But we need to examine it closely to appreciate what it has to offer.

In the following chapter, therefore, we will reflect on the liturgy and its relationship to the world, and thus to social justice, in terms of the relationship between the sacred and the

---

[28] *Dives in misericordia* nos. 119-21, in Carlen, *Papal Encyclicals*, 5:289-90.

[29] Mark Searle, "*Serving the Lord with Justice*," in Mark Searle, ed., *Liturgy and Social Justice* (Collegeville: Liturgical Press, 1980), pp. 15-17.

secular. In chapter three, the social justice implications of the rites of Christian initiation will be examined. Chapters four and five will consider the word of God and social justice, first as this word is presented through the liturgical year in the *Lectionary*, and then as preached in the homily or sermon. The mostly implicit, but not negligible, references to social justice in the liturgy of the Lord's Supper will be studied in chapter six. Crucial for social justice is reconciliation between peoples; chapter seven will consider the liturgy of reconciliation in its relationship to social justice. Ordination and other rituals of appointment to ministry in the church raise questions about the justice of the structures, not of society, but of the church— questions which will be noted in chapter eight on liturgies of ministry and social justice. The liturgical celebration of marriage opens the door to considering in chapter nine a host of justice issues because marriage is a fundamental human reality and one that perdures, or is meant to perdure, for a lifetime and affects the larger community. Chapter ten about the anointing of the sick brings explicitly to the fore human suffering and how social institutions, procedures, and attitudes heal it or cause it. An eleventh chapter focuses on the impact of consumerism on liturgy, with a view to illustrating that liturgical renewal and reform suppose changes in the social order, whereas chapter twelve shows that the social justice effort to change society needs the movement for liturgical reform and renewal.

✻

Bibliography

Brown, Robert McAfee. *Theology in A New Key,* Philadelphia: The Westminister Press, 1978.

> The author explores how we might respond to the issues raised by the theologians of liberation. There is a brief treatment of how liturgy can be an enabling factor.

Cosmao, Vincent. *Changing the World: An Agenda for the Churches*, Maryknoll, N.Y.: Orbis Books, 1984.

> The author analyzes the reasons for continuing under-development in many nations and notes the tendency of societies to settle for inequality and to sacralize it. He then describes how the churches can contribute to the transformation of the world.

Egan, John J. "Liturgy and Justice: an Unfinished Agenda," *Origins* 13 (1983): 245-53.

> This address describes the split between the liturgical movement and the social justice movement in the churches, adduces reasons for overcoming the separation, and proposes future interaction and cooperation between the two efforts.

Fiorenza, Francis Schüssler. "The Church's Religious Identity and Its Social and Political Mission," *Theological Studies* 43 (1982): 197-225.

> After sketching various theological interpretations about how the pursuit of justice relates to the church's religious purpose, the author offers a theology which incorporates work for justice into the church's religious mission.

Harrington, Michael. *The Vast Majority: A Journey to the World's Poor*, New York: Simon and Schuster, 1977.

> Harrington describes his encounters with poverty in India, Africa, and elsewhere. He inserts into this travelogue accounts of how the modern world's poverty developed historically, how current organization of the world aggravates it, and how it might possibly be changed.

Haughey, John C. ed., *The Faith That Does Justice*, New York: Paulist Press, 1977.

These essays thoroughly probe the relationship between faith and justice in the present time, in the church's tradition, and in future directions to be taken, and so contribute to appreciating "the liturgy that does justice."

Kiesling, Christopher. "Liturgy and Social Justice," *Worship* 51 (1977): 351-71.

Emerging from a study group of the North American Academy of Liturgy, this article describes the concerns people have about relating liturgy and social justice, makes precise the questions which arise, and notes ways they can be addressed.

McGinnis, James B. *Bread and Justice: Toward a New International Economic Order*, New York: Paulist Press, 1979.

McGinnis shows the roots of world hunger in patterns of economic and political organization and explains the New International Economic Order which nations of the South have called for but which has been resisted by nations of the North, including the U. S.

Simon, Arthur. *Bread for the World*, rev. ed. New York: Paulist Press; Grand Rapids: Wm. B. Eerdmans, 1984.

This book explains the problem of hunger around the world and in the U. S. and shows how its solution involves such factors as international trade, land ownership, use of water, lifestyles, tariff barriers, and arms production.

Synod of Bishops, Second General Assembly, 1971. *Justice in the World.* In *The Gospel of Peace and Justice: Catholic Social Teaching Since Pope John.* Presented by Joseph Gremillion. Maryknoll, N. Y.: Orbis Books, 1976. Pp. 513-29.

This document affirms work for social justice as integral to the preaching of the gospel, and calls the church to examine and reform its own structures and practices in regard to justice to make credible its call for justice in the world.

2

Liturgy:
A Spirituality of Human Liberation

The Need for a Just Liturgy

That the liturgy is the church's spirituality is now as much a truism as the familiar phrase "liturgy presupposes community." The liturgy is the climactic expression of the spiritual life of the church. It is the way that the Christian community symbolically re-enacts its relationship with God. This liturgical spirituality implies the actual participation in the mission of the church as a means of opening ourselves to the saving power of Christ and the transforming actions of the Spirit. This spirituality is a concrete way of living the gospel under the inspiration of the same Spirit. There is, then, a direct relationship between social justice and the way liturgical spirituality leads the Christian to experiences of transcendence. This is seen in the values affirmed in this kind of spirituality. For instance, one such value is a responsiveness to the signs of the times. This often calls people to awaken the consciences of others with regard to basic human rights. They may demand that world governments respect the rights of minorities, promote racial equality, and move in the direction of the solving of population problems. Another value is personal freedom and responsibility. These are found wherever people accept the task of proclaiming the gospel courageously and with initiative in collaboration with others in a pluralistic society.

There are many other such values. Any list would include:

1) poverty, which witnesses through a sparing and sharing life style and a responsible use of what one possesses; 2) the word of God, in terms of its liberation themes as the basis for one's response and as the criteria for decision-making; 3) the continual conversation with Christ, which includes a deep commitment to discover the hidden roots of selfishness in people in order to move forward to establish community; 4) participation in a faith community, which exists as a sign of love and service to enable persons to receive support and discernment on justice concerns; and finally 5) joy and hope, to sustain others in their struggles as well as to attract to the cause of justice those who are unaware or lack motivation.

Liturgical spirituality presupposes an understanding and experience of what it means to be human and of the inter-relatedness of all reality. This understanding and experience is thematized in the celebration of the sacraments, where the deepest levels of human life and human decisions are grasped and transformed in Christ Jesus. And because the liturgy is composed of social symbols, our human experiences and decisions must be ritualized in the context of the Christian community.[1] This leads to a central element in our liturgical lives, namely, that of the Christian social consciousness, which places a priority on the dignity of the human person and the human rights and duties which protect and enhance that dignity. What makes it possible to have an authentic liturgical celebration is the radical social nature of human existence, the responsibility of the individual to society and vice versa.[2]

The church's mission as sacrament to the world requires that it often be prophetic and counter-cultural in the matter of injustice. The liturgical spirituality of the church should reveal the paschal character of the *human* experience of social justice. It is theologically true that every liturgy brings to expression

---

[1]For a further discussion of the relationship between liturgy and spirituality see James L. Empereur, S. J., "Liturgy and Spirituality," in *Worship Points the Way*, edited by Malcolm C. Burson (New York: The Seabury Press, 1981).

[2]How a lack of this connection between the sacraments and human responsibility has been reflected in a "magical" approach to the liturgical rites has been detailed by John H. McKenna in his article, "Liturgy: Toward Liberation or Oppression?" in *Worship* 56:4 (July, 1982): 297 ff.

those saving actions of Christ which we call the Paschal Mystery, namely, the death, resurrection, and ascension of Christ. But the danger is that Christ's own passover will remain on the abstract level. Liturgy celebrates the dying and rising of Christ when it does so by means of our daily, often quite pedestrian, dyings and risings. Christians who live according to such a liturgical spirituality can be both symbol and cause of God's action in situations of injustice by embodying in their lives the justice and mercy of God. Their sacramental living, then, reveals the meaning in suffering and oppression and calls upon all persons to eliminate the demonic forces which control society.

But is liturgy such a concrete expression of the community's spirituality? So much of the contemporary scene is dominated by ineffective liturgy. On the grass roots levels, is there an integrated experience of liturgical spirituality and justice? Where can one go to participate in a liturgy that does justice? Nathan Mitchell has written about the need to keep liturgy and this world together in our worship of God:

> Liturgy and sacrament are moments when we consciously recognize and ritually respond to the God who acts always and everywhere in the ruddy colors and ruinous catastrophes of this world. The drama of the liturgy is nothing more or less than the drama of human history, permeated by God's presence. One world, one history, one God who acts in them: this is what we confess and celebrate when we assemble for worship. When liturgy becomes a self-absorbed attempt at "religious behavior," or when it calls attention to itself as something "unworldly," it ceases to be worship and becomes an exercise in self-consciousness. Christian worship is inherently worldly. Its primary symbols are drawn from the messiest activities of human life: giving birth and dying, washing and smearing bodies with oil, eating and drinking, unburdening one's heart in the presence of another. All this is the septic stuff of the world's drama—and the stuff of Christian liturgy as well.[3]

[3]"The Spirituality of Christian Worship," *Spirituality Today* 34:1 (March, 1982): 10.

Because liturgy so rarely fulfills Mitchell's description of it, it is no wonder that many of those who work in social justice fields are unaffected by liturgy or at most celebrate it infrequently and informally.

But what is a "worldly" liturgy? The task of this chapter is to attempt an answer to that question. Clearly, it is easier to say what is *not* a liturgy that does justice. It is not, for instance, a liturgy that incarnates injustice in its very structures because it reflects a church which is unjust. Such is the case in certain churches where people are prevented from ministering fully in community. In those several Christian churches where women are excluded from ordained ministry, every liturgy carries with it an element of injustice as long as that situation obtains. Something similar can be said of the Dutch Reformed Church of South Africa as long as it provides *any* basis for the practice of apartheid.

Again, a just liturgy is not one which has intercessory prayers which deal with economic and political tensions, but which continues to employ the kind of imagery and language which sets up a sacred/secular dichotomy in world view and spirituality. A just liturgy is not one which has a sermon on what may be the prevailing social concerns, but which continues to operate according to an institutional model of liturgical understanding. A just liturgy is not one which is celebrated by and for gay/lesbians, women, blacks, or any other oppressed group, but which manipulates symbols, confusing them with signs, creating an imbalance by reducing the total prayer experience to a one dimensional attempt to achieve some political action as a result of the liturgical celebration. Nor is liturgy just if it becomes the opportunity for some angry, conflicted people to avoid the expense of psychotherapy by engaging in free group sensitivity, dominating the ritual with personal agenda.

A liturgy that does justice is not one which calls the worshipers to be just only after they leave their worship and itself does not change ritually and spiritually. Such has been the case of too much liturgy in the past. Nor is the just liturgy one which presupposes that one is just before one comes to it. Such preparation is laudable, perhaps even necessary, but that does not guarantee that liturgy will be just in spirituality and structure. Christians who are sensitive to justice concerns may well be required to worship in an unjust liturgy. Today this is hardly exceptional.[4]

What then is the liturgy that does justice? What is a justice-oriented liturgical spirituality? Such a liturgical experience is one which must possess the qualities of justice which one finds outside of worship. Liturgy as a form of ritual, that is, as patterned symbolic activity, must be permeated by a way of thinking, a way of acting, and a way of relating where individual worth, fairness, rights, and responsibilities are recognized and promoted. Worshipers who engage in this bundle of symbols called liturgy must find themselves within an open-ended situation where they have the opportunity and room to experience justice among themselves and justice within themselves. They must be able to experience a sense of the wholeness of human life in terms of the rite which ultimately speaks of the Paschal Mystery. Through their continual participation they know on all levels, not just the intellectual, what human justice is. A liturgy that does justice certainly makes it easier for people to recognize what forms justice should take in any concrete situation outside of worship. But it does not do this by becoming a recipe book for people working on international issues, or in the inner city, or in the various areas of sexual oppression. Rather it does this by creating the possibility for worshipers to have a justice experience which they can then use as a norm or measure to judge what would be and are the authentic experiences of justice in the rest of life. We cannot know what to do justice-wise simply through analytical study or hortatory instruction. It is important to have other analogous experiences of justice before we can recognize injustice and can facilitate programs for justice.

Perhaps, an example will clarify what is meant here. An art critic is someone who is able to respond to a work of art such as a painting, a sculpture, or a piece of music and judge it to be of high quality, poor quality, or merely mediocre. This skill is not acquired primarily through lectures, reading books, or

---

[4]Some of the limitations of the present situation are discussed by Joseph Gelineau in his article, "Celebrating the Paschal Liberation," *Politics and Liturgy* (Consilium 92) edited by Herman Schmidt and David Power (New York: Herder and Herder, 1974).

seminar discussions. She develops it through continual exposure to art of differing quality. She has enough analogous experiences of good art over a period of time that she can make judgment in any specific case. That is how we become skilled in social justice through the liturgy. The liturgy is the place where we experience often enough the justice of God and our own justice to be able to recognize justice and the lack of it outside the time and place of worship.

It is the purpose of a justice-oriented liturgical spirituality to prevent us from entering the arena of social justice with our own prejudices undiscerned. Too often even social workers, justice consciousness-raisers, feminists, and third world liberators have been motivated by their own inner conflicts and guilt; too often they have laid a trip on other people because they did not really experience themselves as just (lovable) before God. They find this impossible because they do not like themselves, or to put it more biblically, they have not incorporated themselves into the larger story that God has first loved them. William H. Willimon speaks of this:

> We do not worship God to become better people. Christian worship is an intrinsic activity. But as we worship something happens to us. The love we return in worship is, in turn, lovingly forming us for the better. The worship of the church—that predictable, patterned, public, purposeful behavior through which the church tells its story as opposed to other stories, where God is named and praised and let loose in our lives, where the church rehearses and reminds itself of who it is and who it, by God's grace, is becoming— is a major context of moral formation.[5]

A just liturgy, then, is that ritualized Christian prayer which flows from right belief, or a justice-oriented spirituality, and from properly ordered community structures. The just liturgy must articulate the right kind of relationships among God, the individual, the Christian community, and the world of people

---

[5] *The Service of God: How Worship and Ethics are Related* (Nashville: Abingdon Press, 1983), p. 37.

and things outside the community. This liturgy must be built on a properly structured community where people's gifts are recognized. A just liturgy is the result of a just liturgical spirituality and just structures which give form to the spirituality. Rev. Charles Rue, SSC, a missionary from Korea, states it well.

> A just liturgy must be built on the equality, the dignity, and the gifts of every person and group in the faith community. In turn, the structures of the liturgy must reflect and promote the self-worth, the gifts, the call to mutual ministry of each person and group within the community, and likewise of each unique church community within the universal church. Just structures within the community and the liturgy itself are a prerequisite for just liturgy and liturgical experience of justice.[6]

The remainder of this chapter develops the two conditions for a liturgy that does justice: a just liturgical spirituality and just liturgical structures.

A Just Liturgical Spirituality

When we speak of a justice-directed liturgical spirituality we are referring to a certain kind of world view. It implies a context for worship where the community understands and deals with the relationship of the sacred and the secular in a particular way. Often this will demand a revision of Christian spirituality and of the way Christians image their relationship with God. This concretely means a new integration of the way in which the sacred and the secular are perceived and experienced in community. It is no coincidence that the concern for social justice and the liturgy has arisen at a time when there is also a concern about the possibility of worshiping in a secularized age. When the sacred and profane were seen as

---

[6]Maryknoll Regional Catechetical Newsletter: Korea Pastoral Exchange 9:5 (October-December, 1981): 7.

occupying two spheres of reality which were clearly distinct, and as long as this distinction provided the key to the kind of spirituality that surrounded the liturgy, the question of social justice tended to remain suppressed in worship. The other-worldliness of the liturgy was not sympathetic to the social dimension of life and the worshipers who were fed on this kind of spirituality tended to distance themselves from justice issues.

In recent years a more fruitful path to follow for the formation of a just liturgical spirituality has been based on the unity of the sacred and the secular. Such a perspective no longer views the world in terms of a two-storied universe. The identification of the sacred with the other-worldly and the negation of the secular is clearly rejected. It is recognized that our spiritual strivings cannot denigrate the secular values that contemporary people see to be positive. God's working in the world can only be affirmed in faith, but that does not detract from the real human values in the lives of the worshipers.[7]

This more positive approach to the secular seen in terms of its sacred dimensions is based on the Christian understanding of the goodness of creation and the centrality of the incarnation. A redeemed world must remain secular-otherwise it ceases to be this world. Unless redemption is purely accidental and extrinsic, this world is at its heart holy. That is to say, it is the sacred dimension of the secular which gives the secular its real value. The point is that the very meaning of the secular is found in its religious dimension. And what better than the liturgy to bring this to visibility? And when the liturgy does this, it provides the possibility of a justice-oriented experience.

It is the task of liturgical worship to assist us to perceive a sacred presence in secular reality which is really there. Those who maintain the clear-cut distinction between the sacred and profane in human living warn against the projection of a sacrality on this world which is without foundation. Such projection is a real possiblity. But it is precisely liturgical worship which can help us to avoid projecting a holiness on

---

[7]One of the best treatments of what is involved in this change of worldview is that of J. G. Davies in his *Everyday God: Encountering the Holy in World and Worship* (London: SCM Press LTD, 1973). The entire book is highly recommended.

the secular world which is not there. However, that does not imply that one can presume that there is a dichotomy between the two. Rather, those who reject the sacred secular division claim a sensitivity which allows them to discern more readily the sacred dimension of all reality. What is needed is a discernment process and criteria for this discernment. Liturgy can provide a context for this discernment when it is a just liturgy. In fact, the liturgy can be the privileged place for discovering the sacred within the secular. But this can only happen if we begin from the position that liturgy and life must intersect. Years ago Louis Bouyer anticipated this point when he wrote:

> The world into which the liturgy introduces us is not a world in its own right, standing aloof . . . .It is rather the meeting point of the world of the resurrection with this very world of ours in which we live, suffer and die.[8]

How then can the liturgy be the place of this kind of spiritual discernment? It is the way in which humanity is experienced and celebrated in worship. It is in our humanity itself that we can identify the continuity between the sacred and the profane, thus avoiding any opposition between the two. Liturgy is not the place where we turn to an easy sacrality which takes us out of our world and its social concerns. Nor is it a relishing of sacrality itself uncontaminated by the conflicts and struggles of the world. Rather, it should reveal what is fully human and show how this full humanity is the place where the kingdom of God's justice and peace is made alive. In other words, a justice-directed liturgy is a fully human one.

How is it that a fully human liturgy is the one that does justice? How is our humanity the key to a just liturgical spirituality? The answer to these questions is found in the way that our humanity can be an epiphany of God. In our humanness we can experience something ultimate, something that transcends us. When that happens this experience becomes the method of discernment whereby we can discover the sacred

[8]*Liturgical Piety* (Notre Dame: University of Notre Dame Press, 1955), p. 267.

in the secular. We can sense whether any liturgical experience is filled with the justice of God. When our humanity can come to its fullness in liturgy, we can make contact with that sense of ultimacy in our lives that widens our awareness about the justice demanded by the kingdom of God.

But can our humanity come to fullness in liturgy? There are many obvious ways we could immediately point to: a recognizable sense of community, a beautiful and challenging proclamation of the word, a full acceptance of all the ministries through the sharing of ritual roles, and, of course, a Eucharistic experience which is clearly one of eating and drinking in Christ. One could also refer to adequate planning and the quality of the musical dimension. But these are specifically religious in character. The human person comes to fullness in specifically *human* encounters, which, while remaining secular, also have a sense of transcendence about them. For instance, a good meal between friends remains embodied in the secular, that is, it remains meal, but it is also disclosive of a quality of friendship which few people would want to explain in terms of human understanding alone. The same can be said about a good conversation, the experience of loneliness, or the attraction to a potential friend. There is a sense of ultimacy in all these human experiences. And the ultimacy emerges from these differing forms of human encounters precisely as *human*. It is what Sam Keen describes:

> The sacred must be rediscovered in what moves us and touches us, in what makes us tremble, in what is proximate rather than remote, ordinary rather than extraordinary, native rather than imported.[9]

The paradigm of a spirituality of justice is a real human encounter that points beyond itself.[10] And so the liturgy which does justice is the one which is as fully human as possible. It is

[9] *To a Dancing God* (New York: Harper and Row, 1970), p. 159.

[10] Langdon Gilkey has pointed out four ways in which the experience of ultimacy is revealed in the human encounter. It is in relation to our being, in relation to our being in a temporal context, in relation to our consciousness, and in relation to our freedom. See "Addressing God in Faith," *Concilium* 82 (1973).

the one which arises in the context of human encounters, which points beyond itself in this full humanity to a sense and experience of ultimacy. Liturgy is the place to discover the meaning of this secular world in its religious dimension.

It is necessary to do an about face in our perception of the sacred. Rather than drawing such clear lines between the holy and the profane, we must see the sacred as the deeper, fuller, even more authentic dimension of the secular reality itself. When the sacred dimension of every worldly reality, from people to their very environments, is perceived, then the demands of social justice preached by Jesus Christ will be realized. When we give this world's reality its full value, then we will have a glimpse of what kind of justice this world needs. When things we use in worship are real, material, weak, and finite and when they are perceived as such and when we see them as they were meant to be: means of salvation and not idols, we will be able to understand the meaning of justice in the world.[11]

Christians must not worship the work of their hands whether it be the rituals through which they bring their religious experience to expression or the civil society. The temptation is to oversacralize or absolutize the religious dimensions of our lives because in that way it is possible to remain in control. And then we can distance ourselves from such sacred places, persons, and events. Such is the case when people criticize the church when it moves into the political arena. They accuse the church of speaking outside its competence. A spirituality of justice would deny the validity of that accusation because it operates from the conviction that the sacred is sacred to the degree that it is tied to the earth. It both respects the autonomy

[11]Paul Van Buren speaks of five features of secularity, five shifts in emphasis which can help worship become more "worldly," that can help Christians understand that at worship they are not drawing apart from the world, not entering a sacred realm. They are the shifts from permanence to change, from the universal to the particular, from unity to plurality, from absolute to the relative, and from passivity to activity. "The Tendency of our Age and the Reconception of Worship," in *Worship and Secularization* edited by Wieber Vos (Bussum, Holland: Paul Brand, 1970), p. 4ff. See also *Spirituality and Liberation Overcoming the Great Fallacy* by Robert McAfee Brown (Philadelphia: The Westminster Press, 1988), especially chapter 6, "Acting Out the Clue: Liturgy and the Sacraments."

of the secular, the world, and politics but at the same time
demands that it be expressed through that same secularity.
The sacred must be the presence of God in the ordinary and
God's redemption of the ordinary experience. Then social
justice will be perceived as one expression of that presence in a
world still in need of redemption. The U.S. Roman Catholic
bishops in their pastoral letter on the U.S. economy put it this
way:

Worship and Prayer

329. Challenging U.S. economic life with the Christian
vision calls for a deeper awareness of the integral connection
between worship and the world of work. Worship and
common prayers are the wellsprings that give life to any
reflection on economic problems and that continually call
the participants to greater fidelity to discipleship. To worship
and pray to the God of the universe is to acknowledge that
the healing love of God extends to all persons and to every
part of existence, including work, leisure, money, economic
and political power and their use, and to all those practical
policies that either lead to justice or impede it. Therefore,
when Christians come together in prayer, they make a
commitment to carry God's love into all these areas of life.

330. The unity of work and worship finds expression in a
unique way in the Eucharist. As people of a new covenant,
the faithful hear God's challenging word proclaimed to
them—a message of hope to the poor and oppressed—and
they call upon the Holy Spirit to unite all into one body of
Christ. For the Eucharist to be a living promise of the
fullness of God's Kingdom, the faithful must commit themselves to living as redeemed people with the same care and
love for all people that Jesus showed. The body of Christ
which worshipers receive in Communion is also a reminder
of the reconciling power of his death on the Cross. It
empowers them to work to heal the brokenness of society
and human relationships and to grow in a spirit of self-
giving for others.

331. The liturgy teaches us to have grateful hearts: to
thank God for the gift of life, the gift of this earth, and the
gift of all people. It turns our hearts from self-seeking to a

spirituality that sees the signs of true discipleship in our sharing of goods and working for justice. By uniting us in prayer with all the people of God, with the rich and the poor, with those near and dear and with those in distant lands, liturgy challenges our way of living and refines our values. Together in the community of worship, we are encouraged to use the goods of this earth for the benefit of all. In worship and in deeds for justice, the Church becomes a "sacrament," a visible sign of that unity in justice and peace that God wills for the whole of humanity.[12]

But this shift in understanding of the meaning of the sacred on the part of the official church is not new. In 1968, at the meeting of the Latin American Roman Catholic bishops in Medellin, Colombia, church leaders embraced a more balanced and creative approach to the relationship of liturgy and social issues than had been acceptable before. Rafael Avila has done a comparison of the document dealing with the liturgy from this meeting with the *Constitution on the Sacred Liturgy* which emerged from the Second Vatican Council. This comparison makes it clear that a shift in liturgical spirituality has taken place. For instance, whereas the council document on the liturgy sees it as first in intrinsic worth and of primary importance for the life of the church, in Medellin, liturgy is subordinate to the questions of justice and peace. Vatican II still accepted the liturgy as the "summit toward which the activity of the Church is directed; and at the same time it is the fountain from which all its power flows."[13] For Medellin, "the liturgical celebration crowns and nourishes a commitment to the human situation, to development and human promotion."[14] This is more centrifugal and takes the uniqueness of the

[12]*Economic Justice For All: Catholic Social Teaching And the U. S. Economy* (Washington, D. C.: National Conference of Catholic Bishops),in *Origins* 16:24 (November 27, 1986).

[13]*Constitution on the Sacred Liturgy* 10.

[14]Medellin, "Liturgy," 4; English translation, Consejo Episcopal Latinoamericano, *The Church in the Present-Day Transformation of Latin America in the Light of the Council, vol. II Conclusions,* (Washington, D. C.: Latin American Bureau, USCC, 1968).

historical situation more seriously. Liturgy at the Vatican Council is still seen from a dualistic perspective where the church is the subject of a sacred history alongside of secular history. In Medellin, liturgy is the climax of the efforts for development, promotion, and liberation, albeit, in Latin America specifically. Liturgy is that stop along the way where we celebrate our history and its meaning in terms of the Easter event. There is no question of moving back and forth from one history to another, but of recapturing the profound meaning of the only history we have.[15]

Just Liturgical Structures

A liturgy that does justice not only presupposes a just liturgical spirituality, but also must be just in its own internal and external ordering. Liturgical prayer is patterned symbolic activity. It is a ritual which is composed of a structure in the community and in itself. As with certain types of spirituality, these structures are often unjust. When that is the case, the worshipers experience injustice and this despite their efforts to live out of a justice-oriented spirituality. Charles Rue gives examples of unjust liturgical structures:

> 1)"Clericalism" structures into the community and liturgy artificial divisions giving an over importance to the ordained state and an exaggerated sense of dependence among believers.
>
> 2)"Male dominance" structures into the liturgy and community an inequality opposed to a community where there is neither male or female, young or old, etc.
>
> 3)"Power groups" establish a dominant position in the church community from where they push their own particular organization, ideas or agenda, and they often use the liturgy as their personal forum.

[15]For a more fully developed comparison between the two documents of the Second Vatican Council and Medellin, see: Rafael Avila, *Worship and Politics* (Maryknoll: Orbis Books, 1981), chapter three.

4)A "wealthy lifestyle" can be structured into community activity and into buildings and liturgy designed for display.

5)A "reinforcing of society" can be structured into the church community and liturgy when their values and life style merely mirror the society surrounding them.

6)"Intellectualism" can be structured into the community and liturgy through its language and by demanding worldly standards of scholarly achievements for ministries.

7)"Individualism" can be structured into the liturgy when it promotes personal devotions and private celebrations.

8)An "over regard for law" can be structured into the liturgy if it becomes a mere exercise in formalistic rubric keeping.

9)"Standardization" can structure into the liturgy a stifling uniformity which neither encourages nor allows fresh expressions of faith for each community, subcultural group or cultural people.

10)"Architecture" can structure into the liturgy an over-emphasis on divisions of groups, power positions and subservience, lack of spontaneity, other worldliness, individualism, and false security.

11)"Anarchy" can be structured into the liturgy if every celebration has to be completely new and different.

12)"Clubiness" can be structured into the community and into the liturgy resulting in a disregard for the holy, the transcendent, and the future, and causing the worshipers to lapse into merely looking to present happiness, human fulfillment, friendly relations and cheap group therapy.[16]

Unless ritual can call people beyond itself and its structures, it cannot be just. Much of the injustice in today's world comes from the fact that human identity is shaped by society's institutions, roles, and statuses. A liturgy that does justice must provide the opportunity to experience that dimension of life which falls between these structures. The experience of justice is often the experience of anti-structure, or life on the margins. "Liminality," a word which comes from the Latin, *limen*, which means threshold or margin, refers to that specific

---

[16]*Korea Pastoral Exchange* 9:5 (October-December, 1981), pp. 4-7.

quality of symbols that makes such an experience of anti-structure possible. In liminal experiences those things in the structure which define life are left behind and one goes to the fundamental symbols of human life. To live justly is to live liminally.[17]

Liminal ritual allows worshipers to be outside the confines, the constrictions, and defenses of every structure where structure means the accepted way of cultural, political, economic, sexual, familial, vocational, and social living, all of which constitute the conditions of daily existence. For instance, at liminal liturgy there can be no distinction between rich and poor, male and female, and among the races. It is not that structures are unnecessary. They are indispensable for getting things done. But they also confine and regiment people's lives. Aidan Kavanagh has written about the need for liturgy to be anti-structural. He says that liturgy

> like ritual in general, exists to undercut and overthrow the very structures it uses. This is so not because the Gospel is similarly anti-structural, which it is, but because historic human wisdom has detected that human structures ossify and become oppressive or disintegrate when left to themselves . . . The lesson human wisdom seems to have learned is that although we probably cannot do without bureaucrats and bureaucracies, we certainly can do without tyrants and tyrannies. Ritual and liturgical anti-structuralism, therefore exists not to destroy but to renovate social structures, and it does this not as an end in itself but in service to the general social good.[18]

The sacred in the ritual experience is the moment when humans escape their structures, stand over against them, see

---

[17]Liturgists have made extensive use of the concept of liminality especially as it has been described by Victor Turner in his book, *The Ritual Process* (Chicago: Aldine Publishing, 1969). An excellent application of this concept to modern liturgical life can be found in Mark Searle's "The Journey of Conversion," *Worship* 54:1 (January, 1980).

[18]*Elements of Rite: A Handbook of Liturgical Style* (New York: Pueblo Publishing Company, 1982), pp. 4-41.

them as if from a threshold: the moment when they can laugh at them. This experience of living in between the structures of human life is necessary for a justice-filled experience. Although liminality and social justice are not identical, ordinarily the experience of justice is a form of liminality. The liturgy that does justice is one which is enhanced through its liminal quality. It provides the possibility of an experience of God when it helps people to live in the cracks of reality. It is life in the interstices.[19]

We need to find ways to enrich the liminal character of liturgy if it is to be the rendering visible of a liturgical spirituality of justice. Much that was liminal at one time has ceased to be. Nakedness was and can be a liminal experience and attempts are being made to restore this experience to the sacrament of baptism. Clerical dress and celibacy at one time indicated life on the margins. Now they are often simply signs of status or institutional commitment. This institutionalization can weaken the challenge that is often conveyed by the liminal experience. The proclamation of the word of God in the liturgy should carry with it a liminal quality. But this is often inhibited because we have overloaded the Word with words. Thus it is that justice workers who either talk more than they act or who oppress others with their haranguing are inhibiting their effectiveness as promoters of a world where the kingdom of God can break through.

A liturgy that does justice provides for the *experience* of the justice of God as well as the justice of the worshiper or the lack of it. What is there about the liminal experience which makes it an experience of justice precisely as *experience*? One of the reasons is that the liminal is concerned with the pre-rational world. To live liminally is to participate in those dimensions of life which are not controlled by reason alone. Through this liminality we become aware of the experiences which are not

---

[19]For more on Turner's thoughts on the notion of liminality see his article, "Variations on a Theme of Liminality," as well as an article by Terence Turner, "Transformation, Hierarchy and Transcendence: A Reformulation of Van Gennep's Mode of the Structure of Rites de Passage." Both articles can be found in *Secular Ritual*, edited by Sally F. Moore and Barbara G. Myerhoff (Amsterdam: Van Gorcum, 1977).

filtered through the conceptual. Liminality is the opposite of a head trip. The liminal experience is a drive toward unity and so toward justice. The conceptualization of an experience, on the other hand, introduces division and distinction because this means placing strict limits around the experience. But at the very heart of the ritual experience is the sense of striving for oneness with the source and purpose of creation and so with one's fellow human beings. To take a simple example, for someone who experiences difficulty with exchanging the peace in the liturgy, the experience of justice in worship can only be equally or even more difficult.[20]

A second reason that liminality can enhance the experience of justice is that ritual is the combination of spontaneity and programmed activity. Both must be present. In a good human liturgy the structure is the programmed element and the anti-structure of liminality is the spontaneous component. Structures must be present in order that the reality in the cracks may shine through. The liturgy that does justice must be structured or else there will be no experience of justice at all. But even more importantly liturgy must provide for a moment of freedom from the structures of life. That is why liturgy is to be the place where the distinctions of rich and poor, male and female, wise and foolish are suspended, albeit, but temporarily. Moreover, liturgy must be concerned with the poor, the prisoners, the sick and the outcasts because they are liminal people. A purely programmed ritual will never touch these people, nor permit others to enter into their lives.

To put it succinctly, the reason that a liminal liturgy, that is, one that goes beyond the rational and which incorporates the spontaneousness of life, can be the experience of justice is that it is the liminal quality of liturgy which gives the proper perspective on what it means to be a human being. Just as it is in the experience of being human that one discovers the sacred dimension of ordinary human living, so justice begins with the human experience precisely as human. The liminal liturgy is

---

[20]Donal Dorr makes the point that the spirituality of social justice implies con-version on several levels: the religious, the moral, and the political. All are necessary for a balanced spirituality. See chapter one of his book, *Spirituality and Justice* (Maryknoll: Orbis Books, 1984).

the human liturgy is the justice-directed liturgy. Gerard Fourez, S. J., touches on this point when he speaks of the sacraments as celebrating the tensions of modern life:

> To "let the sacraments be" means, through them, to get in touch with the conflicts and contradictions of our societies and our individual lives. At the center of Christian traditions concerning the sacraments a triple dimension is found: confrontation with the gratuitousness of the gift of God, confrontation with evil and injustice, and hope of a global liberation.[21]

There are several ways in which liminality can be present in Christian ritual. First, it would have to be found in the very signs and symbols themselves. Liturgical symbols partake of both structure and anti-structure. Such symbols will both reflect contemporary life as well as use stylized forms. This means, for instance, that liturgical vesture must be recognizable clothing but that does not automatically mean that jeans or the three piece business suit become contemporary liturgical garments. Vestments must be clothing, but of a special type. Another example would be the Eucharist. The Eucharist is a human meal, but not any kind of meal. Sunday liturgy is not the same ritual experience as Sunday brunch.

Secondly, liminality is found where people have the freedom and time to be most themselves, to experience themselves with a certain wholeness and comprehensiveness. People involved in the overt and conscious structure of their lives do not have the time for insightful reflection on their relationship with God in community as well as their responsibility to society and those who are suffering from oppression. But in ritual activity which is liminal, they are placed outside the total system and its conflicts; for a moment they become a people set apart and for a while they are able to contemplate the mysteries that confront all people, the difficulties which beset their own society, their personal problems and the ways in which their

---

[21]*Sacraments and Passages* (Notre Dame: Ave Maria 1983) p. 156

wisest predecessors have sought to deal with them. This can only happen if liturgy does not reinforce anxiety, fear, or does not lay guilt trips or emphasize a negative self-image in the way it deals with sin and injustice. Both social reformers and those who are socially insensitive need liturgy so that they can be themselves for a time, so that they can be for others. In this regard it is important to remove the confusion regarding what liturgy is supposed to do in the matter of social justice. Thomas B. Shephard puts it very well:

> The Liturgical Assembly, then, is the place where justice is proclaimed, but it is neither a classroom nor a political rally nor a hearing. It is more like a rehearsal room where actions must be repeated over and over until they are thoroughly assimilated and perfected—until, that is, the actors have totally identified with the part assigned them. The liturgical action is a rehearsal of the utopian kingdom first enacted upon the human stage in meals that Jesus shared with the outcasts and sinners. In it we learn to understand the drama of God's justice as it unfolds in our world and to identify with the role assigned us so that we can play it effectively in our lives and eventually before the throne of God for all eternity, when his justice will be established beyond all compromise.[22]

Thirdly, a liminal liturgy will be one which is truly incul-turated. This means more than having the symbols of the liturgy reflect contemporary social and political structures. These symbols, because they are liminal, must also participate in anti-structure. The liminal status of symbols means that they are tied to the lives of the poor and the oppressed because they are so obviously exemplars of liminality. But they are not the only marginal people in a society. The sick and the elderly live with the ambiguity of the liminal person. The wealthy and healthy have experiences of liminality too. But we must say

[22]"Liturgy and Social Justice," reprinted in Federation of Diocesan Liturgical Commissions Newsletter 12:5 (September-October 1985), pp. 38-9.

that liturgical symbols cannot be authentic if they prescind from weakness, suffering, and poverty.

What we need to note about this final characteristic of a just liturgy is that the liminal experience of poverty is not to be confused with indigence. One does not create a liminal experience by stripping ritual of beauty, sophistication, and the aesthetically pleasing. In fact, they all enhance the communicative power of ritual. And ritual to be a justice-directed experience must be able to communicate with full symbolic energy. The liminal experience of poverty is of the kind that allows the coming to expression of that experience of separation from our cultural values where there is no distinction between rich and poor, healthy and ill, strong and weak. A liminally "poor" liturgy will never be impoverished in a human way. The irony is that it is usually those coming from situations not ordinarily associated with being oppressed, the white middle-class suburbanites, who want to denude the liturgy in the cause of social justice, claiming that they wish to move away from triumphalism. But colorfully vested black choirs and the lively Hispanic fiesta challenge such a presupposition. It is necessary to look at those usually considered to be marginal to discover the character of a liminally "poor" celebration. Donal Dorr puts it well:

> To make an option for the poor is not to opt for poverty but to opt for people. It is to commit oneself to acting and in a way that respects people, especially those who are not treated with respect in society. It is to proclaim by one's actions that people are more important than the systems that deprive them of their basic rights—the right to eat, the right to work, the right to participate in decision-making, the right to worship according to their conscience, and even the right to life itself.[23]

It has been the purpose of this chapter to detail how the socially committed liturgical assembly can be just in spirituality and in structure. Through its faith and praise it focuses and

---

[23]Dorr, *Spirituality and Justice*, p. 77.

integrates all of its ordinary activities in such a way that it creates a liminal, threshold experience in terms of which it can judge and criticize the world's provisional results as it moves toward liberation.

🌿

Bibliography

Agnew, Mary Barbara. "Liturgy and Christian Social Action," in *Liturgy* 7:4 (Spring 1989).

> This article address the gap between Liturgical theology and Christian ethics regarding the use of the term sacrifice and the conflicts emerging in the moral lives of Christians.

Avila, Rafael. *Worship and Politics*, Maryknoll: Orbis Books, 1981.

> One of the best full length discussions of liturgy and social justice. Avila insightfully moves from the biblical material to the Second Vatican Council to the documents of Medellin to suggest a reinterpretation of the Eucharist. His design for a Eucharist for the future is a contribution to sacramental theology.

Brown, Robert McAfee. *Spirituality and Liberation Overcoming the Great Fallacy*, Philadelphia: The Westminster Press, 1988.

> An excellent book which explores the dualism involved in current understanding of spirituality and liberation. The author examines many manifestations of this and suggests his own model as a solution. Of particular note is chapter 6, "Acting Out of the Clue: Liturgy and the Sacraments."

Dorr, Donal. *Spirituality and Justice*, Maryknoll: Orbis Books, 1984.

This book attempts to resolve the tension between two groups in the church: those concerned about spirituality who react to the perceived over-activism of those concerned about social justice, and those concerned about social justice who react negatively to traditional spirituality because they perceive it as lacking a social dimension. The author offers an alternative approach to this tension.

Fourez, Gerard, S. J. *Sacraments and Passages: Celebrating the Tensions of Modern Life,* Notre Dame: Ave Maria Press, 1983.

The appendix to this book is an excellent statement on the ambiguity of all liturgical celebrations today in the matter of justice.

Meehan, Francis X. *A Contemporary Social Spirituality*, Maryknoll: Orbis Books, 1982.

This presentation of a new social spirituality touches briefly on many topics such as abortion and the arms race. The chapter, "Eucharist and a Spirituality for Justice," is especially recommended.

Pannenberg, Wolfhart. "Sanctification and Politics," *Christian Spirituality*, Philadelphia: Westminister Press, 1983.

This is an attempt to link spirituality to social justice from a specifically Protestant point of view. Pannenberg is extremely critical of liberation theology.

Searle, Mark. "The Pedagogical Function of the Liturgy," *Worship* 55:4 (July 1981).

Convinced that we must use the human sciences to cast light on the meaning of liturgical celebrations, Searle utilizes the pedagogical model of Paulo Freire to reflect on how the liturgy can be an exercise of power by one group over another and how the liturgy might be capable of exercising a critical role in the mission of the church.

Steidl-Meier, Paul. *Social Justice Ministry: Foundations and Concerns*, New York: Jacq Publishing Inc., 1984.

> The author develops first some of the major theoretical aspects of justice such as diagnostic method, relational theology, and the nature of the social experience. Then he takes up several practical areas of concern such as civil authority, poverty, and population. His chapter on spirituality of social justice ministry is good background for linking liturgy and a social justice spirituality.

Willimon, William. *The Service of God: How Worship and Ethics are Related*, Nashville: Abingdon Press, 1983.

> Willimon answers the question: Does Christian worship make any difference to a Christian moral life? The first part of the book deals with the relationship of liturgy and ethics; the second part concretizes that discussion in terms of the Eucharist, preaching, marriage, and the Christian meaning of offering.

Wolterstorff, Nicholas. *Until Justice and Peace Embrace*, Grand Rapids: William B. Eerdmans Publishing Co., 1983.

> This book is written out of the conviction that Western secularism is a passing thing. It is an excellent treatment of social justice themes from a Protestant point of view, in particular, the Calvinistic perspective.

Journal of Religious Ethics 7:2 (Fall, 1979).

> This entire issue is concerned with the relationship of liturgy and ethics. This is a serious discussion by several scholars among whom are Paul Ramsey, Don Saliers, Margaret Farley, and Philip Rossi, S. J. It is a collection of essays to be pondered.

3

Christian Initiation and Social Justice

Two years had passed since Kim's friend Marsha had invited her to attend a parish festival, after Kim had expressed interest in the Catholic faith. At the festival she had been welcomed by several families of the parish. In the month that followed, two of these families had entertained her and Marsha in their homes. On one occasion, they invited her to accompany them to church on a Sunday morning. As a result of the welcome she had received, she came to the decision she had been considering for a year: to become a Catholic Christian.

At a meeting with some parish members, she explained her motives and they had welcomed her decision. At a special ceremony in September, a large number of parishioners were on hand when she and five others were formally admitted into the catechumenate. During the year and a half of the catechumenate, she always felt the concern of Marsha, who was her sponsor, and the families who had welcomed her. When she and the other catechumens met for instruction and prayer, other members of the parish were always present to pray with them and for them, to answer questions, and to provide friendly conversation afterwards, along with coffee and snacks.

Thirteen weeks ago, on the First Sunday of Lent, she had been enrolled among the "elect," those catechumens approved as ready for baptism, confirmation, and first Eucharist at Easter. The six weeks of Lent had been a period of more intense instruction and prayer. The most profound experience

had been, of course, at the Easter vigil. Then, in the midst of
the whole parish, she had been baptized and confirmed and,
for the first time, shared fully in the Eucharist by receiving
Holy Communion. The hearty singing of the gathered community that night seemed a great Amen, Yes, So Be It, to her
becoming one of them.

She and the other newly baptized had special places in the
church during the 10:30 Sunday Mass in the weeks from Easter
until now, Pentecost Sunday. The homilies during these weeks
seemed to be directed to her and the others initiated with her.
The pastor had encouraged the congregation to keep on
renewing their own lives as they continued to journey with the
catechumens and sought to enter with them more fully into
the depths of the Christian mystery celebrated in the paschal
season. Now the special Pentecost Sunday Mass concluding
the lengthy catechumenate was being celebrated. Kim had
tears in her eyes as she recalled the journey she had undertaken
in the past two years. Once she had been lonely, but now she
felt that she belonged to God, experiencing God's love and
care in the welcome of God's people gathered in this church.
As she looked around the church at the many faces which had
become familiar to her, she suddenly realized what no one of
them had ever made her conscious of in all that time—only
her face was Asian.

The story of Kim depicts baptism as we now understand it
in the light of the liturgical revisions inaugurated by Vatican
Council II.[1] Though infant baptism is a more frequent practice,
it is not the norm for understanding baptism; rather, we
comprehend baptism in the context of adult Christian initiation.[2] There baptism is united to confirmation and first
Eucharist in one celebration and situated in the catechumenate,
which precedes the sacraments of initiation to prepare candidates for their celebration, especially at the Easter vigil, and
follows their celebration to deepen the initiates' experience of
the mystery which those sacraments proclaim and actualize.

[1] See *Rites of Christian Initiation*, in *The Rites of the Catholic Church*, vol. 1 (New
York: Pueblo, 1976), pp. 1-334, especially Christian Initiation of Adults, pp. 20-39.

[2] See Aidan Kavanagh, *The Shape of Baptism: The Rite of Christian Initiation*
(New York: Pueblo, 1978), especially pp. 102-25. See also Murphy Center of Liturgical

Christian initiation notably celebrates significant moments of entrance and welcome into a community of faith. It rejoices in much more than that, of course, for it effectively signifies a meeting of God and a person in Christ in the power of the Holy Spirit. But a striking characteristic of Christian initiation is that this meeting occurs in and through a community into which a person enters by stages and which welcomes, instructs, and guides the newcomer.[3] The sacraments of initiation—baptism, confirmation, and first Eucharist—may be received together on one occasion or separately over a period of time. They are always to be understood, however, in relation to one another and as high points of incorporation into a community of faith.

A People Freed from Slavery

How is this community of faith to be defined or described? A basic answer to this question is "the people of God." The usage and importance of this ancient image for the church had been growing for several decades before a Vatican Council II in theological circles.[4] The council fathers decided, then, to devote the second chapter of the *Dogmatic Constitution on the Church* to the notion of the people of God.[5] This image

Research, *Made, Not Born: New Perspectives on Christian Initiation and the Catechumenate* (Notre Dame, Ind.: University of Notre Dame Press, 1976).

[3] See *Christian Initiation of Adults*, especially nos. 4, 11, 12, 19, 27, 37, 39, 40, 41, 49, 82, and *Rite of Baptism for Children*, especially nos. 4, 5, 9, 11, 32, 90, in *Rites of Catholic Church*. The numbers here refer to articles, or paragraphs, in *Rites*.

In the following pages of this book, the word *Rite* with a capital letter, or a title like *Rite of Christian Initiation of Adults* with initial capitals, refers to the printed text of directives and prayers which is a constitutive part of *The Roman Ritual*. The word "rite", or an expression like the "rite of infant baptism", is a general noun or name which refers to an actual ceremony, an implementation of the directives and prayers contained in the printed text.

[4] Kevin McNamara, "From Moehler to Vatican II: The Modern Movement in Ecclesiology," in Kevin McNamara, ed., *Vatican II: The Constitution on the Church* (Chicago: Franciscan Herald Press, 1968), pp. 9-35.

[5] Herbert Vorgrimler, ed., *Commentary on the Documents of Vatican II*, vol.1 (New York: Herder and Herder, 1967), pp. 110, 119. For the significance of this decision, see McNamara cited in note 4, pp. 23-24.

represents a fundamental understanding of the Christian community into which a person is initiated.[6]

But what kind of people is this "people of God"? We begin to answer that question by reaching back to the origin of this people of God recorded in the Hebrew Scriptures before the coming of Christ. There we learn that God's people are those Hebrew tribes who were liberated from slavery in Egypt by God who entered into a covenant with them. During a famine sometime in the early second millennium before Christ, the sons of Jacob migrated to Egypt to take up residence there under the protection of Joseph, their brother, who had found favor with the pharaoh and achieved great influence in the Egyptian realm. The Israelites multiplied in subsequent generations, but new rulers came to the throne of Egypt and the Israelites were eventually reduced to slavery. God, through Moses, liberated them from their oppression, leading them out of Egypt into the desert of Sinai, where God and they struck a covenant together. Thus they were forged into a national entity and eventually entered into, and took over, the land of Canaan, the "promised land."[7]

So God's people are those whose origin is in their liberation from an unjust social system in which some men and women were slaves of others. God's people are those who remember, not merely that they came out of Egypt amidst wonderful acts

[6]Rudolph Schnackenburg, *The Church of the New Testament* (New York: Herder and Herder, 1965), pp. 149-57; Hans Küng, *The Church* (New York: Sheed and Ward, 1967), pp. 107-50, especially p. 119; Doubleday Image Book edition, pp. 147-200, especially p. 162.

[7]Another theory of the underlying origins of Israel is of an eleventh-century "peasants' revolt" against oppressive Canaanite city-states—an origin which was lost to sight in the repetition of the exodus story of some of these "revolutionaries." See Leslie Hoppe, "Biblical Faith and Global Justice." *Spirituality Today* 31 (1979): 6-8 and bibliography in note 4 of the article.

A third theory holds that the settlement in Canaan took place over several generations and was not finished until the time of David. In the beginning there was no military attack on Canaanite cities but only a gradual, nomatic infiltration.

It should be noted that the ordinary expression in the Hebrew scriptures is not "people of God," but "people of Yahweh." See N. Lohfink, "The People of God-The Old Testament and the Central Concept of the Council's Verbal Fireworks," *Great Themes from the Old Testament* (Edinburgh: T. & T. Clark; Chicago: Franciscan Herald Press, 1981), 117-133.

of God, but that they came out of slavery—out of political, social, and economic oppression. "Out of Egypt, that place of slavery" is an expression characterizing God's people that reverberates through the Hebrew Scriptures (Exod.13:3, 14; 20:2; Deut. 5:6; 6:12; 8:14; 13:11; Lev. 26:3; Deut. 13:6; Jos. 24:17; Jud. 6:8; Mic. 1:4; Jer. 34:13).

As a consequence of their origin, God's people, as they are described in the Hebrew scriptures, were, at their best, passionate for justice. The very covenant by which God bound the Israelites together, and specifically the Ten Commandments, concerned just relations between God and God's people. They were to render God the worship rightfully owed to their savior and creator. Just relations among the people themselves were also stressed: you shall not kill, commit adultery, steal, lie, covet—these are commands to respect others' rights; they are basic imperatives for a just social order. Chapters 21 and 22 of the Book of Exodus provide detailed regulations regarding slaves, personal injury, property damage, trusts and loans, and social relationships. The covenant, then, was not a purely "spiritual" bond between God and individual Israelites; it was a bond between God and a whole people and between the members of that people. The bond was incarnate in what for that day and age was a just social order, in contrast to the unjust system from which the Israelites had been liberated. In the collection of laws in the Book of Deuteronomy, the reason of a law is frequently stated: "For remember that you were once slaves in Egypt" (Deut.5:15; 15:15; 16:12; 24:18, 22).

Samuel was reluctant to accede to the people's request for a king. He foresaw that having a king would lead to an unjust social structure. The Lord told Samuel to appoint a king as requested, but to warn the people of what the king would demand of them. So Samuel announced to the people:

> The rights of the king who will rule you will be as follows: he will take your sons and assign them to his chariots and horses, and they will run before his chariot. He will also appoint from among them his commanders of groups of a thousand and of a hundred soldiers. He will set them to do his plowing and his harvesting, and to make his implements of war and the equipment of his chariots. He will use your

daughters as ointment makers, as cooks, as bakers. He will take the best of your field, vineyards, and olive groves, and give them to his officials. He will tithe your crops and give the revenue to his eunuchs and slaves. He will take your male and female servants, as well as your best oxen and asses, and use them to do his work. He will tithe your flocks and you yourselves will become his slaves. (1 Sam. 8:11-17)

Yes, those who had been liberated from slavery to the Egyptians would again become slaves to their own flesh and blood in a society organized for the benefit of an elite.

What Samuel feared, the prophets of later ages decried as the sad plight of God's people. Amos declared:

Thus says the Lord:
. . .they sell the just man (woman) for silver,
   and the poor man (woman) for a pair of sandals.
They trample the heads of the weak
   into the dust of the earth
   and force the lowly out of the way. . .
Upon garments taken in pledge,
   they recline beside my altar,
And the wine of those who have been fined
   they drink in the house of their God.

(2:6-8)

And Isaiah warned:
   Woe to those who enact unjust statutes
   and who write oppressive decrees,
Depriving the needy of judgment
   and robbing my people's poor of their rights,
Making their widows their plunder,
   and orphans their prey!

(10:1-2)

God's people, once liberated from unjust oppression, fell again into the evils from which they had been freed. Israel became a corrupt society. Because of its corruption, God would allow it to be purged by the suffering brought on by its sins. The prophets criticized the Israelites' worship because it was hollow, empty, for it was not accompanied by justice toward fellow human beings (Isa. 1:10-17; 58:2-14; Jer. 6:18-21; 7:2-15; Hos. 6:6; Amos 5:21-25; Mic. 6:6-8).

Out of misery was born messianic hope, the expectation that God would once again liberate God's people from injustice. God would send an Anointed One, the *Messiah*, to free the people from the injustice among themselves in their own nation, and from the injustice they suffered as a vassal nation and slave of foreign powers: the Assyrians, Babylonians, Persians, Greeks, and Romans.

So the history of God's people in the Hebrew scriptures is framed by the theme of social justice and injustice. God's people are those who were liberated from injustice in order to live according to a just social order, who failed, who were punished by the consequences of their sins, but who were continually called to justice by God's prophets and began to look to God to liberate them once again from injustice.

A People Freed by Jesus

The followers of Jesus, after his resurrection, gradually came to see themselves as the people of God.[8] The author of the First Letter of Peter addresses his Christian audience: "You are ... a people he claims for his own... Once you were no people, but now you are God's people..." (2:9-10). Paul writes to the Corinthians: "You are the temple of the living God, just as God has said: 'I will dwell with them and walk among them. I will be their God and they shall be my people'" (2 Cor. 6:16).

The story of this "new" people of God, or, better, this offshoot of God's people once called out of Egyptian slavery, is also framed by the theme of justice and injustice. Their origin was in Jesus of Nazareth, the Just One, whom some Jewish and Roman officials unjustly crucified, but whom God raised from the dead. Jesus as the Just One (or Righteous One) is one of the earliest ways of understanding who Jesus is.[9] In the synagogue of Nazareth he announced himself as

---

[8]Schnackenburg, *Church in the New Testament*, pp. 150-52; Küng, *The Church*, pp. 119-25; Image Book ed., pp. 161-68.

[9]Richard N. Longenecker, *The Christology of Early Jewish Christianity* (Naperville,

fulfilling the prophecy of Isaiah by "bringing glad tidings to the poor, proclaiming liberty to captives, recovery of sight to the blind, release to prisoners, and a year of favor from the Lord" (Isa. 61:1-2; Luke 4:16-21). In him God was again liberating the chosen people.

Mary's canticle recorded in Luke's Gospel is a song of liberation from social injustice. God looked upon Mary, a lowly servant, and the fruit of that mercy is not only her being called blessed for all ages, but the end of injustice, for what God has wrought in her,

> He has deposed the mighty from their thrones
>   and raised the lowly to high places.
> The hungry he has given every good thing,
>   while the rich he has sent empty away.
>
> (Luke 1:52-53)

In these words the early Christian community expressed understanding that the coming of Jesus meant a new social order. They did not have a definite economic plan, or a political program, or specific social reform to offer, but they knew that in Christ there was to be no injustice, no oppression. "You know that those who exercise authority among the gentiles lord it over them; their great ones make their importance felt. It cannot be like that with you. Anyone among you who aspires to greatness must serve the rest" (Matt. 20:25-26). So the early Christians endeavored to live in this new way, although they probably did not succeed in matching the picture which Luke paints of the early Christian community.

> The community of believers were of one heart and one mind. None of them ever claimed anything as his (her) own; rather, everything was held in common ... nor was there any needy among them, for all who owned property or

houses sold them and donated the proceeds. They used to lay them at the feet of the apostles to be distributed to everyone according to his (her) need. (Acts 4:32, 34-35)

If slavery remained among the early Christians, it was to be in a new spirit, as Paul's Letter to Philemon and the Letter to the Ephesians (6:5-9) indicated—a spirit of loving care for another human being redeemed in Christ, not a spirit of exploiting an inferior person for one's own advantage.

Yes, slaves were among the new people of God. In fact, many, though by no means all, converts to the new people of God came from the lower, poorer strata of society. Paul was not simply using rhetoric when he wrote to the Corinthians:

> Consider your situation. Not many of you are wise, as men (and women) account wisdom; not many are influential; and surely not many are well-born. God chose those whom the world considers absurd to shame the wise; he singled out the weak of this world to shame the strong. He chose the world's lowborn and despised, those who count for nothing, to reduce to nothing those who were something, so that humanity can do no boasting before God. (1 Cor. 1:26-29).

The synoptic Gospels contain the early Christians' remembrances of the parables which Jesus told, his activities of healing, his teachings, his discussions with the Pharisees, the Sadducees, and the scribes learned in the law. What did they remember? They remembered that he cared for the "poor," the *anawim*, the "little people," who were looked down upon by the rich and politically powerful Establishment. They recalled his concern for the sick, the crippled, the blind, the mentally ill, and the demonically possessed—the people who are a nuisance to have around. They recollected his care for lepers, who were forced to live outside the city, and the "fallen" women and the "sinners," people who did not, or simply could not, live up to the law regarded as the norm by the Establishment.[10]

---

[10]Albert Nolan, *Jesus before Christianity* (Maryknoll, N.Y.: Orbis books, 1978), pp. 21-29.

They remembered his openness to the hated tax collectors, the publicans, who worked for foreign interests. They portrayed the first people to hear the good news of Jesus' birth as shepherds, lowly people, a group who, in latter times, were assigned a place on Jewish lists of despised employments.[11]

The new people of God, aware of Jesus' concern for the *anawim*, the "little ones," expected to see a new order because of the Christ-event, as the canticle of Mary proclaims. Their expectation of Christ's return, the parousia, was an expectation that soon they would experience a new creation where justice among men and women would reign. Their eager longing for the return of the risen Lord was hunger and thirst for social justice.

The new people of God today still think of themselves, at least theoretically, as "coming out of Egypt, that place of slavery" and existing for the poor. When the conciliar fathers of Vatican II expressed their church's self-understanding for the present era of history, they wrote: "Christ was sent by the Father 'to bring good news to the poor . . . to heal the contrite of heart' (Luke 4:18). . . . Similarly, the church encompasses with her (sic) love all those who are afflicted by human misery and she recognizes in those who are poor and who suffer, the image of her poor and suffering founder. She does all in her power to relieve their need and in them she strives to serve Christ."[12]

Seeking Justice as Members of Christ's Body

The "new" people of God is distinguished from God's people whose story we read in the Hebrew Scriptures because this

---

[11] Joachim Jeremias, *Jerusalem in the Time of Jesus* (Philadephia: Fortress Press, 1969), pp. 305-6, 310. In Luke's reference to the shepherds at Bethlehem, however, Joseph Fitzmyer thinks that Luke's intent was simply to focus on lowly people, and his biblical heritage provided sufficient justification for his associating shepherds with Bethlehem (*The Gospel according to Luke I-IX*, Anchor Bible 28 [Garden City, N.Y.: Doubleday, 1981], p. 396).

[12] *Constitution on the Church*, no. 8, in Austin Flannery, ed., *Vatican Council II: The Conciliar and Post Conciliar Documents* (Collegeville: Liturgical Press, 1975), p. 358.

"new" people is the body of Christ.[13] "You, then, are the body of Christ. Everyone of you is a member of it," Paul wrote to the Corinthians (1 Cor. 12:27). What does this image tell us of the community into which one enters and is welcomed by the rites of Christian initiation? To answer this question, we will reflect on each of the sacraments of initiation.

To enter through baptism into the Christian community as the body of Christ is to participate sacramentally in the death and resurrection of Jesus. We participate sacramentally in the death and resurrection of Jesus insofar as, through the baptismal rite, God graces us, in virtue of the death and resurrection of Jesus, with the Holy Spirit, who henceforth dwells in us and transforms our being, making us a new creation by forgiving our sins, inspiring in us faith, hope, and love, and uniting us in the one body of Christ which is the church, for witness to God's mercy and for service of our fellow human beings.

Certain qualities of life will characterize a people who are graced by this participation in Christ's paschal mystery. They will be a people "dead to sin but alive for God" (Rom. 6:11). That means, on the one hand, that they will strive to root sin out of their lives. Among the sins they will seek to eradicate is injustice of every sort. In the baptismal rite of the United Methodist Church, the candidate is asked: "Do you renounce the bondage of sin and the injustices of this world...?"[14] Those injustices include lifestyles and social structures which give unfair advantage to some over others.

On the other hand, a people "alive for God" will seek to do her will. The great commandments are, of course, to love God above all things and neighbor as self (Mark 12:29-31). But love, compassion, and mercy toward neighbor must respect and promote the God-given dignity and rights of every person. Among the questions in the *Book of Common Prayer* put to candidates for baptism is this: "Will you strive for justice and peace among all people and respect the dignity of every human

---

[13]Schnackenburg, *Church in the New Testament*, p. 142.

[14]*We Gather Together: Services of Public Worship*, Supplemental Worship Resources 10 (Nashville: United Methodist Publishing House, 1980), p. 13.

being?"[15] Such striving and respect includes establishing a social order which reverences and fosters human dignity and rights. To work for a just society is to love others according to God's will. Vatican II could declare that "forms of social or cultural discrimination in basic personal rights on the grounds of sex, race, color, social conditions, language, or religion, must be curbed and eradicated as incompatible with God's design."[16]

Among the baptized a certain egalitarianism is at work primarily in the spiritual order, the realm of God's gift of the spirit, as St. Paul affirms: "All of you who have been baptized into Christ have clothed yourselves with him. There does not exist among you Jew or Greek, slave or freeperson, male or female. All are one in Christ. Furthermore, if you belong to Christ you are descendants of Abraham, which means you inherit all that was promised" (Gal. 3:28-29).

In the course of time, Christians have seen that this egalitarianism extends in some way to the social order also. The primitive Christian community shared their material wealth so that no one was needy (Acts 2:44-45: 4:32-35). Much later in Christian history, slavery, which was long accepted in the church, eventually was seen to be unjust and un-Christian. In our own day we are witnessing a growing awareness of the basic equality (which is not "sameness") of women and men— an awareness testified to in Vatican II's statement: "It is regrettable that these basic personal rights are not being respected everywhere, as is the case with women who are denied the chance freely to choose a husband, or a state of life, or to have access to the same educational and cultural benefits as are available to men."[17]

To enter into, and be welcomed by, God's people through baptism and so share in the death and resurrection of Jesus is to become a member of a community dead to sin, to injustice in all its forms, and alive for God, therefore committed to establishing justice. This justice will be in one's own personal

---

[15] *The Book of Common Prayer* (New York: Church Hymnal Corporation, 1979), p. 305.

[16] *Constitution on the Church in the Modern World*, no. 29, in Flannery, p. 929.

[17] Ibid.

dealings with individuals, in the Christian community's organization, and in the structures of the world to which this Christian community is sent in mission to bring the message and grace of Christ and renew the temporal order.[18]

Baptism has traditionally been called "the sacrament of faith." It expresses the faith of the church and of the candidate. It is the first sacrament sought by a person who comes to Christian faith from unbelief and desires to express his or her faith sacramentally. Before conferring the sacrament, the Christian community expects a profession of faith from an adult recipient and includes a profession in the rite of adult baptism.[19] In the rite of baptism for children, the parents and godparents make a profession of faith immediately before the baptism itself and the presider concludes with the words: "This is our faith. This is the faith of the Church. We are proud to profess it, in Christ Jesus our Lord."[20] The presider then proceeds to baptize the child "in the name of the Father, and of the Son, and of the Holy Spirit"—the very action and formula constituting a profession of faith in the triune God revealed by Jesus and in the gift of the Spirit.

How are we to understand this faith which is signified in baptism? We are not asking here about the object, or content, of the faith, but about the quality of the act of faith. Avery Dulles has shown that different aspects of faith have been emphasized in diverse periods of history or among different groups of Christians.[21] Patristic and medieval understanding stressed the intellectual aspect of faith. Faith was spoken of mainly, though not exclusively, in terms of revelation, know-

---

[18]Vatican Council II, *Decree on the Apostolate of the Laity*, nos. 5-7, in Flannery, pp. 772-75; Francis Schussler Fiorenza, "The Church's Religious Identity and Its Social Political Mission," *Theological Studies* 43 (1982): 197-225.

[19] *Rite of Christian Initiation of Adults*, no. 219, in *Rites of Catholic Church*, p. 99; *Book of Common Prayer* p. 304; *We Gather Together*, p. 14; *The Worshipbook: Services and Hymns* (Philadelphia: Westminister Press, 1972), p. 44 (note also rubric on p. 43); *Lutheran Book of Worship* (Minneapolis: Augsburg 1978), p. 213.

[20] *Rite of Baptism for Children*, nos. 58-59, in *Rites of Catholic Church*, p. 207.

[21]Avery Dulles, "The Meaning of Faith Considered in Relationship to Justice," in John C. Haughey, ed., *The Faith That Does Justice* (New York: Paulist Press, 1977), pp. 10-46.

ing, seeing, light, and truth. At the time of the Reformation among Protestants, and among Catholics today who take a personalist approach, the trust factor in faith has been emphasized—reliance on the power and fidelity of God to effect what he has promised in revelation. More recently, liberation theologians have stressed the commitment factor in faith. This most recent approach focuses strongly on the importance of living the faith that one professes, putting faith into practice. The revealed vision that faith is meant to provide can be seen only if one tries to live what faith points to; the trust and hope involved in faith can be experienced only if one strives to put into practice what God asks. So faith without a corresponding life and practice really cannot be genuine faith. It is defective, even dead.

According to the letter of James, "Faith without works is as dead as a body without breath" (2:26). That statement has long been interpreted to mean faith without love and the deeds of love is dead; now it is being interpreted to include that aspect of love and deeds of love which is justice:[22] faith without active pursuit of justice is dead. So baptism as the sacrament of faith refers to integral faith—faith that is animated by love, as has been said for centuries, but also faith that does justice, as is emphasized in our day when we are so keenly aware of injustice on a global scale.[23]

In view of the origin and call of the community into which baptism initiates a person, the Presbyterian *Worshipbook* appropriately contains a prayer after baptism saying: "God our Father: we praise you for calling us to be a servant people."[24] After the baptism, the minister and an elder representing the session greet the newly baptized member with words indicative of the active pursuit of loving justice upon which she or he has embarked in joining this community: "Welcome to the ministry of Jesus Christ."[25]

---

[22]See Dulles, "Meaning of Faith," pp. 42-44; Christopher Kiesling, "Social Justice in Christian Life according to Thomas Aquinas," *Spirituality Today* 31 (1979): 236-39.

[23]Stanley Parmisano, "Social Justice: The Broader Perspective," *Spirituality Today* 37 (1985): 15-18.

[24]*Worshipbook*, p. 46.

[25]Ibid.

Confirmation complements baptism by manifesting in words and actions the wonderful gift of the Holy Spirit dwelling in God's people through baptism.[26] As a result of the celebration of confirmation, our minds and hearts are opened more fully to the Spirit's influence in our lives. But who is this Spirit whose coming to us is celebrated especially in this sacrament? It is the Spirit of Jesus who, in the synagogue at Nazareth, as we have seen above, declared that he had come to liberate God's people in fulfillment of Isaiah's prophecy (Luke 4:17-21).

The Spirit celebrated in confirmation is, then, among other things, a Spirit of liberation from oppression, injustice, and physical evil. This is the Spirit which is poured out on the newly baptized to strengthen them and anoint them to be more like Christ.[27] This is the Spirit whom God is invoked to send as helper and guide.[28] If the Spirit will give the newly baptized "the spirit of knowledge and reverence,"[29] the purpose, in part, is to enable the newly confirmed to share in the community's mission to evangelize, sanctify, and renew the temporal order.

Through celebration of confirmation, we are made more aware of the heights of holiness to which God invites every Christian and for which God empowers us through God's indwelling Spirit. To become a member of God's people through confirmation is to be quickened by the hope, the great expectation, engendered by the Spirit of Christ. For what is this great expectation?

It is for the final coming of God's reign, when God's will shall be done perfectly on earth as in heaven, when Christ will hand over his kingdom to the Father/Mother and God will be "all in all" (1 Cor. 15:24, 28), when God's designs for creation will be fulfilled. There will be "a new heaven and a new earth" (Rev. 21:1). God shall "wipe away every tear ... and there shall be no more mourning, crying out or pain" (Rev. 21:4).

[26]Christopher Kiesling, *Confirmation and Full Life in the Spirit* (Cincinnati: St. Anthony Messenger Press, 1973), pp.74-79.

[27] *Rite of Christian Initiation of Adults*, no. 229, in *Rites of Catholic Church*, p. 103.

[28]Ibid. no. 230, in *Rites of Catholic Church*, pp. 103-4.

[29]Ibid.

Those who hunger for justice shall be satisfied at last (Matt. 5:6).

We are called by the sacrament of confirmation, then, to strive by our labors to realize the potentialities of nature and humanity and grace; that is our God-given vocation—to work for the betterment of humanity, to tend the garden of nature which God has entrusted to our care (Gen. 1:28; 2:15), and to make fruitful the gifts of grace bestowed on us (John 15:5, 8; 16:16). "That men and women, working in harmony, should renew the temporal order and make it increasingly more perfect: such is God's design for the world."[30]

But the ultimate fulfillment is God's work, not ours. What we can achieve, even with the help of God's grace, is limited because of our finite energies and our sinfulness. The potential of humanity, moreover, what humanity may come to be, is unknown to us; we can never say that we have achieved all that is possible. Furthermore, "eye has not seen, ear has not heard, nor has it so much as dawned on men and women what God has prepared for those who love him" (1 Cor. 2:9, referring to Isa. 64:3). So whatever degree of love of God and neighbor we attain in this life, even though it is by God's grace, there can always be a more perfect love. Likewise, however just the laws and social structures of any society appear to be, however fairly the resources of the earth seem to be shared, there will always be room for improvement. The people of God, therefore, can never rest content with the social, economic, political status quo.

To enter into the people of God through confirmation, then, is to join a community driven by the Spirit of Christ to work ceaselessly for ever more perfect justice in one's own life, in the church, and in secular society, never being content with the current state of affairs, but always striving for a more perfect church and society, until God finally establishes God's reign.

Baptism indicates that the initiates into the Christian community are dead to sin and alive for God. Confirmation

[30]Vatican Council II, *Decree on the Apostolate of the Laity*, no. 7, in Flannery, p. 773.

declares that nothing less than the very Spirit of God is given to dwell in them to help guide them toward an awesome goal—holiness of life. First Eucharist announces that these gifts, their preservation, their growth, and the fulfillment of the promise they contain for the future come through intimacy with Jesus Christ in his death and resurrection, and through communion with his sisters and brothers, members of his body, the church.[31]

In their first Eucharist, the initiates join the Christian community in its most sacred action. They share in the community's *anamnesis* (remembrance-making-present) of Jesus' death and resurrection as the community partakes of the meal of bread and wine which he gave his disciples to celebrate in *anamnesis* of him: "Do this *anamnesis* of me" (Luke 22:19). In faith, hope, and love the initiates eat the bread which is Christ's body given for us and drink the wine which is his blood shed for us. They are most intimately united to Jesus who, having died, now lives and reigns with God in glory. They unite their self-suffering to God with Jesus' self-offering manifested in his death on Calvary, forever accepted by God in Jesus' resurrection, and expressed sacramentally in the Eucharist so that we can be united with it. At the same time, the initiates are united to the members of the Christian community, for they have access to this intimate communion with Jesus only through the community's *anamnesis* in the sacrificial meal; and by union with the head of the ecclesial body they are united to his members.

For our theme, we need to reflect further on this Jesus to whom the initiates—and indeed all Christians—unite themselves in the Eucharist; and we need to consider the union with other Christians effected through communion with Jesus. The Jesus to whom all eucharistic participants are united is the Jesus mentioned by Paul in Philippians 2:7 and 2 Corinthians 8:9: "He emptied himself and took the form of a slave" and "for your sake he made himself poor though he was rich, so that you might become rich by his poverty."[32] Jesus emptied

[31]Kiesling, *Confirmation,* pp. 92-95.

[32]See comments on these passages by J.M.R. Tillard, *The Project of Poverty and*

himself; he claimed no possessions: "The son of man has nowhere to lay his head" (Matt. 8:20). He renounced any show of power in self-defense: "Put back your sword ....Do you not suppose I can call on my Father to provide ... more than twelve legions of angels?" (Matt. 26:52-53). Like a slave, he subjected himself to the will of others. He did not force his message on the people to whom he was sent, but gave them a choice to accept it or reject it. He went further: he allowed himself to be maltreated and crucified. He was poor, both in the spiritual sense of humble, that is, dependent only on God, and in the material sense of not having a lot of possessions.

He was all this for the sake of others, that they might enjoy the blessings of the messianic reign. His poverty of spirit and lack of material wealth were not mere asceticism, self-denial for its own sake, or proof of self-control, or disdain for self and material goods. No, they were embraced so that others might enjoy the justice inherent in messianic fulfillment: "In justice shall you be established, far from the fear of oppression, where destruction cannot come near you" (Isa. 54: 14). As the servant of God introducing the messianic age (Luke 4:16-21), Jesus emptied himself and became poor that we might have justice.

The initiates at the Easter vigil, all of us at every Eucharist, declare ourselves most intimately one with Jesus by eating and drinking sacramentally his body and blood, his bodily self. Our desire, then, will be to think, feel, and act in ways consistent with this sacramental action. We will put on the disposition of heart which Jesus himself manifested. We will strive to empty ourselves, become poor in a biblical sense, for the sake of others. We will seek to be humble, relying not on physical power but upon God for our security. We will limit, even give up, material wealth as a concrete expression of that poverty of spirit. But this dispossession of ourselves will not be simple asceticism or disdain for created reality. As in Jesus' case, its purpose will be that others may benefit in many ways,

---

the Demands of the Gospel (Ottawa, Ontario, Canada: Canadian Religious Conference, 1979), pp. 20-21. This entire essay is especially informative and inspiring in regard to the meaning of voluntary poverty for Christian faith.

indeed, but specifically in their gaining justice. To the extent that we are not grasping for material wealth, are not preoccupied with our own security through physical means, we are free to change our life style, alter our standard of living, and forego our convenience in order that others may have their dignity, their rights, and their fair share of the earth's resources, which is now denied to them in the present world order. To identify with the eucharistic Jesus is to be transformed in our innermost being to become radically agents of social justice.

Kim, whose story opened this chapter, did not experience racial discrimination in the community into which she was initiated. Racial discrimination—or any other sort of injustice—has no rightful place among God's people. Indeed, God's people are called to promote God's reign of justice, not only among themselves, but in the whole world. That is the community into which we are incorporated by the liturgy of Christian initiation.

※

Bibliography

Boff, Leonardo. *Liberating Grace*, Maryknoll: Orbis Books, 1979.

> Boff places the traditional understanding of the key theological concept of grace in a liberation theology context. Because grace is so closely associated with the sacraments of initiation, what Boff says of grace applies to these sacraments.

Duggan, Robert, ed. *Conversion and the Catechumenate*, New York: Paulist Press, 1984.

> This collection of essays deals with the various aspects of conversion which are either presupposed by, or which

accompany, adult initiation. James Dunning in particular describes the social dimensions of conversion.

Egan, John P. with Colford, Paul D. *Baptism of Resistance and Blood and Celebration*, Mystic, Conn: Twenty-Third Publications, 1983.

This is a popular and personal statement by a priest activist about baptism and Christian witness. Egan warns of the suffering that will come to those who live out their baptismal promises to fight against injustice.

Fourez, Gerard S.J. "Baptism: Liberated or Crushed by Human Community," *Sacraments and Passages: Celebrating the Tensions of Modern Life,* Notre Dame: Ave Maria Press, 1983.

The sacrament of baptism as a rite of passage is the celebration of hope in an oppressive society. Baptism speaks of community solidarity in its symbols and its challenges to the Christian.

Ganoczy, Alexander. *Becoming Christian: A Theology of Baptism as the Sacrament of Human History*, New York: Paulist Press, 1976.

The author maintains that baptism makes most sense when it is seen as the sacrament of human history. Thus, the sacrament is placed in the context of a movement toward individual and social freedom. Ganoczy says we must include social progress and self-actualization as part of the salvific process.

Happel, Stephen. "Rites of Initiation and the Politics of Cooperation," in *Liturgy* 7:4 (Spring 1989).

In this article the author explores the relationship between the sacraments of initiation and the social dimension by focussing on the specific meaning of sacramental cooperation.

Haughey, John C., S.J. "The Eucharist and Intentional Communities," in *Alternative Futures for Worship: Vol. 3: The Eucharist*, edited by Bernard J. Lee, S.M., Collegeville: The Liturgical Press, 1987.

> This is an analysis of the eucharist and intentional communities from the perspective of the North American church. It proposes a eucharistic paradigm, in dialogue with Paul and the Corinthian community, which calls for a change of consciousness that moves from self interest to the formation of communitarian individuals.

O'Hare, Padraic, ed. *Education for Peace and Justice*, San Francisco: Harper and Row, 1983.

> This series of essays deals with the various aspects of social justice and religious education. They are important for the ways in which they bring to our attention what must follow upon the celebration of the sacrament.

Segundo, Juan Luis, S. J. *The Sacraments Today*, Maryknoll: Orbis Books, 1974.

> This classic application of liberation theology to the sacraments applies cogently to our initiation practices today. To be noted, is the author's answer to the question: infant baptism: is it still meaningful?

Wainwright, Geoffrey. *Christian Initiation,* Richmond: John Knox Press, 1969.

> This ecumenical discussion of initiation concludes with a chapter on initiation and mission. Although it is somewhat dated, it still raises some important pastoral issues.

White, James F. *Sacraments as God's Self Giving*, Nashville: Abingdon Press, 1983.

> James White, an eminent Protestant liturgist, includes in this book a chapter on sacraments and justice. His discussion of baptism and justice is concrete and to the point.

_____. *Worship* 56:4 (July 1982).

This issue contains John McKenna's article, "Liturgy: Toward Liberation or Oppression?" as well as several others on the RCIA. These latter serve as necessary background for a discussion of the relationship of social justice to Christian initiation.

4

The Lectionary:
Justice in the Liturgical Year

In the Roman rite of the baptism of a child, among the ceremonies following the washing with water, the presider, touching the ears and then the mouth of the newly baptized (cf. Mark 7:32-35), says: "The Lord Jesus made the deaf hear and the dumb speak. May he soon touch your ears to receive his word, and your mouth to proclaim his faith, to the praise and glory of God the Father."[1]

Christian initiation thus leads to hearing the word of God and to bearing witness to the faith affirmed in baptism. To nourish themselves on the word of God and to express their belief publicly, the members of the Christian community assemble on Sundays for the liturgy of the word and the Eucharist. On these occasions the word of God is presented in the church's *Lectionary*, the book which distributes biblical passages to be read throughout the year.[2] Does the word of

---

[1] *Rite of Baptism for Children*, nos. 65-66, in The *Rites of the Catholic Church*, vol. 1 (New York: Pueblo Publishing Company, 1976), p. 210. In the *Rite of Christian Initiation of Adults*, the same ritual is entitled "Rite of Ephphetha or Opening of Ears and Mouth" (nos. 200-2, in *Rites of Catholic Church*, p. 91). In the rite for adults, this ceremony is offered as a preparatory rite which may be performed on Holy Saturday before the Easter vigil.

[2] For an understanding of the origin and structure of the *Lectionary*, see William Skudlarek, *The Word in Worship: Preaching in a Liturgical Context* (Nashville: Abingdon, 1981), especially pp. 11-64. References to the lectionary in this chapter refer to the *Roman Lectionary*.

God addressing us through the *Lectionary* in the course of the
year speak to us about social justice? Before answering this
question, let us first note carefully what we are dealing with
here, namely, the word of God.

Characteristics of the Word of God

The word of God is not merely some words printed in a
book. We are reflecting, rather, on a word of God proclaimed
in public reading in the assembly of Christians. We are looking
at the Christian community's activity announcing the good
news of God's love intervening in history, fully revealing itself
in the death and resurrection of Jesus, and moving toward the
fulfillment of the promise of a new creation. In the community's activity, *God* is active. Through the proclamation
which touches our ears, quickens our imaginations, arouses
our memories, and disposes us for insights which discern God's
message for us, God acts upon us. Simultaneously God acts
within us through the indwelling Spirit both to enlighten us, so
that we grasp God's word for us, and to strengthen us, so that
we may respond in deeds.[3] We are inquiring, then, about a
contemporary, living word from God now in this our day (cf.
1 Cor. 10:11; Rom. 15:4; 2 Tim. 3:16).[4]

This word, moreover, expresses *the* word of God incarnate,
Jesus Christ. Jesus Christ addresses us in the church's proclamation. Through the witness of the apostolic writings, we
encounter Jesus Christ himself calling us to conversion, even
as he called the Jewish people of Palestine nearly two thousand
years ago (Mark 1:14-15). The message he offers is himself:
"Come, follow me" (Mark 1:17, 2:14).

[3]Cf. Thomas Aquinas, *Summa Theologiae*, II-II, ques. 6, art. 1. See Vatican Council
II, *Constitution on Revelation*, nos. 2 and 5, in Austin Flannery, *Vatican II: Conciliar
and Post Conciliar Documents*. (Collegeville: Liturgical Press, 1975), pp. 750-52.

[4]For a comprehensive theological appreciation of the word of God, see Karl Rahner
and others, *The Word: Readings in Theology* (New York: P. J. Kennedy, 1964),
especially the essays by Rahner, Latourelle, Leonard, A.Q: Boff, Schillebeeckx, and
Semmelroth. See also Vatican Council II, *Constitution on Divine Revelation*,
especially chapter 6: "Sacred Scripture in the Life of the Church," in Flannery, pp.
762-65.

The liturgy's proclamation of the word, then, is not simply conveying some information which it may be convenient or "nice" to know but which, whether we know it or not, makes no real difference in our lives. No, this word presents us a choice which we cannot avoid and which has consequences for our lives. "Here, then, I have today set before you life and prosperity, death and doom. If you obey the commandments of the Lord, your God, ... you will live ... if, however, you turn your hearts and will not listen ... you will certainly perish (Deut. 31:15-18; cf. Matt. 7:24, 26).

Because the word of God we are concerned with in the liturgical assembly is a living word of God and not simply a written text or bulletin of information, those who read the scriptures are called upon—in justice to the community—to study and meditate upon the passages they are to read in order that they may hear the Word of God, Jesus Christ, speaking in the scripture—and speaking a message of social justice. If readers do not hear the One who speaks and grasp his message, how can they proclaim it to others? Beyond that, readers must prepare for their actual verbalization of the text before the assembly. Their pace of pronunciation, tones of voice, and emphasis can make clear the message or obscure it, make it a "living and effective word" of God (Heb. 4:12) or the clumsy recital of meaningless words.[5]

To answer the question now whether the word of God presented in the *Lectionary* throughout the year challenges us to pursue social justice, let us examine some selections from the *Lectionary*. No attempt is made here to do an exhaustive study of the *Lectionary* and how it contains a call for social justice. What follows is intended to suggest how one can discover a justice-oriented spirituality in the liturgical readings.

The Ugly Reality of Injustice

Chapter 21 from the First Book of Kings provides the first

---

[5]An excellent help for readers of the word of God which takes into account not only the meaning but also the manner of reading is the book *Celebrating Liturgy: The Book for Lectors and Gospel Readers*, published annually by Liturgy Training Publications, Archdiocese of Chicago, 1800 N. Heritage Ave., Chicago, IL 60622.

scripture reading for Monday of the eleventh week in even numbered years. It is about Ahab, king of Samaria. He wanted the vineyard of Naboth in Jezreel for a vegetable garden, since it was next to the royal palace. In exchange, Ahab offered Naboth a better vineyard or a suitable amount of money. But Naboth could not bring himself to give up his heritage and refused the king. Ahab was angry. When Jezebel, his wife, asked him why he was so angry, he recounted his offer to Naboth and his refusal. Jezebel scoffed at him for giving up so easily. She assured him she would see that he got the vineyard of Naboth. Using Ahab's name and royal seal, she sent letters to the elders and nobles of Naboth's hometown. She directed them to assemble the people for a fast, get two scoundrels to accuse Naboth of cursing God and the king, then stone Naboth to death. The elders and nobles did as Jezebel directed them and sent word to Jezebel that Naboth was dead. She informed Ahab that he was now free to take possession of Naboth's vineyard because he had died. Ahab then took over Naboth's property for his vegetable garden.

This story is not pleasant. We would hardly call it inspirational. But like so many biblical passages, it confronts us boldly with the world in which we live—a world full of nature's wonders and of human warmth, but also a world full of injustice and a host of related vices. It challenges us to respond to this world, respond both to its loveliness and to its moral corruption, as Jesus responded and would respond today.

A reading from the prophet Amos (8:4-7) on the twenty-fifth Sunday of the year, cycle C, is not as graphic as the passage from First Kings in portraying injustice in our world, but it does refer straightforwardly to those "who trample upon the needy and destroy the poor of the land," who are eager for the Sabbath or any religious feast to be over, so that they may sell their produce and cheat others; they will "buy the lowly man (woman) for silver and the poor man for a pair of sandals." In the example of the steward who saves his own neck by cheating his employer—the Gospel (Luke 16:1-13) for the twenty-fifth Sunday, cycle C—Jesus acknowledges the uncanny cleverness with which injustice insinuates itself into society.

The excessively luxurious life of the rich is criticized in

Amos 6:1,4-7, read on the twenty-sixth Sunday of the year, cycle C, along with the Gospel of Luke's account of Lazarus and the self-centered rich man (16:19-31), "who dressed in purple and linen and feasted splendidly every day. At his gate lay a beggar named Lazarus who was covered with sores. Lazarus longed to eat the scraps that fell from the rich man's table." But Lazarus was ignored.

Favoritism, failure to meet the bodily needs of a brother or sister, and roots of injustice like uncontrolled desires and envy—all of which maladies become ingrained in the social system and propagate themselves from one generation to the next —are excoriated in the reading from the Letter of James in the B cycle for the twenty-third to the twenty-fifth Sundays of the year (2:1-5; 2:14-18; 3:16-4:3).

John the Baptizer's admonitions to the crowds, the tax collectors, and the soldiers about their just behavior are recalled in the Gospel of Luke 3:10-18 on the third Sunday of Advent, cycle C. The sharing of goods by the members of the early Christian community at Jerusalem, so that there was no one needy among them (Acts 4:32-35), is recounted in the first reading of the second Sunday of Easter in the B cycle.

In the pericopes noted so far, the question of injustice or justice is on the surface. Often, however—too often, indeed— we have to dig for a message of justice in the *Lectionary*. But the message can be found. The Letter to the Ephesians 3:2-3, 5-6, for example, which is the second reading for the feast of Epiphany, teaches that "in Christ Jesus the Gentiles are now co-heirs with the Jews, members of the same body and sharers of the promise." This unity in Christ between Gentiles and Jews can be respected and fostered only by just social organization of the Christian community. The Gospel of Matthew 25:31-46, read on the last Sunday of the year, the feast of Christ the King, cycle A, contains Jesus' description of the final judgment, when the sheep will be separated from the goats on the basis of whether or not they cared for the hungry and thirsty, the stranger, the naked, the ill, and the imprisoned. This passage calls not only for compassion, love, mercy, and generosity, but also for social justice, because the call is not simply to relieve misery, but ultimately to root out its causes by reorganizing society.

The love which Jesus commands—"Love one another as I have loved you"—in the Gospel of John 15:9-17 for the sixth Sunday of Easter, cycle B, is the motive of Christian justice. This inter-Christian love inspires just action and insures that it is done in a way which respects the total dignity and welfare of others and does not sacrifice them to some "system" purporting to be just.[6] The love of enemies, of which Jesus speaks in the Gospel of Matthew 5:38-48 for the seventh Sunday of the year, cycle A, or the Gospel of Luke 6:27-38 for the same Sunday, cycle C, impels us to seek justice even for our enemies.

When Jesus advocates learning of him because he is gentle and humble of heart, as he does in the Gospel of Matthew 11:25-30 for the fourteenth Sunday of the year, cycle A, he is urging us to assume qualities which free us from self-centered-ness and so facilitate our behaving justly toward others, even changing our standard of living for the sake of social justice for those now deprived of basic necessities of life. Likewise, Paul's exhortation in Romans 13:11-14, read on the first Sunday of Advent, cycle A, to "live honorably as in the daylight; not in carousing and drunkenness, not in sexual excess and lust, not in quarreling and jealousy," instructs us to behave in ways that are necessary conditions for acting justly toward our neighbor.[7]

Isaiah's messianic vision is contained in the first reading (Isaiah 2:1-5) for the first Sunday of Advent, cycle A: "They shall beat their swords into plowshares and their spears into pruning hooks. One nation shall not raise the sword against another, nor shall they train for war again." Peace, whether between individuals, groups, classes, or nations, is a conse-quence of social justice, as contention is an effect of social

---

[6]See Pope John Paul II, encyclical letter *Dives in Misericordia*, 30 November 1980, nos. 119-22, 145-48, 151-52, in Claudia Carlen, *The Papal Encyclicals 1958-1981* (New York: McGrath Publishing Company, 1981), pp. 289-90, 293.

[7]Thomas Aquinas' correlation of the cardinal virtues and charity can help us see the connection of many virtuous attitudes and activities with social justice. See Christopher Kiesling, "Social Justice in Christian Life according to Thomas Aquinas," *Spirituality Today* 31 (1979): 231-45.

injustice.[8] Paul's prayer in Romans 15:4-9, read on the second Sunday of Advent, cycle A, that God may enable his hearers "to live in perfect harmony with one another according to the spirit of Christ Jesus," also presupposes social justice, for that is fundamental to "perfect harmony."

Thus the theme of social justice is found in the *Lectionary* sometimes by contrast to the injustice of the world portrayed in the scriptural passages, sometimes in biblical examples of just conduct or in precepts of justice, sometimes in scriptural exhortations to the virtuous attitudes and conduct which accompany and entail just social activity. If our examination of the *Lectionary* had included readings from the days of the week as well as from Sundays, considerably more passages would have been noted that dealt with justice and injustice. The week days of the first portion of Lent, for example, and many readings from the Hebrew Scriptures throughout the weeks of the year, from both the prophetic books and historical books, set the issue of social justice before us.

A revision of the *Lectionary* is needed, however, to provide scriptural passages which more forthrightly address social justice, especially on Sundays during the ordinary time of the year. A different set of principles ought to be used for selecting readings, so that they reinforce each other, rather than introduce disparate themes, thus weakening the impact of the proclaimed word.

Our Model: Jesus, the Servant of Justice

The Christian proclamation of God's word through the *Lectionary* presents our model of life, Jesus Christ, in a context of hoped-for social justice and as the liberator from social injustice. The anniversary of Jesus' birth in the past becomes the occasion for the church to anticipate the risen Jesus' future coming in glory. So the Advent season tells us whom we are expecting to come.

[8] Vatican Council II, *The Church in the Modern World*, nos. 78 and 83, in Flannery, pp. 986-87 and 993.

Advent

The readings of the first Sunday of Advent announce the full breaking-in of God's reign over creation and history. They attempt to capture the utter blessedness of that time, the awesomeness of the great event, the final condemnation of wickedness, and the need to live now in readiness for the moment. Social justice has a place in all of this. The first reading in cycle A, Isaiah 2:1-5, speaks of the peace that will prevail. As we have already noted, justice is a fundamental ingredient of peace. The second reading of cycle A, Romans 13:11 -14, indicates the dispositions we need to cultivate in order to make justice possible. The reading from Isaiah 63:17-19; 64:2-7 in cycle B expresses this hope: "Would that you God might meet us doing right." "Doing right" surely includes keeping the commandments of God, most of which concern justice toward neighbor.[9] The first reading for the first Sunday of the C cycle is from Jeremiah 33:14-16. This passage prophesies God's raising up for David "a just shoot, he shall do what is right and just in the land." The coming of this "just shoot" will make Judah and Jerusalem safe and secure. Consequently, people will refer to Judah or Jerusalem as "The Lord Our Justice." Here is a particularly powerful suggestion that the Jesus we await is the Just One (or Righteous One) who will definitively establish justice, including social justice, in God's creation and in history.[10]

The readings for the second Sunday of Advent continue the same general themes, but they add John the Baptizer's heralding of Jesus. The first reading for cycle A is a prophecy from Isaiah 11:1-10 about the coming savior. "The spirit of the Lord shall rest upon him" with a plenitude of gifts. As a result,

[9]For an appreciation of the concreteness of such terms as *right, just, righteous, justice, judgment,* and related words in the Bible and their reference to historical social justice, that is, to justice in this world and not another world and not only as metaphors for moral goodness, see José Miranda, *Marx and the Bible* (Maryknoll, N.Y.: Orbis Books, 1974), especially pp. 35-199; also John R. Donahue, "Biblical Perspectives on Justice," in John Haughey, ed. *The Faith That Does Justice* (New York: Paulist Press, 1977), pp. 68-112.

[10]See John Haughey, "Jesus as the Justice of God," in Haughey, ed. *Faith That Does Justice,* pp. 264-90.

"not by appearance shall he judge, that is, declare what is right, or just, nor by hearsay shall he decide, but he shall judge the poor with justice, and decide aright for the land's afflicted." Indeed, "justice shall be the band around his waist." The first reading in cycle B, again from Isaiah (40:1-5, 9-11), alludes to God's coming to put things right, rewarding the good and the just, correcting the wicked and unjust. The prophet Baruch (5:1-9) in the first reading of cycle C, sees the new Jerusalem "wrapped in the cloak of justice from God" and "named by God forever the peace of justice, the glory of God's worship"; God leads *God's* people "by the light of his glory, with his mercy and justice for company." All these prophecies present the Jesus who is to come as the one who will finally establish justice for all.

The responsorial psalms of the second Sunday, except cycle C, sing of the justice of the coming savior and his kingdom. The refrain for Psalm 72 in cycle A is: "Justice shall flourish in his time, and fullness of peace forever." Of the future savior the psalm sings:

> God, with your judgment endow the king,
> and with your justice, the king's son;
> He shall govern your people with justice
> and your afflicted ones with judgment.
> Justice shall flower in his days
> and profound peace, till the moon be no more . . . . For he
> shall rescue the poor man (woman) when he cries out
> and the afflicted when he has no one to help him.
> He shall have pity for the lowly and the poor;
>> the lives of the poor he shall save. (1-2, 7-8, 12-13, 19)

The theme of justice also occurs in the responsorial psalm (85) for cycle B on this second Sunday of Advent: ". . . justice and peace shall kiss . . . justice shall look down from heaven . . . justice shall walk before him."

The second reading of the second Sunday of Advent, cycle B, is 2 Peter 3:8-14. It contains a helpful summary of the context in which we expect to see the risen Jesus coming again: "What we await are a new heaven and a new earth where, according to his promise, the justice of God will reside."

On the third and fourth Sundays of Advent, the readings tend to recall the events of the past which are the basis for our present expectation of what will be in the future. But the theme of social justice does not disappear entirely. It is evident in the responsorial psalm (146:6-7, 8-9, 9-10) of cycle A of the third Sunday of Advent: the Lord "secures justice for the oppressed, gives food to the hungry ... sets captives free ... loves the just." The first reading from Isaiah 61:1-2, 10-11 in cycle B contains verses which, according to Luke 4:16-21, Jesus used in the synagogue at Nazareth to refer to his own ministry as one who has come to set affairs right once again. The passage goes on to say that God has "wrapped me in a mantle of justice." Further it says: "The Lord God will make justice and praise spring up before all the nations." The responsory for this third Sunday in cycle B is Mary's canticle recorded in the Gospel of Luke. The theme of justice prominent in that canticle is recalled in the line: "The hungry he has given every good thing, while the rich he has sent empty away."

Christmas

At midnight mass on Christmas, the first reading from Isaiah 9:1-6—the same for cycles A, B and C—evokes memories of Israel's exodus from Egypt as it rejoices in the Lord who comes: "For the yoke that burdened them, the pole on their shoulder, and the rod of their taskmaster you have smashed." Peace is at hand: "For every boot that tramped in battle, every cloak rolled in blood, will be burned as fuel for flames." The "child born to us is called 'Prince of Peace'" and "his dominion is vast and forever peaceful." His kingdom "he confirms and sustains by judgment and justice both now and forever." The responsorial psalm (96) reminds us that "he shall rule the world with justice."

The second reading from the Letter to Titus 2:11-14 speaks of the savior whom we await as the one who "sacrificed himself for us, to redeem us from all unrighteousness and to cleanse for himself a people of his own, eager to do what is right." The

Gospel of Luke 2:1-14 at midnight mass describes the angel of the Lord announcing the good news of Jesus' birth to the shepherds near Bethlehem. The first announcement of Jesus' birth is made to the lowly people in society.[11]

In the mass at dawn, the responsorial psalm (97) declares that "the heavens proclaim his (the Lord's) justice" and "light dawns for the just." The latter are encouraged: "Be glad in the Lord, you just." In the Gospel of Luke 2:15-20, the shepherds appear again.

The responsorial psalm (98) for the mass during the day announces that "in the sight of the nations he (the Lord) has revealed his justice"—in the Word made flesh, Jesus, the subject of the prologue to John's Gospel which is proclaimed at that liturgical assembly.

Epiphany and Baptism of Jesus

The feast of the Epiphany not only recalls Jesus' revelation to the magi but looks forward to the complete manifestation of the glory of Jesus at the end of time. As a responsory is Psalm 72, which is the same one used on the second Sunday of Advent, cycle A, and which clearly declares the work of justice that the coming Christ will accomplish for the poor and the afflicted, the victims of injustice.

The Advent-Christmas-Epiphany cycle comes to a conclusion with the commemoration of Jesus' baptism.[12] The Gospel reading for this feast is one or another of the accounts of Jesus' baptism by John (Matt. 3:13-17; Mark 1:7-11; Luke 3:15-16, 21-22). In all accounts, after Jesus' baptism, the skies

---

[11]As already noted, Joseph Fitzmyer, *The Gospel According to Luke I-IX*, Anchor Bible 28 (Garden City, N.Y.: Doubleday, 1981), p. 396, sees sufficient grounds in biblical literature for associating shepherds with Bethlehem and enabling Luke to show his predilection for the lowly. Later rabbinical lists of despised occupations included shepherds with gamblers, usurers, tax collectors, publicans, and some others. See Joachim Jeremias, *Jerusalem at the Time of Jesus* (Philadelphia: Fortress Press, 1969), pp. 303-12.

[12]The introduction to the *Lectionary* lists the Feast of the Baptism of the Lord under the Christmas season (no. 12.1 at the end; cf. no. 15.1). See also the directive, or "rubric," at the end of the reading for the Baptism of the Lord, or the Sunday after January 6 (no. 21 in the body of the *Lectionary*); also the directive under the title "Season of the Year" (before no. 65); and the directive after no. 212.

open and the Spirit descends on him in the form of a dove; then a voice from heaven says: "You are my beloved Son. On you my favor rests" (Matthew uses the third rather than the second person). The heavenly words echo Isaiah 42:1: "Here is my servant whom I uphold, my chosen one with whom I am pleased." So the Jesus whose coming we anticipate is the servant of God. What is the ministry of this servant?

The first reading for the feast of Jesus' baptism in all the cycles of the liturgical year is Isaiah 42:1-4, 6-7. It declares: "I, the Lord, have called you for the victory of justice." This justice entails not simply personal holiness, a personal right relationship to God, but also justice to fellow human beings in society, for the former cannot exist without the latter. The refrain for the responsorial psalm is "The Lord will bless his people with peace"; and the second reading, Acts 10:34-38, refers to "the good news of peace." We have seen the necessary connection between peace and justice.

Thus the Jesus presented to us in the Advent-Christmas-Epiphany readings is the servant of God who has come, comes now, and will come in order to establish justice in the fullest sense of the word—a justice which includes an intimate union with God in faith, hope, and love; but a justice which also includes the right relationships among men and women, individually and socially. Jesus saves, that is, he liberates, from injustice the poor, the oppressed, the deprived, the needy. Yes, he brings a new sort of love into the world—a love beyond the demands of any purely rationally conceived justice and characteristic of the kingdom which he heralds and indeed incarnates. But that love and the compassion, mercy, and beneficence which it entails assume specific, concrete, historical embodiment in deeds of justice and just social orders. This Jesus is our model for our lives; and we are the members of his body through whom he wishes to be active now to move the world toward that plenitude of justice for which he comes.

The Easter Cycle

When we come to the celebration of the paschal mystery beginning with the Mass of the Lord's Supper on Holy

Thursday and extending to Easter Sunday, the Jesus presented to us is, again, the servant of the Lord.[13] The Gospel read at the Mass of the Lord's Supper is John 13:1-15, the opening of the Johannine account of the Last Supper. It tells of Jesus' washing the feet of his disciples. When he finishes that task, he makes clear to his disciples who he is and who they are to be: "If I washed your feet—I who am Teacher and Lord—then you must wash each other's feet. What I just did was give you an example: as I have done, so you must do. I solemnly assure you, no slave is greater than his master; no messenger outranks the one who sent him" (John 13:14-16).

This powerful gospel message is backed up liturgically by a rite in which the pastor (or bishop, or pope) literally washes the feet of men and women whom he is appointed to serve. Although the ceremony may at times appear to be somewhat contrived, still there is a moving reminder here of what Christianity is all about when we see someone in a "high place" from a worldly point of view on his knees washing the feet of "ordinary" people.

The second reading for the Mass of the Lord's Supper is from Paul's First Letter to the Corinthians 11:23-26. Paul recounts Jesus' institution of the Eucharist which proclaims the death of the Lord until he comes. Paul gives this account not simply for the sake of passing on historical information or doctrine to be believed. He does it to remind the Corinthians that they must love one another and share their food with one another. The rich must not ignore the poor. They cannot treat one another unjustly[6]and with clear conscience share the one loaf and the one cup which are the body and blood of the Lord.[14]

The liturgy of Good Friday does not let us forget Jesus as the servant of God who shall bring forth justice to the nations.

---

[13]The original inspiration for the interpretation here of the readings for the Easter Triduum was provided by Robert Lott in a presentation to the Liturgy and Social Justice Group at the annual meeting of the North American Academy of Liturgy, Washington, D.C., January, 1980.

[14]Jerome Murphy-O'Connor, *1 Corinthians* (Wilmington, Del. Michael Glazier, 1979), p. 114; William F. Orr and James Arthur Walther, *1 Corinthians*, Anchor Bible 32 (Garden City, N.Y.: Doubleday, 1976), pp. 273-74.

The celebration of the Lord's passion begins with a reading of the fourth of the Servant Songs, Isaiah 52:13-53:13. The passion of Jesus is read according to the Gospel of John. The Gospel portrays vividly the innocence of Jesus which Pilate recognizes, tries to defend, but, in the pinch, sacrifices to his personal interests in the Roman imperial system and to the aims of the Jewish establishment by an unjust judgment to death.

The background of the Easter vigil is the story of the exodus—God's liberation of the people from oppression as slaves under the pharaohs of Egypt. A new exodus is celebrated in this vigil—Jesus' liberation from death, mortality, and his establishment in the justice of God. But Jesus' liberation, the paradigm of ours, is not only a "spiritual" event, leaving unaffected our bodies, our temporal existence, the world in which we live. For the risen body of Jesus is part of that bodily, material creation about which we read in Genesis 1:1-2:2. This passage of Genesis is the first and non-optional reading at the Easter vigil liturgy. Jesus' liberation, his victory, expressed by his resurrection from the dead, entails the liberation of all creation, of all history, and of all humanity. In Jesus, God's reign has indeed broken into history and God's power, creative of social justice, is at work in us, if we do not rebel against it.[15]

The image of Jesus, God's servant, liberating God's people and our model of life, expressed in the paschal celebration, can be carried forward into Lent and beyond to Pentecost. Other aspects of who Jesus is are more dominant in the Lenten and Easter periods, but it is the same Jesus; and the message of the *Lectionary* in these periods will often have at least an implicit dimension of social justice. On Pentecost we celebrate, of course, the gift of the Holy Spirit who anointed Jesus the servant, sending him on a mission of liberation of society's oppressed. Since the Advent-Christmas-Epiphany season and the Lent-Easter-Pentecost season reveal so clearly Jesus the servant, we can also detect that same Jesus during the so-

[15]See Albert Nolan, *Jesus Before Christianity* (Maryknoll, N.Y.: Orbis Books, 1978), pp. 82-85, 140-41.

called ordinary time of the year. Whatever the explicit content
of liturgical readings may be, the Jesus who addresses us
through them is always the liberating servant of the Lord, the
Just One, who comes for the victory of justice.

A Liberation Theology

Finally, we note that the *Lectionary* presents the mystery of
Christ over the course of the year in such a way that it leads us
to theologize in a pattern like a theology of liberation.[16] It
guides us to reflect on, and evaluate, not only our private,
interior lives, but also our world and our involvement in it, in
the light of God's coming kingdom.

The Advent-Christmas-Epiphany cycle looks forward to
Christ Jesus manifested in his full glory, with wisdom, power
and that judgment which establishes what is right. We are
made aware of the "not yet," The Day of the Lord, the
consummation of history. We have already noted the second
reading for the second Sunday in Advent, cycle B, namely, 2
Peter 3:8-14, which reads: "What we await are new heavens
and new earth, where, according to his promise, the justice of
God will reside." The first reading of the C cycle, Baruch 5:1-9,
as we have seen, speaks of Jerusalem "wrapped in the cloak of
justice from God, ... named by God forever the peace of
justice with his mercy and justice for accompaniment."

As we look forward to the new heaven and new earth and
the promised justice of God, we are simultaneously recalling
the beginnings of the motive for our expectation: the incarnation of God's Son in Jesus. That mystery brings us "down to
earth"; it reminds us of Zachary and Anna, Mary and Joseph,

---

[16]The classic expression of liberation theology is by Gustavo Gutierrez, *A Theology of Liberation* (Maryknoll), N.Y.: Orbis Books, 1973). For an explanation and critique of liberation Theology, see Avery Dulles, "Faith in Relationship to Justice," in Haughey, ed., *Faith That Does Justice*, pp. 32-44. See also Dermott Lane, *Foundations for a Social Theology* (New York: Paulist Press, 1984), pp. 19-29. The Congregation for the Doctrine of the Faith has issued a criticism of *certain forms* of liberation theology, but not of liberation theology generally, nor of its goal, namely, to aid the poor by overcoming their oppression: *Instruction on Certain Aspects of the "Theology of Liberation,"* in *Origins* 14 (September 1984): 193-204.

pregnancy, travel to be registered in a census, a crowded inn, childbirth, shepherds, the slaying of innocent children by a paranoiac puppet king. There is a large gap between the world in which we live and the new heavens and new earth which we expect. The social arrangements in which we live fall far short of the justice with which God will wrap Jerusalem. We cannot rest with the status quo in the world. There is always room for improvement of the social, economic, and political orders toward justice for all.

In the Lenten liturgy, Jesus invites us to go with him into the desert and with him empty ourselves for service to others as servants of God. Lent is a time of penance and recon- ciliation, a time to look deeply into ourselves and around our world, to see there the radical goodness which God's love brought forth, and to note the obstacles we have placed, often more or less deliberately (sin), to the divinely intended fulfill- ment of that creation. During Lent we can examine our patterns of social life, seek out their flaws, weigh our complicity in perpetuating injustice, and have "a change of heart", "a conversion", so that we become servants, not obstacles, to the coming reign of God with its social justice.

This period of *metanoia* flows into the Easter-Pentecost celebration with its heightened consciousness of new life in the risen Christ through the gift of his Spirit. God's justifying love has broken into history in Jesus and overcome our greatest enemy—death—and therefore all our enemies, all the forces acting against us, including the spirit of selfishness and injustice which infects the human race. God has poured out the Spirit of Christ upon us, that we, like Jesus, may live and die for the kingdom of God's justice. We have the power of God within us to cast down the barriers to justice discerned in Lent— barriers that stand in the way of the justice dreamed of, and hoped for, in the Advent-Christmas-Epiphany season.

The joy of new life during the fifty days of the Easter Pentecost period refreshes us for the long, demanding, often discouraging work of establishing social justice in our world. That work takes dedication, which can be renewed each Sunday of the year when we assemble to remember again God's promises and the anticipated fulfillment of them in Jesus risen from the dead. The word of God during the Sundays of the year reminds us and encourages us, sometimes explicitly, to pursue social justice in our society; but more often the readings implicitly or indirectly promote our seeking social justice by nourishing other features of Christian life which prepare the ground for just social action, or remove obstacles in us to such action, or inspire us to undertake it, or which can flow only from social justice.

As we begin, perhaps, to grow weary in the struggle, the end of the year comes again with the feast of Christ the King which recalls that he is, and has been, at work in the world through his Spirit, and in him our victory is assured. "Already" the reign of God is in the midst of us, but it is "not yet" fully here. That fact is set before us once again as we enter the Advent-Christmas-Epiphany season. We hear anew the prophetic words promising that "justice and peace shall kiss . . . and justice shall look down from heaven" (responsorial psalm, second Sunday of Advent, cycle B). Again we recall the coming and going of simple people, the *anawim*, living in twisted, corrupt, oppressive societies, deprived of dignity, rights, and freedom. We see the gap between what God promises and our actual condition. We turn one more time in Lent to examine our consciences, repent, and discover again at Easter the power of the risen Christ within us to continue working to change society.

From God's Word to Our Word

The word of God calling us to social justice can make us aware of how often, and how much, the word of women and men embodies and carries on social injustice in society. The falsity of advertising is apparent to many, but we cannot overlook the fact that the words of advertising in our consumer society shape the world which our children grow up believing is the true world; and we adults are often unaware of how subtly those words work on our value system and support the social classes, economic disparities, political disenfranchisements, and cultural alienations which exist in our nation and around the world. Through propaganda, governments generate prejudices and hatred among peoples, rob nations of their resources, reduce countries to vassalage, while pretending that such ideas, feelings, and situations are simply the way things are, perhaps even the work of the Creator.

Far more than we appreciate, the human word begets, sustains, and transmits unjust social structures, attitudes, and behavior patterns. The evening TV news and the morning newpaper must be heard and read critically in the light of God's word. The hearers of God's word, moreover, have a mission to speak out with the truth on every subject, so that justice may more and more inform society. Only truth can be the foundation of social justice.[17] A "letter to the editor" may be more than a way to pass the time or vent anger. It may be a contribution to the justice of God's coming kingdom. Government commissions to watch over "truth in advertising" or to protect consumers from dishonest business practices are not burdens upon citizens but their instruments to provide for social justice in anticipation of the future reign of God. Speaking and doing justice are, in the final analysis, a fundamental response to God's word. They are the necessary presupposition for the authenticity of our worship. Our God has declared: "It is mercy I desire and not sacrifice." (Hosea 6:6; Matt. 12:7; cf. 1 Sam. 15:22). It is that mercy which alone adequately does justice to neighbor.

❧

Bibliography

Burghardt, Walter A. "Preaching the Word," in Mark Searle, ed. *Liturgy and Social Justice.* Collegeville: Liturgical Press, 1980. Pp. 36-52.

> The author gives the theological basis for preaching on justice and doing it in the context of the liturgy. He offers some principles to consider in approaching sensitive issues.

---

[17]Pope John XXIII, encyclical letter *Pacem in Terris*, nos. 35-36, in Carlen, *Papal Encyclicals*, pp. 110-11.

Gonzales, Justo and Gonzales, Catherine. *Liberation Preaching: The Pulpit of the Oppressed*. Nashville: Abingdon, 1980.

An excellent presentation of how to approach the Scriptures, derive from them God's word for the freedom of men and women from oppression and proclaim that word for the powerless and powerful.

Happel, Stephen. "Worship as a Grammar of Social Transformation," in *The Catholic Theological Society of America Proceedings* 42 (1987).

This is an interesting study of language and sacraments. The author draws upon the ideas of Paul Ricoeur and David Power and treats the transformative dimension of a sacramental rhetoric and its place in the political, economic, and social world.

Haughey, John C. "Jesus as the Justice of God," in John C. Haughey, ed. *The Faith That Does Justice*. New York: Paulist Press, 1977.

Pp. 264-90. From an examination of Jesus' Jewish heritage, the Evangelists' images of him, his own teaching, and Paul's doctrine, this book justifies viewing as the justice of God the Jesus who is celebrated liturgically in word and sacrament.

Hessel, Dieter T., ed., *Social Themes of the Christian Year: A Commentary on the Lectionary*, Philadelphia: The Geneva Press, 1983.

This is the most extensive work dealing with the social themes of the Christian year. The various authors develop the aspects of social justice found in each season of the year by concentrating on a central theme. A more wholistic approach to each season of the year follows these more specific thematic essays.

Kellermann, Bill. "Seasons of Faith and Conscience," in *Sojourners*, vol. 14 (1985).

> In a series of six articles in the course of the year, beginning in January and concluding in December 1985, the author reflects on the implications for social justice and political involvement which are latent in major liturgical seasons and feasts of the year.

Miranda, José. *Marx and the Bible.* Maryknoll, N.Y.: Orbis Books, 1974. Pp. 35-199.

> The three central chapters of this book have little to do with Marx but can help discern the social justice implications of the *Lectionary* readings because they examine in great detail the notions of justice in the Bible and their reference to everyday life.

Nolan, Albert. *Jesus Before Christianity.* Maryknoll, N.Y.: Orbis Books, 1978.

> This book brings to light social justice implications of Gospel passages as it examines Jesus' milieu, his preaching and healing ministry, his death, and, in all this, his effort to get at the roots of injustice through conversion to, and faith in, the kingdom of God.

Porteous, Alvin. *Preaching to Suburban Captives.* Valley Forge, Penn.: Judson Press, 1979.

> Aiming at a perspective in liberation theology which addresses the situation of middle-class suburban Americans, this work offers a profile of such Americans, an interpretation of the Gospel message as liberating them, and strategies for communicating this message in preaching.

Skudlarek, William. *The Word in Worship: Preaching in a Liturgical Context.* Nashville: Abingdon, 1981.

This book provides a history of the *Lectionary*, the principles behind the selection of the biblical passages included in it, and proposals on how to use it in preparation for preaching. Its scope is general, however, not focused on social justice.

Sweazy, George. "Controversial Preaching" and "Preaching on Social Morality." In his book *Preaching the Good News*. Englewood Cliffs, N.J.: Prentice-Hall, 1976. Pp. 213-25, 247-56.

The author suggests techniques and ways of proceeding when one needs to face issues on which there is disagreement, and he offers reasons for preaching on social issues for action.

5

Preaching and the Transformation of the World

Liturgical Preaching and Social Justice: A Dilemma

Not all preaching is liturgical. A distinction often made is that the homily refers to preaching in a liturgical setting, while the sermon is a more comprehensive term which applies to all the occasions of developing the richness of God's word for others. Homilizing is a specific occasion of preaching so that the word of God may be intelligible and enlightening to the worshipping community. There are a number of characteristics of liturgical preaching which define its place and function in the setting of worship.

(1) Liturgical preaching is a "Word-Event" in which the truth of the hearer's existence is revealed. As in the case of the scriptures, preaching proclaims God's gracious work in Jesus Christ. It is a proclamation which frees the hearer to love.

(2) Liturgical preaching is contextualized by the liturgy itself. It is the "eighth sacrament." It too is a symbol, an action of grace, the way the spiritual reality of salvation is contained in the perceptible reality of human communication.

(3) Liturgical preaching is an ecclesial event. It is always of the church and in the church. It is never directed to the individual alone. It is not problem-solving for the isolated Christian. It is to build up the church as do the other sacraments. It is also one of the identifying gestures of the Christian community.

(4) Liturgical preaching is an act of "memorial" in the sense of effectively recalling the past and really anticipating the future. It is the link between events of Christ's redemption and his final return. For the members of the community it connects their past incorporation into the church with their eucharistic experiences which anticipate the return of the savior in glory.

(5) Liturgical preaching is an integral part of the liturgy. It is not an element to be dispensed with as non-essential or secondary. Thus, the homily has theological significance and is not some kind of pedagogical insert. Along with the rest of the liturgy, preaching proclaims the story of the history of salvation to the community. The homily reminds the worshipers that they must respond to the gracious actions of God. Such preaching is more than a subjective analysis of personal faith or a presentation of some objective moral system of thought.

The question is how can liturgical preaching achieve these pastoral ends and yet be related to social justice? The dilemma is:

> how one could be prophetic without alienating a congregation; and second, how one could be prophetic without impairing one's role in pastoral care. In other words, is it possible for one to be a pastor and a prophet at the same time? Can one stand "over against" a congregation in the tradition of a prophet and proclaim the unequivocal "thus saith the Lord" while at the same time being identified with the congregation in the tradition of a priest and mediating the comfort of grace.[1]

This is one of the major challenges facing preachers of the gospel in our society. They are pulled toward two extremes. There are ministers who are committed to certain social justice issues and every homily proclaims their position. Such preachers force the lectionary to say what they wish it to say. At the other extreme are the preachers whose desire to be approved

---

[1]Norman Neaves, "Preaching in Pastoral Perspective," in Edmund A. Steimle, Morris J. Niederthal, and Charles Rice's *Preaching the Story* (Philadelphia: Fortress Press, 1980), pp. 111-112.

by the congregation is so great that even when the biblical readings clearly confront a particular social justice issue, they avoid confronting the people of God with the responsibility of the gospel imperative.

But as has already been demonstrated earlier in this book, if the struggle for justice is indispensable to the church's mission, and if liturgy is tied to the fulfillment of this mission, then there can only be one answer to the question: should the preacher preach justice? Listen to the words of the preacher, Walter Burghardt, S.J.:

> And so I must speak to this people's needs, this people's hungers. If they need to act justly or if they hunger for justice, a liturgy that expresses and molds their faith-experience forbids me to keep silent. To say nothing is to say something.[2]

Nor is this advice something peculiar to the contemporary church. Mark Searle observes:

> The close continuity between liturgical celebration and social action is evident in the early history of the liturgy. It is the role of the bishop not only to preside at the liturgy and *to preach* (italics mine) but also to oversee the general welfare of his people and to involve himself directly in settling disputes, feeding the poor, caring for the sick, providing for orphans and widows.[3]

And in our own time, the Roman Catholic Bishops have reemphasized this connection:

> Action on behalf of justice and participation in the transformation of the world fully appear to us as a constitutive dimension of the preaching of the gospel, or in other words,

---

[2]Walter J. Burghardt, S. J., "Preaching the Just Word," in *Liturgy and Social Justice* edited by Mark Searle (Collegeville: The Liturgical Press, 1980), p. 45.

[3]Mark Searle, "Serving the Lord with Justice," in *Liturgy and Social Justice*, p. 20.

of the Church's mission for the redemption of the human race and its liberation from every oppressive situation.[4]

Justice in the Scripture

Liturgical preaching flows from the scriptures, and in particular, the selections proclaimed as assigned over the course of the year in the lectionary. We have already noted how the lectionary presents us with a program of a spirituality of justice. No attempt is made here to review the previous chapter. However, there are several general observations highlighting the presence of social justice in the biblical readings which the homilists can use as the foundation of their own preaching and preaching preparations.[5]

First, the Hebrew bible is an expression of the faith experience of an oppressed and powerless people. It is the story of the deliverance of this people. Their whole history has been summed up in the paradigmatic event of the exodus. The justice of the Hebrew Scriptures is seen in terms of the relationship of the Israelite to Yahweh, to fellow Israelites and to the land. Old Testament justice has a social character because its results are described in terms of peace and harmony among people, the gifts of the earth, freedom and hope for others. Justice is contextualized by the Hebrew covenantal relationship to God. And in the concrete treatment of the poor, the widows and the orphans, the Israelites found the measure of the observance of that covenant.[6]

The thematizing experience of the exodus of the Hebrew people finds its counterpart in the New Testament in Jesus,

---

[4]*Justice in the World* (Synod of Bishops, November 30, 1971), paragraph 6. In Joseph Gremillion, *The Gospel of Peace and Justice* (Maryknoll: Orbis Books, 1976), p. 514.

[5]We have already recommended the excellent treatment of the theme of justice in the bible and its relationship to social justice by John R. Donahue, S. J., "Biblical Perspectives on Justice," in *The Faith That Does Justice* edited by John C. Haughey, S. J. (New York: The Paulist Press, 1977).

[6]Ibid., pp. 77-78. For another treatment of justice in the Hebrew Scriptures consult John Topel, S. J., *The Way to Peace: Liberation Through the Bible* (Maryknoll: Orbis Books, 1979).

and especially in his call for the establishment of the kingdom of God. Out of the experience of oppression, the biblical presentation of Jesus is that of someone who is in the service of God's kingdom. He proclaims the gospel of a new order (Lk 1:46-55). Thus, there is the paradox and scandal of God who takes the form of a servant and makes Godself one with others. Speaking of the New Testament revelation of God's justice, John R. Donahue says:

> Faith frees people to be people of compassion because they have received compassion; it frees them to care for the weak and prodigal because they have been accepted by God though weak and prodigal.
>
> The cause of the poor, the hungry and the oppressed is now the cause of Jesus. He is the Son of Man, present in the least of his brethren. Christians are called to bear one another's burdens. This is to fulfill the law of Christ, to be a just people.[7]

While the kingdom of God is an eschatological reality, it is also a vision of this world being saved now. There is no contradiction between these two events for there is only one history. Our worldly history is our salvation history. God is the Lord of all history. It is history itself which serves as medium between God and ourselves and makes God available to us. Thus, as already noted in chapter two, in that sense there should be no dichotomy between the secular and the profane. Creation, salvation, and the coming of the kingdom of God are aspects of the one process of God and this world in relationship. What may be scandal and enigma to those who do not see with faith, becomes for Christians *the* example of what God is doing in Jesus Christ, namely, inaugurating God's kingdom in the lives of the oppressed and marginalized.

Secondly, the bible as a religious reality is always a call to action. This call is defined by the scripture itself in terms of the

---

[7]Donahue, "Biblical Perspectives," p. 109.

context of the exodus and the kingdom of God. It involves actions which are specifically directed toward helping the oppressed, the needy and the lonely. But more than that, it is directed toward changing social structures and systems which oppress. We are to cooperate with God in God's plan of salvation, which is liberating all areas of oppression in our world. We need to work with each other to realize this salvation. From a justice-oriented perspective, to cooperate with others is to cooperate with God. Preaching the justice of the scriptures means to point out the directions in which this cooperation may take place. Donahue speaks to this point when he says:

> The bible proclaims what it means to be just and to do justice: it is less interested in what justice is in the abstract. It gives concrete instances of justice and injustice in the lives of people. The task of translation is to make alive in our present age the vision of justice which formed the lives of the biblical writers. Interpretation of the bible is always determined by the social context of the interpreter. Luther wrestled with the late medieval problem of a just God and sinful creation and translated the God of justice into a God of love. The task of our age may well be the reverse—to translate the love of God into the doing of justice.[8]

The bible is a call to action because the word of God is. The Hebrew, *dabar*, which is translated as "word" has many meanings, one of which is "action." That is why New Testament preaching and action go together. Often the apostolic preachers were described in terms of their actions of healing, raising the dead, and the giving up of their lives. Raymond Brown notes that the God of Israel is one both of action and speaking. Both aspects convey a truth which is at the heart of justice in the bible.[9] As the scriptures record the

---

[8]Ibid., p. 108.

[9]Raymond E. Brown, S.S., "Preaching in the Acts of the Apostles," in *A New Look at Preaching* edited by John Burke, O.P. (Wilmington: Michael Glazier, Inc., 1983), p. 61.

development of belief in God and God's kingdom, there is ever present the leitmotif of justice as both a gift and a demand. And it is justice with a direction because the full realization of God's justice is a matter of future hope. The call to action is characterized by the realism of eschatological hope. The believers living in the "between times" are challenged to confront the structures of injustice and yet to present a vision that hints at the final coming of the kingdom of God.

Thirdly, the bible is essentially communitarian. It is the story of the history of a people, how they were formed, how they rose and fell from power. It is the story of how these people together saw God acting in their lives. The bible is also the story of the birth of Christian community. Although the New Testament does not clearly depict Jesus as forming the church as an organized society as we know it, the early Christian preachers presumed a social movement initiated by Jesus. Baptism was the way in which such a visibly structured community came about. Raymond Brown says: "For the author of Acts, baptism involves acceptance into a community and Christianity is a communitarian religion."[10] Jesus saves not individuals but a people. The connection so often made between baptism and social justice is a specific instance of the communitarian faith portrayed in the scriptures. To be a person of the bible is existentially synonymous with belonging to a community. In the case of Christians, this is a community entered by means of baptism.

What lies behind the various New Testament theologies of baptism is a new community called church which is the creation of the Spirit. This church envisioned in the New Testament identifies with the poor and oppressed in an attitude of solidarity by assuming the mantle of servanthood. It provides an alternative social reality whereby Christians are called to view systems, societies, cultures, and institutions (including the church) from the point of view of their *victims*. As noted in chapter three, the Christian community, formed and shaped through baptism, has a unique and perpetually revolutionary

[10]Ibid., p. 70.

role in history, i.e. that the kingdom of God is not a territory, but a *new* order.

Yet even the exploration of justice in the bible must always be under critique. Father Gerard Sloyan puts it well:

> The paradox is that we can be led astray by the very things we most count on as our allies: a knowlege of how God acts in a universe marked by order, a knowledge of how God has acted with the people of the bible, Israel, a knowledge of the promises made to the covenantal community we know the Church to be.[11]

Prophetic preachers who proclaim the demands of biblical justice to others must be less concerned to preach *to* them than to struggle *with* their congregation. The bearers of the message of justice cannot prescind from the complexities of global problems. We need less naive certainty and more struggling reflection in the pulpit. This is not to say that preachers cannot be clear, make use of dramatic images, or call for responsible action. But the rhetoric must be matched with thoughtful questioning and some agony of searching.

Preaching as an Event

Liturgical preaching is the proclamation of the Good News to worshipping Christians. It is a concrete, linguistic event which both reflects and creates the experience of Christian salvation.[12]. Through this proclamation, the Gospel is integrated into human society. As a creative event, preaching brings to awareness the presence of God in our lives here and now. Preaching should be the locus of a saving encounter between the worshipping community and its God. In liturgical

[11]Burke, "Introduction,"*A New Look at Preaching*, p. 159.

[12]For more on preaching and liturgy as word-events, see Gerhard Ebeling, *Word and Faith* (Philadelphia: Fortress Press, 1963) and James L. Empereur, S. J., "Liturgy as Proclamation," in *Modern Liturgy Handbook* edited by John Mossi, S. J. (New York: Paulist Press, 1976).

preaching, the context is always an ecclesial one because the word of God is spoken to the church. The homily as a language event is not to people as individuals, but to people forming the community of believers. One helpful working definition of preaching has been provided by James A. Forbes, Jr. in his response to a paper on the meaning of preaching by William J. Hill, O.P.:

> Preaching is the kerygmatic re-interpretation or represen-
> tation of the word of God in an ecclesial form and context,
> in which the preacher mediates a saving encounter of the
> believer with the living God, through the New Testament
> message of Jesus as proclaimed in the Church. It is grounded
> in present experience and is empowered by the Holy Spirit.
> As such preaching is revelation from God.[13]

Thus, preaching as an event of the Good News releases the meaning of our lives which is open-ended and not clearly defined. It is a communal meeting with God where we allow ourselves to be interpreted by what we hear. It is "a speech event drawing others into the circle of new understanding."[14] As event, liturgical preaching exists on the level of symbol rather than the one dimensional sign, which means that it must be a personally transforming meeting of world views. As Leander E. Keck puts it:

> Preaching which occurs at the intersection of the world and
> gospel will be an interpretative event, a hermeneutical act
> which exposes profound choices which the hearer is invited
> to make and to make repeatedly. Such preaching goes far
> deeper into the issues of life than do homilies which merely
> exhort a course of action.[15]

Preaching as an event takes on the character of the scriptures as proclamation. This means that ordinarily homilies will be

---

[13]Burke, "Introduction," *A New Look at Preaching*, p. 127.

[14]Ibid., "Response," Forbes, p. 128.

[15]Ibid., "Biblical Preaching as Divine Wisdom," Keck, p. 156.

oriented to the narrative, the story. They will also include an explicitly prophetic element. And this implies that there are certain forms of preaching which should not be the dominant modes of homilizing. Preaching in a worship context should not be primarily doctrinal, didactic or moralizing. That liturgical preaching employs the narrative form of communication does not mean a mere reiteration of the biblical material and language. In fact, preaching needs to forge a new language, which is appropriate to the changing cultural contexts in which the preaching is taking place. The implication in the narrative form of preaching is that this mode of proclamation has more power to confront present problems.[16] This will avoid an escapist approach to preaching and will situate the proclaimer in the midst of the human situation. Stories work only if they can be understood and if they resonate with life experiences.[17]

But the preacher's stories also come to listeners who are overly inculturated in their societies. Homilists are preaching to those who have over-adapted to the world's structures. Thus, the narrative needs to be prophetic. This demands "an attitude of critical negativity toward the structures and the spirit of secular existence, avoiding all conformity to the mores of bourgeois society and conventional piety in the forgetfullness that we are a people of unfulfilled promise."[18] To preach from the hearer's context is not to identify faith and ideology. No structures, even those of the church, in their historical forms, are absolute.

Moralizing is contrary to the narrative form of preaching. To moralize is to reduce the gospel to simple imperatives. The homilists moralize when they extricate from the liturgical lessons a list of suggestions for better living, principles for

---

[16]A helpful reference here is *Storytelling and Christian Faith, Chicago Studies* 21:1 (Spring 1982). See especially the article, "The Demands of a Truthful Story: Ethics and the Pastoral Task," by Stanley Hauerwas.

[17]More on storytelling and the imagination, human experience, and faith commitment can be found in the works of John Shea: *Stories of Faith*, (Chicago: Thomas More Press, 1980), *Stories of God* (Chicago: Thomas More Press, 1978) and *The God Who Fell From Heaven*, (Allen, Texas: Argus Publications, 1979).

[18]William J. Hill, O.P., "What is Preaching? One Heuristic Model From Theology," in Burke, *A New Look at Preaching*, p. 123.

Christian behavior, or duties to be met by the worshipers. But to do this is to domesticate the gospel, to equate it with a privatized, pietistic morality. In the moralizing sermon the narrative style and form become little more than a place to mine for moral precepts. Everything has a message. Parables, biblical personalities, and events of salvation history all contain ethical advice. Sometimes this is a throwback to medieval allegorization; sometimes it is an unabashed reading *into* the text. Willimon summarizes the matter well:

> The function of the sermon as a liturgical act is not primarily exhortation, dissemination of information, or instruction on correct doctrine—though these functions may be performed from time to time in sermons. The primary function is proclamation—again and again naming the Name, telling the story, keeping time, rehearsing the truth, stating the way things are now that God has come among us, announcing the facts of our adoption as children and heirs. Any ethical payoff from the sermon must derive from this essentially theocentric function. Ethos must not be allowed to precede logos—We do not need a sermonic set of rules for action, we need a story that helps us make sense out of the conflict that circumscribes our moral experience, a story complex and tragic as life itself. Without this sustaining narrative, action is impossible.[19]

Just as all liturgy is the articulation of the spirituality of the Christian community, so preaching, as a liturgical action, helps to bring to expression the self-image of the universal and local church. For liturgical preaching to participate in this enormous task, it must proceed from an enlightened theological understanding of the faith. It depends upon an informed re-reading of the word of God as it is lived in the Christian community. It is based on a theological reflection which is rooted in the historical process. In the concrete today, this will mean the process of liberation within the world of the poor, the oppres-

---

[19]William H. Willimon, *The Service of God: How Worship and Ethics are Related* (Nashville: Abingdon Press, 1983), p. 151.

sed, and the marginalized. It must be the logical outcome of a theology which involves a commitment to create a just and social world of mutuality between men and women. In other words, theology comes after involvement. It is the "second act" referred to by the liberation theologians.

To help the Christian community achieve its spiritual identity, the liturgical homily announces the Good News of the love of God for all men and women without exception, a love revealed and made flesh in Jesus Christ. Redemption has been accomplished through this love which has been made available through the death and resurrection of Christ and the gift of the Holy Spirit. But now it must be made historical. Preaching can do that by calling people to live in communion with the trinitarian God, by urging the love of Christ in terms of solidarity with the poor, by offering the hope and motivation that we can live as brothers and sisters in Christ within a just society.

The preaching which helps the community to re-interpret itself calls 1) for a change of heart and 2) for the re-reading of scripture. Often the *metanoia* or "conversion" spoken of in connection with preaching is seen in terms of individual repentance or a call to change one's personal way of living. The presupposition is that the hearers are caught in an attitude of sin and need to experience a reversal of life-style and moral perspective. But, in fact, most liturgical preaching today is not addressed to people who would be classified as serious sinners. Rather, change of heart is demanded in a particular way of religious people, those of us who think we know what God wants. The call to conversion is not that of moving away from an orientation of personal sinfulness, but one which involves a recision of present religious convictions. As Raymond Brown so poignantly observes:

> We remember that Jesus had few problems with sinners; they seem to have been relatively open to his message. His greatest problem was with religious people who knew already what God wanted and were therefore offended by hearing a different message from Jesus.[20]

[20]Burke, "Introduction," *A New Look at Preaching*, p. 68.

The homilist helps us reread the scriptures proclaimed in the assembly. Although this is a complicated process, what this means for the community as a whole can be summarized according to the four moments of the "hermeneutic circle" as described by Segundo.[21] They are: 1) the raising of consciousness by becoming suspicious of an ideological view of reality; 2) the questioning of the status quo by applying the ideological suspicion to larger superstructures and to theology in particular; 3) the re-reading of the bible in light of this new way of experiencing reality; 4) the formation of a new hermenuetic, or new way of interpreting scripture in the light of new insights into reality. The hermeneutical circle presumes and demands an ongoing praxis on the part of *both* the preacher and the congregation. It is not enough for the preacher to re-read *for* the community. Although this chapter focusses on the homilist primarily, much that is said of the preacher applies also to the congregation.

Preaching as an Event of Justice

Since liturgical preaching is rooted in the biblical perspective, and since this is one which is essentially directed to the marginated and the powerless and their experiences of freedom, preaching itself must be an experience of justice. It cannot prescind from the life and concerns of the elderly, the poor, gay/lesbians, racial minorities and women. But while preaching is proclaiming Good News, an event bringing to the worshipers' awareness experiences of liberation and the need for this liberation, it also calls them to celebrate the liberty that has been and is being achieved. Preaching justice in worship is not to be the occasion for the homilist to display unresolved anger or to paint an optimistic, but fundamentally false, picture. Preaching will never be a justice-event as long as it is true that "far too much preaching today claims to be prophetic when it is merely hostile."[22]

---

[21]Juan Luis Segundo, S. J., *The Liberation of Theology* (Maryknoll: Orbis Books, 1976), p. 9.

[22]Keck, in Burke, *A New Look at Preaching*, p. 155.

Preaching will not provide imaginative options for the oppressed unless preachers are aware of multiple ideologies in society and in the world. To presume that faith is transcultural and transhistorical here would be fatal. Homilists must be cognizant of other societies and how the gospel finds a home in these societies while challenging them concomitantly. The world is always larger than the preacher's personal experience. Even liturgical preaching cannot be limited to the world of the lectionary. At times significant passages may have been left out or cut up. This requires compensation and adaptation. Nor can preaching in the liturgy expect to achieve its full effect if it is not complemented with preaching in other contexts. Many of the truly marginated people have been alienated to the point where they are not present at the Sunday service. Preaching the justice of God must be made available to them. Perhaps, in such a situation more preaching will need to be done by lay people. Overcoming the barrier between clergy and lay will enhance liturgical preaching as an experience of justice.

Because the liturgy is for all Christians and because preaching cannot be directed to only a part of the Christian community, preachers must preach to both the oppressed and the (often unwitting) oppressors. Both are found in the congregation. Accordingly, homilizing must be the articulation of the experiences of the people of God and not only of the homilists or of some segment with whom their sympathies lie. If preaching is for the *whole* assembly, it will become a justice-event for the marginal ones so preferred by the New Testament. Why? Because it is not the case that some individuals are marginated and others are not. Margination is part of everyone's life. And unless liturgical preaching can mobilize the needs and areas of marginality in those who are usually considered to be the oppressors, these will never respond in turn to those who are usually considered to be the oppressed. What Regis Duffy says about the biblical symbols is especially relevant to liturgical preaching in this matter:

> The rich biblical symbols of hunger and thirst for the feast and of the food of the satisfied will be useless if they do not evoke from us our own experience and its symbols. The

resulting new awareness of our redemptive needs will help us to redefine our service to others. These needs, in turn, can never be simply our private concerns. For our needs should redefine the discipleship of others even while those same needs call out our gifts for the other. When we re-examine our own stories, what are the symbols of our false abundance that might urge us to be better listeners of those parables against false satiety? What instances in our cyclic passages through life would point to a hunger and thirst for God's righteousness? When did the need of others re-key our own?[23]

Often, then, the preaching of justice to publicly recognized oppressors will not at first make them aware that they are oppressing others. It will rather be to assist them to recognize their own needs so that they may become more sensitive to the needs of others. Good preaching in this situation will aim to produce a resonance between the needs among individuals, although these needs will not be identical. Good preachers do not prescribe, do not tell the believers what they ought to do. Truly good preachers lead the faithful on a journey through images, symbols, and other imaginative creations where they may encounter God by making decisions that make a difference for them.

All this should not weaken the fact that the homily will usually be a kind of narrative prophecy which calls for action. That, of course, means that it will often be confrontational. One of the truisms that has been passed along in the Christian tradition is that the word of God constitutes an offense. Offense implies some kind of disturbance which results from some call for action. Too often this offense was seen as the call to sinners to change their ways. But it is also a challenge to the reigning system of the pious and dutiful. Thus, moral conversion as a form of action moves into the public area where just wages,

---

[23] Regis Duffy, O. F. M., "Symbols of Abundance, Symbols of Need," in Searle, *Liturgy and Social Justice*, p. 77.

the possibility of nuclear holocaust, and governmental ideology must be subjected to a Christian critique.[24]

This prophetic character of preaching usually implies an element of urgency. If this preaching is going to be eschatological, which seems to be an essential aspect of prophecy, then there must be some summoning to decision here and now. The present order can never be absolute. It can have no final power over the worshiper. Historical though we are, we cannot find our identity in the past (even the Christian tradition) alone. Yet we cannot be so caught up into the future or the new order we wish to usher in, that the present is emptied of all meaning. Christian preaching must remind us that temporality is not a superficial prelude to a new heaven and a new earth. Just because the kingdom of God cannot achieve consummation in this world is no excuse to delay working at it now.

Preaching as narrative prophecy is not the same as communicating theological views and conclusions. As narration, it will be more experiential, and in both preparation and execution, praxis will have a priority over theory. The call to action, of which the call to conversion is a part, flows from the telling of the Christ story as a way of following after Christ. It is more than information about Christ. William Hill puts it well:

> I would be reluctant to suggest that ongoing conversion is less necessary for the theologian than for one entrusted with preaching. But conversion for the former serves as reflective understanding whereas it is more immediately oriented toward witness on the part of the preacher.[25]

Liturgical preaching is to be seen as community interaction and a collaborative effort. It arises out of and helps to build an

---

[24]For a fuller discussion of the relationship of social action and the various levels of conversion, see Edward K. Braxton, "Preaching As Food For Thought And Action In The Church," Burke, *A New Look at Preaching*.

[25]Burke, *A New Look at Preaching*, p. 124.

integral sense of community. The insights of the members of the community should be drawn on by the preacher, if those who are involved in the struggle for liberation and those who are oppressed are to have a voice. A practical implication could be the consideration of such participatory modes as the sharing of reflections, dramatizations, and dialogue. These activities would be either part of the preparation for the homily or a part of the preaching itself.

If liturgical preaching is to assist the community in its formation of a self-image in terms of justice, it will continue to ask it to grapple with questions of power:

-Who has authority over whom?
-Who is an "insider"; who is not?
-How does God enter into these relations?
-How does God respond to power and to powerlessness?

Such questions will only be significant if they are asked and responded to within the imaginations of the listeners. For instance, the homily will call into question the position of the hearers by asking them to examine their lives from the point of view of identification with the "enemies" of Jesus rather than with the "converted." In what ways are the Pharisees, the Romans, the High Priests, the rich—enemies of Jesus?

The community out of which preaching as a justice-event arises contains both the powerless and the powerful. Such preaching will, in particular, aim to assist the rich and the powerful to a personal attachment to a loving, provident, personal God in whom they can find real identity and liberation from their false selves and from an identity around possessions, power and prestige. Such preaching will help the powerless to articulate the needs and hopes in the ongoing process of their liberation. The oppression reflected on will not be just that of distant places, but that which exists in one's own country, city, neighborhood, home, and heart. But the formation of community is not only raising up social limitations, it is also a celebrative event. In the end, preaching is only liturgical when it becomes an important part of the convening of the community of faith for celebrating the authentic moments of liberation.

The Preacher as an Event of Justice

Preaching is not a thing or an object. It is a human event. In liturgy it is not possible to separate the preaching from the preacher. And so homilists must be events of social justice also. But how are they to become this? How can homilists move beyond the limitations of personal experiences as well as the confines of their own role in society? Elisabeth Schüssler Fiorenza suggests a way:

> I would suggest that in such a restrictive ecclesial situation the homilist has not just the function to articulate his own experience of God as a very particular experience but must also seek to articulate publicly the learning process and experiences of the people of God as well, since they are for the most part excluded from public proclamation. In order to be able to do so the homilist must become (1) self-critical, (2) attentive to the experience of others not like himself, (3) seek the involvement of those others in the task of preaching and proclamation and (4) develop dialogical modes and styles of preaching.[26]

The remainder of this section spells out these four points in greater detail.

Self-Critical

The basic point here is that the homilists must resist the temptation to substitute their own experience for that of the people to whom they are preaching. Most people preaching today are from the groups with power—not the powerless. Preachers must recognize their own areas of power and power-lessness and speak words of liberation from them. Preaching begins with a suspicion about where the power really is in one's own life situations. Homilists must recognize their own relationship to powerful and oppressive social structures. If

[26]Ibid, pp. 45-6.

the preachers come from the white middle class, they need to realize they can be oppressed by their own system. In the case of minority preachers, they can be the oppressors of other minorities.

Self-critical preachers will use language that is inclusive of both men and women. They will use language that is highly affective, while still clear-headed and precise. Such preachers will be conscious that their life-style can be as liberating as the words. After all, one's life, rather than one's doctrine, is the acid test of faithfulness to scripture.

Being self-critical will prevent homilists from identifying social justice with one political viewpoint or party. Christianity is larger than any one political idea. It is much better to find themes of justice in every political persuasion and then urge the congregation to be *more* inclusive in their notion of justice. The preacher of justice will befriend each member of the community present no matter what their political affiliation. There will be exceptions in those countries where a political party openly espouses an unjust goal.

Self-critical preachers will build up hope and instill a confidence that people have power to imagine and act. Such preachers will avoid making people feel guilty for past, ancient, and unjust social structures. They will not presume willing cooperation on the part of the hearers. We are as much the victims as the perpetrators of injustice. Self-critical preachers will be insistent and repeat frequently an exegesis of scripture which presents the gospel ideal of justice. They will gradually start to make applications which are concrete and limited, first to history and then to the present. They will not overwhelm people at first with incomprehensible, insoluble problems. They will not avoid the more difficult scriptural passages, whether they be ones which are too obviously confrontational or too easily abused by misinterpretation.

As an event of justice, preachers will build up a vision of the kingdom based on love and equality. They will highlight the experience of that vision within the liturgical event. Worship is a way of coping with "getting there but not quite yet." Sometimes liturgy itself leads to freedom through confrontation or by sharing a prejudice openly. Preachers will introduce a practical situation in which to concretize the movement to action. They will explicate the liturgy as a foretaste of the eternal, heavenly banquet, then ask if there will be anyone or any group we would be embarrassed to meet there. Finally and most importantly, self-critical preachers will love whom and what they criticize or shut up. Even oppressors are due the justice of loving concern, especially when they know not what *they do* or are trapped in situations extremely difficult to escape from.

Attentive to the Experience of Others

Homilists might well pose to themselves two questions in the beginning: what human struggle have I encountered this month in my family? What human struggle of the larger world-family has been presented to me this month? Homilists need to listen carefully to others so that they will not project their own fears and problems onto the congregation. They must relativize their own experiences. They must "sit where the people sit." There is no substitute for interacting with the members of the community on a daily basis whereby a rapport and trust level can be established which will enable preachers to confront and at the same time be with the people in the struggle for social justice. The key seems to be able to trust the freedom of the gospel and also trust the Spirit to empower people to responsible action.

To attend to the experience of others, not one's own, is to recognize that preaching should always be done in the context of the community, not just as a community of individuals with isolated needs and interests, but as a community of faith that shares in the struggle for greater freedom and happiness. Such attention to others' experiences is to recognize the total humanity of other persons with a respect for their personal gifts and talents and how they contribute to the community. It is to be sensitive to their educational, cultural, and spiritual backgrounds. It is a way to allow them freedom to exercise their own rights. To base one's preaching on what one hears from the community is already to begin the process of social integration because it lessens manipulation and discrimination. And ultimately it is a very concrete way to help people respect each other as brothers and sisters in Christ.

Seeking the Involvement of Others
in the Task of Preaching

As already noted, this presumes the involvement of people in the preparation for proclamation. But this does not suffice. It means that preaching cannot remain a clerical preserve. Preaching cannot be so absolutely tied to ordination, at least as ordination is presently understood. As E. Schüssler Fiorenza observes: "While the ordained is responsible that the word of God is proclaimed, such responsibility does not require that he himself always preaches but that he enables others to do so."[27]

This is not the place to develop with any comprehensiveness the arguments in favor of lay preaching. This has been done in *Preaching and the Non-Ordained*, edited by Nadine Foley, O.P.[28] In his essay Edward Schillebeeckx presents the historical argument for the right of Christians to speak from their evangelical experience. The juridical mission is not the only source of the right to proclaim the gospel. Sound theological training is also one. But ultimately, "the evangelical power to preach is to be found in the evangelical way of life."[29]

Sandra Schneiders in her essay convincingly argues that 1) the New Testament data does not automatically exclude anyone, including women, from the ministry of the word, 2) the New Testament ordering of ministries by competent authority is for the sake of effective proclamation of the word and not to limit the freedom of Christians in the exercise of their gifts, and 3) authentic preaching cannot be judged by institutional criteria alone. Vocation, assimilation of the

[27]Ibid, p. 49. At the present time in the Roman Catholic Church liturgical preaching is restricted to the priests and deacons. However, there are some provisions for lay participation. Most dioceses will allow lay persons to make remarks after the closing prayer of the liturgy, before the blessing and dismissal. Lay persons can make remarks before the opening of the liturgy. Unfortunately, the occasions for these remarks are limited to such times as funerals, religious professions, or other special situations. In the United States the prohibition against lay preaching is interpreted more or less benignly in individual liturgical assemblies.

[28]Collegeville: The Liturgical Press, 1983.

[29]"The Right of Every Christian to Speak in the Light of Evangelical Experience 'In the Midst of Brothers and Sisters,'" p. 37.

mystery of Christ, and the gift of the Spirit are also to be considered as criteria for apostolic preaching.[30]

Drawing upon the liturgical tradition, Mary Collins makes the point that it is possible "for the one who presides within the liturgical assembly by office to engage another believer to lead them all together into deeper communion with the mystery of Christ by the power of the Word, and that this collaborative ordering does not fracture the sacrament of unity."[31]

Speaking as a canonist, James H. Provost concludes that "From a careful reading of the revised Code, it seems that a lay person could on occasion preach in place of the ordinary or extraordinary minister who would usually provide a homily. The conditions under which this could be done would depend on the physical or moral unavailability of the ordained, ordinary or extraordinary, minister and could arise from pastoral need."[32] What will be of continuing significance in the matter of lay preaching is that since the Second Vatican Council, the legal basis for preaching has shifted from jurisdiction to baptism. All the baptized have the responsibility to proclaim the gospel in the world.

In the Roman Catholic Church, there has been some extension of the preaching ministry with the presence of the permanent deacon. However, until present institutional policies change, greater involvement in preaching will be most realistically realized in the last of E. Schüssler Fiorenza's points.

Developing Dialogical Modes and Styles of Preaching

Dialogue homilies and communal homilies have been with us for some time and will continue in certain situations.[33]

---

[30]"New Testament Foundations for Preaching by the Non-Ordained," p. 85-86.

[31]"The Baptismal Roots of the Preaching Ministry," p. 130.

[32]Ibid., p. 150. See also: William Skudlarek, "Lay Preaching and the Liturgy," *Worship* 58:6 (November, 1984).

[33]In the Roman Catholic Church at the present time dialogue homilies as we understand them are forbidden. *The Third Instruction On The Orderly Carrying Out of The Constitution On The Liturgy* (September 5, 1970) states in section 2: "The congregation is to refrain from comments, attempts at dialogue, or anything similar." This statement should be understood in its context, namely, a reaction to abuses in

What is proposed here is one method for greater involvement in the process of proclamation, one, hopefully, which will be an example of justice in the liturgy. It is an adaptation of a process explained by Thomas Groome in his book *Christian Religious Education*.[34] What is envisioned here is the presence of a group or team with whom the homilist interacts as part of the preparation for preaching in the liturgy. There are five basic movements in this shared praxis approach.

(1) Naming Present Action.

The participants are invited by the facilitator to name their own activity concerning the topic being considered. For instance, the question to begin with could be: what is the primary message you are hearing from next Sunday's scripture readings? What is your action as a result of what you are hearing? This action includes what the people are doing physically, spiritually, emotionally and intellectually. The point to this first movement is to get people to move into the concrete. What can they name in their lives now that which suggests or implies a connection between the scriptures and actions of justice?

(2) The Participant's Stories and Visions.

The participants are invited to reflect critically on why they do what they do and what are the likely or intended consequences of their actions. Here they are to become aware of their social conditioning, their biases, and presuppositions. They are invited to imagine the future consequences of their present actions. What memories and hopes are triggered by the biblical material on which they are reflecting? What are the reasons for their present actions and what are the consequences of them in terms of their justice commitments? Sometimes the

this matter where the congregation's participation overwhelmed the role of the presider. When such abuses are not foreseen and when the presider continues "to preside" over this part of the liturgy, a more benign interpretation of this restriction seems to be inorder.

[34](San Francisco: Harper and Row, 1980). Gilbert Ostdiek, O.F.M., *Catechesis for Liturgy* (Washington, D.C.: The Pastoral Press, 1986).

difference between what is done and what is desired comes up. But this can be the motivation for change.

(3) The Christian Community Story and Vision.

The preacher makes present to the group the Christian story concerning the topic at hand and the faith response that it invites. This is the catechetical moment when the scriptural texts need to be exegeted so that the theological meanings of the readings can be fitted into the larger Christian story. Hopefully, in this third movement, light is shed on the lessons for a particular Sunday by seeing their location in a liturgical season or their place in the liturgical year. This movement is to enable the group to encounter the story and vision of the Christian tradition, especially as it is the Good News of liberation. Often this can be done by juxtaposing the biblical readings with current theological writings on faith and justice.

(4) Dialectical Hermeneutic Between the Story and the Participants' Stories.

The participants are invited to appropriate the Christian story to their lives in a dialectic with their own stories. How does this larger story affirm, heal, and support our own? There will always be limitations in our stories and the community's story will bring them to light. This should not be a negative experience. It can be a liberating critique and a creative process. The group here should gain greater insight into the scriptures and hopefully see what is, or is not, feasible as a response in social justice. There is a going back and forth between the justice of God and the justice we live out. It is a bringing together of the faith tradition and the faith experience.

(5) Dialectical Hermeneutic Between the Vision and the Participants' Visions.

At this point the present actions of the reflection group are placed in the specific perspective of the kingdom of God. What are the signs of the kingdom already present among us? How does the kingdom still need to be realized? How shall we act in the future? This is the time when we critique our own visions in terms of the vision of the kingdom of God. This is the opportunity for the group and individuals in the group to respond in faith. This last movement is where concrete actions of justice will especially emerge, possibly providing options which might be presented to the congregation. But such concreteness also means that not all in the group will always agree on the specifics of justice. But that is part of the Christian vision.

This process can serve as the structure for a group from the parish (with changing membership) which meets with the homilist for the preparation of homilies. It could provide the format for small group liturgies of the word. It could also be incorporated in various kinds of prayer services. In this latter case, lay preaching would be possible. But even in those main Sunday liturgies where people are invited to share briefly with those near them, Groome's method might well be employed.

The use of this method of engaging small groups of the congregation in homily preparation at any given time can gradually educate the assembly to ways of listening to preaching. Concrete involvement in the process makes preaching a shared event. Worshipers sensitized by this approach will be more likely to derive benefit from the Sunday homily, even when it less than adequately fulfills the qualifications for good liturgical preaching

꙳

Bibliography

Academy of Homiletics. *Preaching and Worship,* Princeton: Princeton Theological Seminary, 1980.

> These papers come from the 1980 meeting of the Academy of Homiletics. While the essays deal with various aspects of preaching and liturgy, there is much material here that is relevant to the issue of social justice.

Brown, Robert McAfee. *Unexpected News,* Philadelphia: The Westminster Press, 1984.

A well written and engaging book that takes ten scripture stories and reexamines them from a contemporary, liberation perspective. The author's treatment of scripture can serve as a model in approaching preaching from this perspective.

Burghardt, Walter, S.J. "Preaching the Just Word," in *Liturgy and Social Justice,* edited by Mark Searle, Collegeville: Liturgical Press, 1980.

Burghardt's essay is a good introduction looking at the relation of preaching and justice from the points of view of theology, liturgy, and homiletics.

Burke, John, O.P., ed. *A New Look at Preaching,* Wilmington: Michael Glazier, Inc., 1983.

The volume treats of preaching as a contemporary experience in the Church, suggesting ways to make it vital and at the center of Christian life. The section most explicitly dealing with social justice is Elisabeth Schüssler Fiorenza's response to the paper by Walter Burghardt.

De Clercq, Bertrand. "Political Commitment and Liturgical Celebration," in *Concilium 84: Political Commitment and Christian Community,* edited by Alois Muller and Norbert Greinacher, New York: Herder and Herder, 1973.
This is a good, but too short, statement of the relationship of the political dimension of life and liturgical celebration.

Donahue, John R., S.J. "Biblical Perspectives on Justice," in *The Faith That Does Justice,* edited by John Haughey, S. J. New York: Paulist Press, 1977.

This competent and comprehensive study of justice in the Old Testament, the Intertestamental Period, and the New Testament is highly recommended.

Krieg, Robert A. "The Funeral Homily: A Theological View," *Worship* 58: 3 (May 1984).

Although this article is not explicitly on social justice, it does provide a basis for how the preacher might incorporate the aspect of justice in this humanly critical situation.

Llopis, Joan. "The Message of Liberation in the Liturgy," in *Concilium 92: Politics and the Liturgy,* edited by Herman Schmidt and David Power, New York: Herder and Herder, 1974.

This article analyzes the relationship between the words of the liturgy and the political dimension of Christian faith. Although brief, it presents a fine summary of the need for proclamation to maintain a concrete historical setting and to have a liberating relationship to the past, present and future.

Marty, Martin. *The Word: People Participating in Preaching,* Philadelphia: Fortress Press, 1980.

Marty's point is that preaching is not the domain of the preacher alone but is an act in which the people participate. They do so when they receive, share and act upon the word.

National Conference of Catholic Bishops. *Fulfilled in Your Hearing: The Homily in the Sunday Assembly,* Washington, D.C. United States Catholic Conference, 1982.

This is an excellent introduction to the meaning of liturgical preaching. It contains a fine method for homily preparation.

Willimon, William H. "Preaching: Responding to the Word," in his *The Service of God: How Worship and Ethics are Related,* Nashville: Abingdon Press, 1983.

In this chapter Willimon is primarily concerned with the tendency in Protestantism to turn preaching into forms of moralizing.

6

Social Justice in the Liturgy of the Eucharist

In our consideration of Christian initiation, we saw that first Eucharist has implications for social justice because it unites us intimately with the risen Jesus who sacrificed himself for us, who emptied himself, taking the form of a slave for our liberation from slavery, and who, though he was rich, became poor, so that we who are poor might become rich. Every Eucharist unites us to that same Jesus and has implications for social justice. But more can be said about the significance of the eucharistic liturgy for social justice.

The Assembly

On Sunday morning we observe people converging on the parish church. We *assemble* for the Eucharist. We do not go by ourselves into the privacy of some room as we may do for other forms of prayer. The very need to assemble for the Eucharist is a reminder that we are social beings; we live, work, play and pray with others. If we are social beings, we are called to justice, for only in loving justice can men and women live socially in a way commensurate to the dignity of each one.

We recall here what was said about the community into which the rite of Christian initiation introduces us: that community is made up of a people freed from oppression and possessing a passion for social justice. If we are called together, moreover, it is to acknowledge anew our mission from Jesus Christ to announce the good news of God's salvation, which includes the establishment of social justice in human society.

In the church we see all sorts of people: rich and poor, healthy and disabled, young and old, business executives and employees, office workers and factory hands. The only distinctions that can be made in the eucharistic assembly are those arising from liturgical functions or due occasionally to civil authorities in accord with liturgical law.[1] We are reminded of the basic equality and dignity of every person vis-à-vis God and, therefore, the rights of every person to a fair share of the earth's and society's resources which are God's gifts for all her children.

As we gather in a particular church, we may be struck by the fact that there are very few poor people present. Or the opposite may be true: we see few people whose clothes obviously come from the city's better stores or whose automobiles are new every year. On the other hand, the congregation may be composed of both the economically well-off and those who are barely managing to live. In any case, we find that our social order comes into church and sits in the pews with us. Any assembly reminds us that there are many unjustifiable inequalities in our world.

We often accept our society uncritically as "simply the way things are," the Creator's order rather than humanity's disorder. As a result, we do not notice the social injustice that reveals itself in our eucharistic assemblies. When we look around at the congregation gathered from the neighborhood, however, we may be prompted to wonder whether there are written or unwritten covenants among people to exclude certain ethnic groups from renting or purchasing homes in the area, or whether local banks are redlining, that is, refusing loans or investments in the district to force neighborhood

---

[1]Vatican Council II, *Constitution on the Sacred Liturgy*, no. 32. in Austin Flannery, ed., *Vatican Council II: Conciliar and Post Conciliar Documents* (Collegeville: Liturgical Press, 1975), p. 11.

decline and eventually cheap property to be bought at low prices and resold for substantial profits.[2]

At the beginning of the Sunday liturgy the presider and other ministers may process down the center aisle from the rear of the church. The participants in that procession remind us of social justice. Does the procession consist only of the priest and an "altar boy" or are other people involved? Are there any women and girls among the ministers, or are they all men and boys?[3] In fact, we will have encountered ushers while assembling before the liturgy began. Any women among them? And when the procession reaches the sanctuary, where do the laity and especially women take their positions? Is the church in its visible actions a sacrament, an effective model, for society of a truly just social organization, or does it cling to unjust societal patterns which it absorbed from the world?

Sunday worship commonly begins with a hymn. What about the language of that hymn and of the greetings, invitations, prayers, and readings which will be spoken as the liturgy progresses? Is the language sexist? Does the congregation profess in the Creed that "for us men and for our salvation" the Word of God came down from heaven? Does the presider announce in the fourth preface for Easter in the Roman sacramentary that in the risen Christ "a broken world has been renewed and *man* is once again made whole"?

The question of sexist language is complex. There is little excuse, however, for perpetuating today masculine terms like "brother," "man," "mankind," "he," "his," "him" in a generic sense when large portions of the population do not interpret them in that way and are offended by them, and when no

---

[2]On discrimination in housing, see, for example, Denis Woods, "Housing Discrimination: An Analysis of Social Structures, "*America*, 18 August 1981, pp. 49-53; Allen J. Fishbein, "Redlining Revisited: The Myth of Competition in Urban Mortgage Markets," *Journal of Retail Banking* 5 (Summer 1983): 69-76; for arguments that redlining does not exist, arguments Fishbein refutes, see David and Marily Oblak, "The Charge of Mortgage Redlining: Discrimination Against Logic, *Journal of Retail Banking* 5 (Summer 1983): 59-68; see also Robert Drinan, "Is a Fair Housing Law a Forgotten Dream?" *America*, 7 April 1984, pp. 257-60.

[3]See Sandra Schneiders, "The Effects of Women's Experience on Their Spirituality," *Spirituality Today* 35 (1983): 101-3; John Huels, "Female Altar Servers: The Legal Issue," *Worship* 57 (1983): 513-25.

conceivable harm can come to those who still accept them in an inclusive sense.[4] The more delicate problem is language referring to God.[5] Simply omitting titles such as "Father" or "Son" does not solve the problem, nor does feminizing the Holy Spirit. Some names for God are part of revelation as the vehicle of that revelation; they say something God intends us to hear. In preaching, however, and eventually in liturgical texts, we certainly can and should balance the masculine names and references with feminine terms found in scripture and also meant to tell us something about God.

In about the year 150, St. Justin Martyr wrote that, after the reading of the memoirs of the apostles and the exhortation of the president of the assembly, "then we all stand up together and offer prayers."[6] To restore active participation by the faithful in the liturgy, this practice was reestablished in the Roman liturgy by the incorporation of the General Intercessions (often called the Prayer of the Faithful). Here, according to the General Instruction of the Roman Missal (no. 45), the faithful intercede for the church, civil authorities, the salvation of all, and "those oppressed by various needs." The General Intercessions are meant to broaden the vision of the local assembly, to lift the gathered people beyond their own immediate problems, worries, and needs, to make them conscious of all God's children scattered far and wide over this planet,

[4]Barbara Beckwith, "Why Sexist Language Doesn't Belong in Church (or Anywhere Else)," *St. Anthony Messenger* 88 (February 1981) 22-26; Jacki Kelly, "The Justice of Inclusive Language," *Modern Liturgy* 11:5 (June/July/August, 1984): 27. Carol Schuck, "Christians Shouldn't Use Sexist Language," *U. S. Catholic 49 (April 1984): 12-13 (reprinted from Salt).*

[5]Gail Ranshaw Schmidt, "Lutheran Liturgical Prayer and God as Mother," *Worship* 52 (1978): 517-42; idem, "*De Divinis Nominibus*: The Gender of God: A Contribution to the Conversation," *Worship* 56 (1982): 231-38; Elizabeth A. Johnson, "The Incomprehensibility of God and the Image of God, Male and Female," *Theological Studies* 45 (1984): 441-65; Mary Collins, "Naming God in Public Prayer," *Worship* 59 (1985): 291-303. For more of Gail Ramshaw's work on language in the liturgy see her *Worship: Searching for Language*, Washington, D.C.: The Pastoral Press, 1988.

[6]St. Justin Martyr, *First Apology*, 67, cf. 65, in Paul Palmer, *Sources of Christian Theology I: Sacraments and Worship*(Westminster, Md.: Newman Press, 1955), p. 40, cf. p. 3.

millions of them suffering hunger, malnutrition, ignorance, homelessness, political imprisonment, torture.[7]

A danger in the General Intercessions is that they can become simply words. We hear a petition for the starving people of the African Sahel and respond, "We pray to the Lord." But we are not really engaged in the petition. We have no thoughts about, or feelings for, the people mentioned in the prayer; we are not interested in trying to do something to change the situation. It may well be true, of course, that we in our location and circumstances are praying precisely because we are up against a limit to our capacities to effect change which we truly want and are willing to do something for. This is an appropriate motive, but it does presuppose a desire to help those in need. If, then, the General Intercessions are going to be authentic prayer, social justice must be a consciously cultivated aspect of our Christian lives.[8]

The Gifts We Offer

At the presentation of the gifts, two, three, or four people leave their places in the pews to pick up the gifts and then process with them down the aisle to the ministers in the sanctuary. We ordinarily pay little attention to this action. We can think to ourselves: "Somebody must bring the gifts up to the table, so those few people may as well do it. And it's so nice if a family does it!"

But more is involved here than simply transporting the gifts.

---

[7]Vatican Council II, *Constitution on the Sacred Liturgy*, no. 53, in Flannery, p. 18; Gail Ramshaw Schmidt, *God's Food: The Relationship Between Holy Communion and World Hunger* (Philadelphia: Lutheran Church in America, 1984), p. 21. Examples of intercessions pertinent to justice in our world may be found here and there in the Litany in the *Lutheran Book of Prayer* (Minneapolis: Augsburg, 1979), pp. 169, 171; in *The Book of Common Prayer* (New York: Church Hymnal Corporation, 1979), pp. 387-90; in *Worshipbook: Services and Hymns* (Philadelphia: Westminister Press, 1972), pp. 31-32, 105-31.

[8]For authentic petitionary prayer, see Jerome Murphy O'Connor, "Prayer of Petition and Community," in idem, *What is Religious Life?* (Wilmington, Del.: Michael Glazier, 1977), pp. 31-40.

All of us gathered to celebrate the death, resurrection, and future coming of Jesus Christ bring those gifts to the table. Those two, three, or four people are our representatives: *we* are carrying those gifts to the table.

What do we bring? The fruits of the earth and the vine—God's gift to us of his creation. We bring God the beauty and bounty of her creation —golden fields of wheat and fat clusters of grapes. The fruits of God's earth are for all men and women, not just some of them. Pope Paul VI noted clearly that the right to private property is not an absolute right, allowing one to use it any way one wishes, even to destroy it; but all property is to be used in a way which benefits the common welfare.[9] So when we—not only the few people who physically carry the gifts—present them at the table, we are handling the common patrimony of God's creation. To be worthy of presenting those gifts, we must be women and men intent upon the fair sharing of the fruits of the earth among all the globe's inhabitants.

But we bring to the table more than the fruits of the earth: we bring "the work of human hands."[10] We bring the products of human effort, indeed, social effort. For it is not simple stalks of wheat plucked from the field or whole grapes from a vine that we bring, but bread and wine. The field and the vine, moreover, are not wild strands of wheat or wild olives, but cultivated fields and vineyards. Immense amounts of human thought, decision, and muscular energy have been invested in that wheat and those grapes. Decades—in fact, centuries—of human cultivation have improved the quality of the grain and grapes. During their growing period they are nurtured, watched over, protected from insects. Then there is the work of harvesting the grain and fruit, transporting them to where

[9]Pope Paul VI, *On the Development of Peoples,* 16 March 1967, nos. 22-24, in Joseph Gremillion, *The Gospel of Peace and Justice* (Maryknoll, N.Y.: Orbis Books, 1976), pp. 393-94.

[10]See Gustave Martelet, *The Risen Christ and the Eucharistic World* (New York: Seabury, 1976), pp. 31-36; Enrique Dussel, "The Bread of the Eucharistic Celebration as a Sign of Justice in the Community," in Mary Collins and David Powers, eds. *Can We Always Celebrate the Eucharist?* Concilium 152 (New York: Seabury Press, 1982), pp. 60-61; also John A. T. Robinson, *Liturgy Coming to Life* (Philadelphia: Westminster Press, 1960), pp. 33-37.

they are processed. Again, long hours, much ingenuity, care, and social organization are devoted to transforming the raw material into bread and wine. Once the transformation is accomplished, many people are further involved in packaging, shipping, distributing, selling, and buying these products, so that they finally appear in the assembly as gifts brought up to the table in worship. Highways and telephones and mail services are required in this distribution process. Accountants and secretaries also play roles. Simply speaking, the whole economic and social organization of our society is symbolized in the bread and wine which we bring to the table. But, in fact, we can only bring them because God has first brought them to us. Bread and wine are first symbols of God and then symbols of our lives.

As we offer our world to God, can we fail to be concerned about the social injustice that corrupts that world, that taints our gift? At the price of what oppression do we carry up to the table gifts of bread and wine? Who has been hurt in the long process in which that bread and wine have made their way from the fields and the vines? Migrant workers and their children?[11] Who else? Dare we offer to *our God* moldy bread and sour wine—moldy and sour not because of some bacteria, but because of the social injustice suffered by so many of the men, women and children through whose efforts this bread and wine come to be here in the midst of this assembly? We ask God to forgive the mold and sourness, our social injustice, and to transform our imperfect gifts and return them to us as the risen Just One. Dare we then partake of these consecrated elements if we are indifferent to the cries of the poor locked in

[11]For illustrative reports on the conditions of migrant workers, see, for example, Mark R. Day, "Aliens' California Suite: Rats and Ravines," *National Catholic Reporter*, 31 July 1981, p. 1; John T. Berfuss, "Worker's Death Peak of Iceberg," ibid., p. 2. For more complete studies, see Joy Hintz, *Poverty, Prejudice, Power, Politics: Migrants Speak about Their Lives* (Columbus, Ohio: Avonelle Associates, 1981); Jacques Levy, *Cesar Chavez: Autobiography of La Causa* (New York: W. W. Norton, 1975); Ronald B. Taylor, *Sweatshop in the Sun: Child Labor on the Farm* (Boston: Beacon Press, 1973). For further studies, Beverly Fodell, *Cesar Chavez and the United Farm Workers: A Selective Bibliography* (Detroit: Wayne State University Press, 1974).

the cages of unjust social, economic and political structures?

A collection is often taken up at Sunday worship.[12] The collected funds are frequently brought up to the table with the gifts of bread and wine. Christians have always made contributions of goods for the needs of the church and the poor. When, from the eleventh century, money became a more prominent gift, the interpretation of what was occurring at this point of the celebration became quite pragmatic. But it ought not to be so; the gift of money is an offering of self, of one's labor and time, and is an expression of concern for the church and the poor.

The collection of "filthy lucre" in worship is a powerful reminder that our Christian life is not angelic but very much in the midst of this world of our human making. Our savior is God *incarnate*; through our humanity we journey to eternal life. Part of St. Paul's ministry was concern for a collection to be taken up throughout the churches of Greece and Asia Minor for the poor church in Jerusalem (cf. Acts 24:17; Rom. 15:25ff.; 1 Cor. 16:1ff; 2 Cor. 8:1-9, 15; Gal. 2:10).

The collection at worship is also a potent reminder that we are entwined in the economic, social and political orders of our nation as we, God's people, endeavor to provide for what we need to live out our Christian faith: Sunday liturgy, funerals, schools, relief agencies, hospitals, homes for the elderly, and so forth. We can easily get caught in the injustices that warp the economic, social and political spheres of our society. Christian institutions exercise considerable purchasing power and investment potential which can be directed to support businesses that strive to be just in all their operations, rather than those which exploit people, or are indifferent about the social consequences of their activities. Parishes, hospitals and other church agencies hire people; they have an obligation

---

[12]For history and meaning of the collection, see Edward J. Kilmartin, "The Sacrifice of Thanksgiving and Social Justice," in Mark Searle, ed., *Liturgy and Social Justice* (Collegeville: Liturgical Press, 1980), pp. 53-71. Kilmartin includes discussion of Mass stipends; for more on that topic, see M. Francis Mannion "Stipends and Eucharistic Praxis," *Worship* 57 (1983): 194-214; and John M. Huels, "Stipends in the New Code of Canon Law," ibid., 215-24.

to pay just wages.[13] There is the delicate matter of recognizing unions.[14] The simple "ritual" of dropping money into the basket at Sunday worship recalls our responsiblity to seek social justice in exercising the stewardship over this world's goods which God entrusts to us.

The Prayers of Thanksgiving

Even eucharistic prayers contain subtle pointers to social justice. In Eucharistic Prayer II of the Roman rite, the presider prays: "May all who share in the body and blood of Christ be brought together in unity by the Holy Spirit." In Eucharistic Prayer III the petition for unity is slightly different: "Grant that we, who are nourished by his body and blood, may be filled with the Holy Spirit and become one body, one spirit in Christ." Even the ancient Eucharistic Prayer I pleads for unity before the narrative of institution: "We offer them [the gifts] for your holy Catholic Church; ... grant it peace and unity throughout the world." In the *Book of Common Prayer*, the Great Thanksgiving of the Holy Eucharist, Rite II, begs God that the faithful be sanctified "to serve you in unity, constancy and peace." Jesus' prayer was, according to the Gospel of John, that "all may be one ... So shall the world know that you [God] sent me and that you loved them as you loved me" (17:21-23). The unity of Christ's disciples is to be the sacrament of the unity of all men and women with God and among themselves.[15] So the unity of Christ's followers is fundamental to the divine intent and to the fulfillment of the Eucharist.

Unity, however, implies several components. It entails a certain equality among the disciples of Christ: "All of you who have been baptized into Christ have clothed yourselves with him. There does not exist among you Jew or Greek, slave or freeperson, male or female. All are one in Christ" (Gal. 3:27-

---

[13]Synod of Bishops, Second General Assembly, 1971, *Justice in the World*, no. 41, in Gremillion, *Gospel of Peace and Justice*, p. 522.

[14]See, for example, Adam Maida, ed. *Issues in the Labor Management Dialogue: Church Perspectives* (St. Louis: Catholic Health Association, 1982).

[15]Vatican Council II, *Constitution on the Church*, no. 1, in Flannagan, p. 350.

28; cf. Col. 3:11). But this unity also embraces a variety of gifts, ministries and works: "There are different gifts but the same Spirit; there are different ministries but the same Lord; there are different works but the same God who accomplishes all of them in everyone" (1 Cor. 12:4-6; cf. vv. 14-30; Rom. 12:3-8; Eph. 4:11). Finally, unity implies the harmonious inter-action of these equal, but variously endowed, persons who constitute Christ's ecclesial body: "Through him the whole body grows, and with the proper functioning of the members joined firmly together by each supporting ligament, builds itself up in love" (Eph. 4:16).

To pray for the unity of the church, therefore, is to pray for all of the factors which make up unity and all the virtues required to make them possible, including social justice. Without social justice in the church, the equality of persons will not be acknowledged in fact; the diversity of gifts, ministries and works will not be utilized; and harmonious interaction will be replaced by favoritism, conflict and smoth-ering of some members' gifts. In a word, without ecclesial social justice, the divine intent for the body of Christ and fulfillment of the Eucharist will be frustrated.

The church's purpose in the world, moreover, will be crip-pled. Unless there is social justice in the church essential for its unity, the church cannot be an effective model or credible prophet to the world of the unity and, implicitly, the social justice to which humanity is called. We are not speaking now only of attitudes and deeds of individuals, but of the very way the church—the local parish, the diocese or presbytery or district, a church school or hospital—is organized and carries on its activities. Does the church in its structures as well as the habitual attitudes and actions of its members follow the social status quo of society, or does it challenge society with an example of social justice and unity? Are women treated more justly in the church than in secular society? Does the church serve as a model to the world for the treatment of minorities? Is the church a leader in the way it provides for disabled persons?

Eucharistic Prayer III of the Roman rite includes the inter-cession: "Lord, may this sacrifice, which has made our peace with you, advance the peace and salvation of all the world."

This peace with God includes, of course, peace with fellow human beings, for peace is the fruit of love of God and that love is inseparable from love of neighbor (1 John 4:20-21). Peace both with God and neighbor implies justice. We "owe" God something, namely, reverence, worship and service—acts of the virtue of religion. We owe our fellow human beings something: respect for their persons, their reputations, their property, their share of the material and cultural goods requisite for a decent human life, and an organization of society which insures all forms of justice. In this intercession of the third Eucharistic Prayer, then, we pray that Christ's sacrifice, which has established justice and so also peace between us and God, may also bring about justice and peace among men and women of all the world.

God, however, is not going to answer this prayer apart from our efforts. The Incarnation reveals that God effects salvation through the human being, Jesus. Jesus is the pattern of how God intends to bring justice and peace into the world: through our graced human activity in the service of his free gift of salvation. We do not presume on miracles as answers to our prayers. This prayer for the advance of the peace and justice "of all the world" is not offered to make a need known to God, as if she did not already know our miseries. It is offered to inspire us to work toward that goal as co-operators with God in her saving work, while placing trust in her that she will provide where we fall short or run into seemingly insurmountable obstacles; and then she will provide, not a miracle, but by her grace new human insight, right judgment, deliberate choice, and responsible action.

In the narrative transition in Eucharistic Prayer IV, the presider prays on behalf of the community: "Father ... you sent your only Son .... To the poor he proclaimed the good news of salvation, to prisoners, freedom, and to those in sorrow, joy .... He sent the Holy Spirit from you, Father, as his first gift to those who believe, to complete his work on earth and bring us the fullness of grace." The words about proclaiming the good news to the poor, to prisoners, to those who mourn, echo the passage from Isaiah, chapter 61, quoted in the Gospel of Luke, chapter 4, and are, as we have seen, filled with implications for social justice.

The prayer goes on to recognize that Jesus gives his first gift of the Holy Spirit to believers in order to "complete his work on earth." This phrase may be interpreted to mean only by the gift of the Spirit does the risen Jesus achieve the goal toward which his earthly activities were directed. The concluding phrase, "bring us the fullness of grace," can be interpreted as defining, so to speak, what the completion of this earthly work is, namely, the gift of the Spirit, God's very being, "the fullness of grace," bestowed on us.

But to "complete his work on earth" can also mean to continue to carry on the mission which he began while he was "on earth" in our midst, the mission of announcing the good news to the poor, freedom to prisoners, and joy to mourners. He sends the Holy Spirit to believers to make them his ecclesial body in space and time and to inspire them to carry out this mission, *his* mission. Jesus, through his members, brings the fullness of grace to men and women down through the ages and ultimately through the consummation of creation on the Last Day. A significant factor in "completing Jesus' work" is, as we have noted before, struggling for social justice, even as it implies love, humility and other virtuous attitudes and activities. So even in the heart of the Eucharistic Prayers we find notable, though implicit, references to social justice.

The Our Father

The Our Father is especially rich in its implications for social justice. Michael H. Crosby, a Capuchin priest, has written a book unfolding the meaning of the Our Father in relation to our contemporary economic, social and political world—*Thy Will Be Done: Praying the Our Father as Subversive Activity.*[16] The following paragraphs attempt to give the gist of his thought but are no substitute for the original. Understandably, there are serious difficulties today with the application of the name, Father, to God. However, in the best

---

[16](Maryknoll, N.Y.: Orbis Books, 1977).

of all possible worlds where we would be fully inclusive in our language about God and would be calling God both Father and Mother, there would presumably be some significance to speaking of God as Father.

Addressing God as "Our Father" draws us out of ourselves. It reminds us that we are a part of the human family, to whom God has given creation, so that every human being has a right to life and the riches of nature and human invention. The title "Father" reminds us that our God is Father, Son and Holy Spirit, a community of knowing, loving, caring "persons," sharing one divine being. We are called to share in this common life of Father, Son and Holy Spirit and to reflect this divine community in our human community, which can happen only through truth, love, social justice, peace and freedom.

"Hallowed be thy name" is prayer, or even a declaration of faith, that God's name, God's being, will be recognized and revered among all men and women. God's name, or being, includes her intentions, her purposes. Among these is that we human beings be images of the divine being, freely exercising dominion over creation. God's name cannot be hallowed where men and women live in oppression, denied access to the sources of life which have been entrusted to the stewardship of all the human family.

"Thy kingdom come" affirms that God's justice is what we desire, not the "justice" that human authorities set up, be they ancient Roman emperors, medieval lords, baroque monarchs, modern presidents and premiers, parliaments and houses of representatives, soviet republics, national or international business communities, or academies of science or literature. However perfectly just our world may seem, if we examine it closely, we will find it short of the justice of God's reign.[17]

"Thy will be done on earth as it is in heaven." God's will is his plan for creation. This plan is that all women and men, sharing in the divine life of the Trinity, reflect the triune divine

---

[17]It may be appropriate to note here that the ancient Near Eastern concept of "kingdom" understood the king as providing for the marginated in the community. In the prologue of the Code of Hammurabi there is mention of the king as the provider of the widows and orphans.

life in their human social life and in their caring for creation and enriching it as co-workers with God. This plan includes, therefore, liberating women and men from oppression of every sort, so that they may attain to the fullness of life destined for them by God. Unjust social structures and ways of doing things are obviously contrary to God's will.

If the petition "Give us this day our daily bread" is understood to refer to the Eucharist, we must remember the ancient prophets' criticisms of the Israelites' worship and sacrifices because they did not accompany their worship of God with social justice in their daily lives. To be remembered is Paul's warning to the Corinthians (1 Cor. 11:29) to recognize "the body" when partaking of the Eucharist. Although this warning may refer to recognizing that the bread and wine are the body and blood of Jesus, it also refers to recognizing that to share the bread and wine with others is to profess a bond of unity with them in Christ, so that to act unjustly toward them while at the same time communicating in the Eucharist is hypocricy.[18]

"Forgive us our trespasses as we forgive those who trespass against us" alludes to the Year of Jubilee prescribed in the Mosaic law (Lev. 25). In that light, the word *debts* rather than *trespasses* or *wrongs* or *sins* captures the down-to-earth, everyday material realities implied here. For in the Jubilee Year, every fiftieth year, all debts were to be cancelled, Israelite slaves freed, land returned to its original owners, and the farms left uncultivated.[19] The forgiveness of God we seek, then, is in proportion to our willingness to lift burdens from people, free them from oppression, ensure a just distribution of wealth in the world, and enable men and women to enjoy freedom for play and prayer.

When we pray "Lead us not into temptation," the temptation we seek to avert is not merely unacceptable urgings of the flesh, or feelings of pride, envy, jealousy, anger, impatience, or

---

[18]Jerome Murphy-O'Connor makes a strong case for interpreting "the body" in the First Corinthian text as an allusion to the community as the body of Christ. See his "Eucharist and Community in First Corinthians," *Worship* 51:1 (January, 1977): 67-8.

[19]See Vincent Cosmao, *Changing the World: An Agenda for the Churches* (Maryknoll, N.Y.: Orbis Books, 1984), p. 64.

the lure of money, prestige, or power; it is also participation in distorted, inhuman, unjust economic, social and political systems and their legitimizing ideologies, attitudes and ways of doing things. We ask not to be "led" into temptation because we can be caught in the web of these evils without our being aware of it. As children we accept the world as presented to us by our elders; as adults, we accept it as presented by the leaders of our society; often we never see fundamental injustices built into that world. So it is that we ask God to "deliver us from evil" to liberate us from our blindness and the web of injustice in which we have become entangled without realizing it, both supporting it and being victimized by it at the same time.

The prayer for social justice implied in the Our Father is continued in the prayer which follows in the Roman liturgy: "Deliver us, O Lord." We realize now that the "every evil" from which we ask to be delivered includes not only personal sins, mental and bodily ills, but also distorted social structures which deprive people of their human and religious dignity, rights and development. If we ask God for "peace in our day," much more than interior tranquillity of soul is meant. We pray that God protect us from all "anxiety." The Latin word for "anxiety" is translated as *perturbatio*, which signifies confusion, disorder, disturbance. It does not have the exclusively psychological meaning that the English word *anxiety* carries. So this petition strongly suggests, in its original Latin version, that the surrounding social world in which we live is chaotic, twisted, disordered, inhibits human life and is, therefore, an imperfect, unjust social system—clearly a source of personal anxiety.

Making Peace

When St. Justin Martyr explained the Christian Eucharist around 150 C.E. in his *First Apology* (no. 65), he noted that after the general intercessions, before the bread and wine were brought to the president of the assembly, the people "greet one another with a kiss." This gesture of peace clearly issued from Jesus' words in the Sermon on the Mount: "If you bring your gift to the altar and there recall that your brother or sister has anything against you, leave your gift at the altar, go first to be reconciled with your brother or sister, and then come and offer your gift" (Matt. 5:23-24). In later centuries this gesture of reconciliation was moved back in the Roman Mass ritual to before Holy Communion, but it remains as the conclusion of the liturgy of the word in many Christian worship services. In any case, what we have come to realize in the course of this chapter is that the peace which Christ desires to give us, which we pray for, and which we wish for one another in symbolic action, means not only inner quiet of the soul, not only harmony between individuals, but also a social order in which each person enjoys a fair share of God's gifts to humanity in creation. Our gesture of peace with people around us in church or chapel is superficial, if it is not accompanied by a willingness and appropriate action to provide justice for all in our parishes, neighborhoods, cities, nation and world. The Hebrew word for peace, *shalom*, implies a fullness of blessing and happy relationships, all of which entails a just social order as a requisite element.[20]

This theme is echoed again in the antiphon sung during the breaking of the bread: "Lamb of God ... have mercy on us ... grant us peace." The action of breaking and distributing the bread is rich in symbolism (cf. 1 Cor. 10:14-22). Among its many meanings is our duty to share God's blessings with others, not only the "supernatural" blessings of grace in Christ, but through social justice, the blessings of creation and human inventiveness, such as and especially those basic goods necessary to sustain life in a way compatible with human dignity— food, clothing, shelter, education, work. The Eucharist was connected in the minds of the New Testament disciples with Jesus' feeding hungry crowds of people, as in the account of the multiplication of loaves (Mark 6:32-44; 8:1-9).[21] To sup-

[20]Xavier Léon-Dufour, ed. *Dictionary of Biblical Theology* (New York: Desclee, 1967), pp. 364-65. See also: National Conference of Catholic Bishops, *The Challenge of Peace: God's Promise and Our Response*, nos. 27-54 (Washington, D.C.: United States Catholic Conference, 1983), pp. 9-17, for biblical understanding of peace in both Testaments.

[21]Monika Hellwig, *The Eucharist and the Hunger of the World* (New York: Paulist Press, 1976), pp. 31-32. Albert Nolan, *Jesus Before Christianity* (Maryknoll, N.Y.: Orbis Books, 1978), pp. 51-52.

port economic, social, and political systems which prevent the sharing of the blessings of creation and civilization and, at the same time, to communicate in the body and blood of Christ is, ultimately, to engage in the sort of hollow worship the prophets of Israel castigated.

At the conclusion of the liturgy we are bidden: "Go in peace." In light of what has been said above about the content of peace, those parting words do not mean only "Go in the tranquility which has filled your heart as a result of this worship." They also mean "Go in that happy relationship to God and your sisters and brothers in Christ to work with Christ to bring peace and therefore justice, including social justice, to the world in which you live." "Go in peace," the conclusion of Sunday worship, is not only a statement about what may have occurred personally in the course of the celebration just completed; it is also the beginning of a mission, or the renewal of a mission, to seek that social justice which corresponds to God's reign on earth as in heaven.[22]

As the eucharistic liturgy unfolds, therefore, it reminds us of numerous social justice issues. Assembling from our homes in the neighborhood prompts us to think of the housing needs of the poor and elderly and calls to mind discriminating practices in renting and selling property. The entrance song and procession lead to awareness of sexism, discrimination against women in a wide variety of ways in many spheres of contemporary life. We are made conscious of human rights in the general intercessions pleading for those who are political prisoners, inhumanly incarcerated criminals, or oppressed minorities.

The right to just wages and the sin of defrauding workers

---

[22]On peacemaking, pacificism, and conscientious objection, see Gordan C. Zahn, *War, Conscience, and Dissent* (New York: Hawthorn Books, 1967); Hans-Werner Bartsch, "The Foundation and Meaning of Christian Pacificism," in Martin E. Marty and Dean G. Peerman, eds., *New Theology No. 6* (New York: Macmillian, 1969), pp 185-98; Geoffrey Nuttall, *Christian Pacificism in History* (Berkeley, Cal.: World Without War Council, 1971; original copyright 1958); Thomas A. Shannon, ed., *War or Peace? The Search for New Answers* (New York: Macmillan, 1980; National Conference of Catholic Bishops, *Challenge of Peace*, nos. 111-21, pp. 34-37. On relation of all this to the Eucharist, see Carol Frances Jegan, "The Eucharist and Peacemaking: Sign of Contradiction," *Worship* 59 (1985): 202-10.

come to mind during the collection. When the gifts are presented, we can wonder about our economic system which produces these gifts—a system which seems incapable of full employment and overcoming vast pockets of hungry and poor people in the midst of the most affluent nation in the world.[23]

The Eucharistic Prayers' vision of the unity of all women and men raises questions about the international economic order, where certain developed nations hold other nations in economic dependence, so that the citizens of the former can enjoy luxuries to which they have become accustomed, while citizens of the latter are deprived of their labor's fruits, which are siphoned off by the economic colonialists.[24]

The Our Father reminds us that all women and men are God's children for all of whom God created the earth—including future generations whom we can unjustly deprive of their heritage by polluting land, sea and air and recklessly consuming and wasting natural resources. The prayer for, and sign of, peace are occasions to recall the scourge of injustice inflicted on innocent children, women, and elderly by war, and the robbery committed against the poor by the vast sums of money, labor and natural resources poured into making weapons of war.[25] Holy Communion evokes the image of Jesus feeding the hungry crowds. By partaking of the consecrated bread and wine, his body and blood, we claim to

[23]National Conference of Catholic Bishops, *Catholic Social Teaching and the U.S. Economy*, first draft, nos. 8, 161-66, 187-204, in *Origins*,15 November 1984, pp. 342, 359-60, 362-64.

[24]See Michael Harrington, *The Vast Majority: A Journey to the World's Poor* (New York: Simon and Schuster, 1977), pp. 48-53, 129 -51; James B. McGinnis, *Bread and Justice: Toward a New International Economic Order* (New York: Paulist Press, 1979), pp. 57-75; Arthur Simon, *Bread for the World*, rev. ed. (Paulist Press, 1984), pp. 45-54, 115-27.

[25]"We declare once again: The arms race is one of the greatest curses on the human race and the harm it inflicts on the poor is more than can be endured" (Vatican Council II, *The Church in the Modern World*, no. 81, in Flannery, p. 991).

"The arms race is an act of aggression which amounts to a crime, for even when they are not used, by their cost alone, armaments kill the poor by causing them to starve." Statement of the Holy See on Disarmament, 7 May 1976, in United Nations' document *Strengthening the Role of the United Nations in the Field of Disarmament*, in *The Nuclear Challenge to Christian Conscience: A Study Guide for Christians, 2: The Response of Faith* (Washington, D.C.: Sojourners Magazine, 1977), p. 5.

identify ourselves with him; yet we in the United States fill our garbage containers to overflowing while untold numbers suffer from malnutrition or die of starvation in our world.

The parting farewell, "Go in peace," sends us forth to work for a condition of human life and society which can be achieved only if we citizens vote conscientiously for political leaders who are dedicated to fashioning just economic, social and political structures in our society and in the international community.[26]

≫

Bibliography

Balasuriya, Tissa. *The Eucharist and Human Liberation,* Maryknoll, N.Y.: Orbis Books, 1979.

> The author shows how the forms of celebration of the Eucharist in the course of the centuries and in various cultures reflect the social order, sometimes confirming the injustices inherent in it, and how, on the other hand, the Eucharist can be a force, creative of freedom from oppression.

Beckwith, Barbara. "Why Sexist Language Doesn't Belong in the Church (or Anywhere Else)." *St. Anthony Messenger* 88 (February 1981): 22-26.

> The author gives three reasons for revising liturgical texts to nonsexist language: it confronts the sexism of society, shapes thought about the worth of each sex, and insures clarity of expression.

---

[26]Paulist Press has granted permission to make use of some of the material that appeared in Christopher Kiesling's article, "Social Justice and the Eucharist," *New Catholic World* (July/August, 1981) in the writing of this chapter.

Corbon, Jean. *The Wellspring of Worship,* New York: Paulist
    Press, 1988.

> In this work the author develops the relationship between
> the Incarnation and poverty. The author suggests the model
> for the future of the church is that of compassion. There is
> no communion or community without entering into the
> compassion of Jesus who suffers with the poor. See Chapter
> 9, Compassion, the Liturgy of the Poor."

Collins, Mary, O.S.B. "Eucharist and Justice," in *Worship:
    Renewal to Practice,* Washington, D.C.: The Pastoral,
    1987.

> Collins points to the significance of anamnesis in the matter
> of liturgy and justice. For a justice oriented eucharistic
> praxis, she suggests the model of the four fold eucharistic
> action: take, bless, break, eat.

Crockett, William R. *Eucharist: Symbol of Transformation,*
    New York: Pueblo Publishing Company, 1989.

> This book first of all traces the evolution of the various
> cultural traditions of the eucharistic celebration. These tra-
> ditions then become the context for exploring the relation-
> ship between eucharist and justice. The author develops the
> notion that eucharistic anamnesis is a subversive memory
> because it calls into question the present order of things in
> light of the death and resurrection of Jesus.

Crosby, Michael. *Thy Will Be Done: Praying the Our Father
    as Subversive Activity,* Maryknoll, N.Y.: Orbis Books,
    1977.

> This fine book enlightens the reader not only about the
> meaning of the Our Father and of prayer generally, but also
> exposes the various injustices which infect the world in
> which we live and the pertinence of our prayer and action
> to them.

Cummings, Owen, F. "The Eucharist and Social Justice," *The Clergy Review* 71:6 (June, 1986).

> A brief and clear summary of the reasons for the divorce between liturgy and social justice, emphasizing the sacred/secular dichotomy. The author locates in scripture and the history of the church the close connection betwen justice and Eucharist. He points to the importance of the memory of suffering to establish this connection.

Dussel, Enrique. "The Bread of the Eucharistic Celebration as a Sign of Justice in the Community." In Mary Collins and David Powers, eds. *Can We Always Celebrate the Eucharist?* Concilium 152. New York: Seabury Press, 1982. Pp. 56-65.

> Dussel explores the various meanings of bread—as fruit of labor, as substance of eucharistic offering, as the body of the prophet. He discusses the links among bread, economy and Eucharist. The emphasis on offering bread to God in the Eucharist represents a somewhat dated theology.

Fiorenza, Elisabeth Schüssler. "Table Sharing and the Celebration of the Eucharist." In Mary Collins and David Powers, eds. *Can We Always Celebrate the Eucharist?* Concilium 152. New York: Seabury Press, 1982. Pp. 3-12.

> An examination of Paul's words on the Eucharist in 1 Corinthians, chapters 10 and 11, which shows that his thinking about the worth of the Eucharistic celebration requires the abandoning of societal discrimination among those who partake of the body and blood of Christ.

Hellwig, Monika. *The Eucharist and the Hungers of the World*, New York Paulist Press, 1976.

> In this small volume, the author explains in simple language the intimate connection betwen the Eucharist and our caring

for suffering, oppressed people near at hand and around the world in their physical, psychological, and spiritual needs.

Johnson, Elizabeth A. "The Incomprehensibility of God and the Image of God, Male and Female," *Theological Studies* 45 (1984): 441-65.

The author describes the inadequacy of simply bringing out the feminine characteristics of the God of male imagery, and the deficiency of feminizing the Holy Spirit, and calls for the use of both male and female imagery to provide a balanced view of the one God who is beyond the grasp of any one image-and indeed all images.

Kiesling, Christopher. "Social Justice in the Eucharistic Liturgy," *Living Light* 17 (1980): 21-29.

This article indicates how the Eucharistic liturgy offers expression to principles of social justice which are enunciated in Pope Paul VI's encyclical *Populorum progressio* as urgently in need of implementation in our times.

Wolterstorff, Nicholas. "Liturgy, Justice, and Tears," in *Worship* 62: 5 (September, 1988).

This essay explores the connection between liturgy and justice by examining the affinity among human suffering, praise and lament. The author develops the relationship between God's suffering and human suffering.

7

Reconciliation and Justice in the Church and in the World

Reconciliation as a sacramental experience in the churches is still in a state of ambiguity. Both theological understanding and pastoral practice are trying to free themselves from an excessively individualistic imaging of the sacrament inherited from the Middle Ages. Emphases which were evident before Vatican Council II, but certainly more clearly obvious after that Council, have highlighted the sacrament's social and communal character. While the immediate goal of the Council's reforms dealt with textual revisions and ritual clarifications, the larger challenge was to see the sacrament of penance as linking reconciliation with God to reconciliation with the church in order to contextualize the specific sacramental rite in the more universal pastoral mission of the church. No longer could this sacrament be described as confession, as if the telling of sins to a duly delegated priest was its primary function in the community.[1] Nor could the sacramental experience be

[1]"Reform of Penance," by Christopher Kiesling, O.P., in *America* (June 20, 1970), p. 657. See also: "The Many Ways to Reconciliation: An Historical Synopsis of Christian Penance," by Nathan Mitchell, O.S.B., in *The Rite of Penance: Commentaries, Background and Directions*, vol. 3 ed. Nathan Mitchell, O.S.B., (The Liturgical Conference, 1978). Concrete evidence of this move to a more communal understanding of the sacrament is found in the rite for *Corporate Confession and Forgiveness* in the *Lutheran Book of Worship* (Minneapolis: Augsburg Publishing House, 1978), p. 193; the penitential orders for Rites I and II in *The Book of Common Prayer* (The Seabury Press, 1977); *Rite for Reconciliation of Several Penitents with Individual Confession and Absolution* and *Rite for Reconciliation of Several Penitents with General Confession and Absolution* in *The Rites of the Catholic Church* (New York: Pueblo Publishing Co., 1983).

reduced to the formula of absolution which implies that reconciliation is foremost in what happens between God and the individual Christian through the mediating power of the priest.[2]

The reforms of the rites of reconciliation in the churches have been in place for some time. These new liturgies, however, give little hope or evidence for a revitalization of the experience of ongoing conversion in the Christian community. The purpose of the liturgical celebration of forgiveness through Christ as described in the introduction to the *Rite of Penance* from the Roman Catholic Church seems still far from being achieved.

> In order that this sacrament of healing may truly achieve its purpose among Christ's faithful, it must take root in their whole lives and move them to more fervent service of God and neighbor.[3]

Despite the shortcomings in the liturgical rites of reconciliation and their failure to bring back the long lines of penitents so characteristic of a former time, there has been a widening of the meaning of reconciliation in the church.[4] Typical of much of the speaking on reconciliation by church officials, pastoral theologians, and religious educators is this statement from "Reconciliation and Penance in the Mission of the Church," a preparatory document issued before the 1983 Synod of Roman Catholic bishops in Rome:

> To the extent that Christians are thankful and faithful to God for the great gift of reconciliation received, they become

[2]The evolution of this sacrament in the Roman Catholic Church from the period of Trent up to the 1983 Code of Canon Law and the 1983 Synod of Bishops in Rome has been succinctly described by James Dallen in his article, "Church Authority and the Sacrament of Penance: The Synod of Bishops," in *Worship* 58:3 (May, 1984).

[3]Introduction II, 7:b.

[4]Even the fact that the Roman Catholic rites offer three possibilities, two of which are communal in character, helps to move reconciliation and the celebration of forgiveness of our sinfulness into a more public arena. For an expanded notion of the meaning of reconciliation see *Towards Reconciliation* by Walter Burghardt, S.J. (Washington, D.C.; USCC, 1974).

living witnesses and founts of reconciliation in everyday existence. Reconciliation with God is thereby put forward as a source of brotherly (sic) reconciliation—in the ecclesial community and in human society—which is both grace received and responsibility assumed by Christians in the world.[5]

There is still considerable conflict in official church documentation, in theological writing, and in pastoral practice regarding the communal and individual character of reconciliation, but the sacrament's relationship to social justice is in place and it is the intention of this chapter to make explicit what is often only hinted at in liturgies, preaching, and catechesis. This will be done by reviewing and re-examining the major theological and liturgical elements presently connected with cultic reconciliation. And this will be done by discussing in order these elements in terms of the new structure of the sacrament as it is now found in the Roman Catholic *Rite of Penance* as promulgated in December of 1973. That structure, especially as reflected in the *Rite of Several Penitents* (Form II) contains:

1. Introductory rites of greeting and reception of the penitents;
2. The celebration of the word of God, including an examination of conscience;
3. The Rite of Reconciliation, which includes the confession of sins, acts of satisfaction, absolution, a proclamation of praise, and prayer of thanksgiving;
4. The concluding rites of blessing and dismissal.

It is not the purpose of this chapter to examine the liturgy as such or to provide a theology of reconciliation. What is presented here is a look at the liturgy of reconciliation from a social justice perspective.

[5] *Origins*, vol. 11:36 (Feb. 18, 1982), #42.

Introductory Rites:
Christian Initiation and Reconciliation

One of the opening prayers of one of the suggested penitential services from the *Rite of Penance* relates this sacrament to
the grace of baptism:

> Lord Jesus,
> You redeemed us by your passion
> and raised us to new life in baptism.
> Protect us with your unchanging love
> and share with us the joy of your
> resurrection,
> for you live and reign for ever and ever.[6]

At the most fundamental level the relationship of the sacrament
of reconciliation and social justice is based on the meaning of
Christian initiation. The very process of initiation moves a
person from an individualized to a communitarian existence.
It is because Christians are members of a community and it is
because they find their salvation through community, that
reconciliation with God presupposes reconciliation with
church. In this sacrament they meet a human community
which understands and forgives them. And at the same time,
such a community's response becomes a model for how they
are to bring justice to the world.

The document "Reconciliation and Penance in the Mission
of the Church" (see footnote five) calls baptism the primary
and fundamental sacrament of reconciliation. The sacrament
of penance, as it is still called, is more properly named second
reconciliation. Both sacraments symbolically enact the conversion process. Introduction into the life of the church and
rebirth into Christ are here the images of radical conversion.
"The victory of Christ over sin 'shines out above all in
baptism.'" The document continues:

---

[6]Appendix II, 1. "Penitential Celebrations During Lent," #9.

> Baptismal reconciliation of its very nature is total and definitive, constituting the Christian "holy." It is therefore necessary to keep ever in mind the baptismal origin of Christian penance—it is in baptism that the Christian receives the fundamental gift of "metanoia."[7]

From baptism comes the meaning of every other sacramental reconciliation. But more to our concern regarding social justice, the document notes that "every act of penance of the Christian is profoundly linked to the reconciliation of baptism."[8]

The church is the *place* of reconciliation. This mission of Jesus is carried out in the church in many ways, only one of which is the sacrament of penance itself. There is also the Lenten/Easter season which is the outstanding penitential structure in the liturgical year. This season as a process of repentance and as the joyful celebration of reconciliation with Christ is based on a renewal of baptismal commitment. And thirdly, there is the continual proclamation of the reconciling gospel in our daily lives in the church. This is especially where reconciliation takes place on a social dimension for baptized Christians. As the RCIA makes clear, there is to be "a progressive change of outlook and morals ... together with its social consequences."[9] The gospel of reconciliation is concretized in every encounter of Christians among themselves, in their mutual ministries, in their ongoing support and encouragement of each other.

But the initiatory rites call for more than a supportive and loving community. They look to changes in outlook and in community living. The place of reconciliation is a church which is a community called to justice. The community of the church is called to a responsibility to cooperate with God's liberating activity in history. The church is a symbol of God's recon-

---

[7] II. 1. 32. There is also a sense in which the Eucharist is the primary sacrament of reconciliation. All sacraments point to the Eucharist. But because initiation is the fundamental sacrament in a way that even Eucharist is not, it can be considered the primary sacrament of reconciliation.

[8] Ibid.

[9] RCIA #19.

ciliation in the world when it is committed to breaking down all alienating structures. To be baptized into the church is to find a home where liberation is a religious experience. To participate in Christ's victory over sin is to struggle for the kingdom of God, which is the overriding symbol of our call to justice and of the reconciliation of alienating structures. Finally, it is by means of initiation, especially adult initiation, that the church is asked to recognize that its own communal structures are not yet the kingdom of God and so they participate in the sinfulness of society. The church, while a symbol of reconciliation, is also in need of reconciliation.

The Celebration of God's Word: Reconciliation and Repentance

The introduction to the *Rite of Penance* indicates that:

> Readings should be chosen which illustrate the following: a) the voice of God calling men (sic) back to conversion and ever closer conformity with Christ; b) the mystery of our reconciliation through the death and resurrection of Christ and through the gift of the Holy Spirit; c) the judgment of God about good and evil in men's lives as a help in the examination of conscience.[10]

What the liturgy of the word promises us is the possibility of reconciliation and what it calls us to is a deeper experience of repentance. The following is an attempt to make explicit the relationship of social justice to the reconciliation and repentance celebrated through the proclamation of the word.

What is meant by reconciliation?[11] To be reconciled indicates that one has overcome some kind of estrangement. There has been a healing of personal and/or societal fragmentation and

---

[10]Introduction #24 a, b, c.

[11]For a discussion of the Pauline notion of reconciliation see J. A. Fitzmyer, S.J., "Reconciliation in Pauline Theology," *No Famine in the Land: Studies in Honor of J.L. McKenzie* (eds. J.W. Flanagan and A. W. Robinson; Missoula: Scholars Press, 1975).

inner distancing. Those dimensions of human living which have been alienated and which were warring with each other have been integrated. Humanization has taken place in the bridging of what may have been formerly perceived as irreconcilable differences. New life is emerging through this human growth and this victory over the enmity that is found in self and the world.

The reconciliation which is celebrated in this sacrament takes place on many different levels. In point of fact, all these levels should be touched by the ritualization of this sacrament in the Christian community. It is questionable whether the sacrament of penance can address itself only to a single aspect of this human experience of reconciliation. One of the problems with the penitential practices of the past several centuries is that the reconciliation identified with the sacrament has been too one-dimensional in character.

The most obvious area of reconciliation that comes to mind for most people when dealing with this sacrament is the overcoming of one's estrangement from God. Often people saw this as the only form of alienation in need of healing. If this alienation from God, or sin, were more comprehensively understood, it would be less problematic. But far too many understand sin as an offense against God or, more specifically, as a violation of some divine legislation. Here one is guilty because one has broken a positive law, one has legally trespassed, one has stepped out of the proper order, one has destroyed the harmonious relationship in this world which has been established by God. Reconciliation here tends to be the restoration of a harmony in the world originally planned by God. But this is not usually seen as a social reality. Rather, it is the overcoming of the estrangement that one experiences between oneself and one's creator. What the sacrament ritualizes is the reordering of one's life to conform to a pre-established pattern of responding to an ideal relationship between God and oneself. Such a perspective rarely does justice to the social nature of sin.[12] It is not on this level that reconciliation is experienced as the sacrament that does justice.

[12]"The Sacrament of Penance Today I," by Charles Curran in *Worship* 43:9 (November 1969), p. 516.

A fuller and less extrinsic approach to reconciliation would see it as overcoming self-estrangement. Self-alienation is the product of the kind of self oppression which takes place when one introduces dualisms into one's life. It may be placing an excessive chasm between one's intellectual understanding and feelings; it may be the old body/soul dichotomy with a resulting denigration of the material or fleshy dimension of one's existence. It may be an alienation of one's sexuality from the total personality.[13] In any event, there is a loss of self-identity and suppression of one's true self image. Self depreciation and denegration on the one hand or the assumption of some kind of false self-image, such as the pious or spiritual type, are harmful and bring into one's life a separation from oneself that is truly alienating.

One can speak of this estrangement from oneself in terms of sin and offense against God. But it is equally valid to see this as being out of contact with one's feelings and emotions and living under the imperialism of a negative self-image. However, this experience may be described, it is in need of sacramental healing because it is not only psychological; it also has a religious dimension. It is sin insofar as it is freely chosen or allowed to dominate. If it is not the result of personal choice, then it is the result of the sin of the world. It is the concrete reality which is the foundation of a wrong relation to God; it is the concrete reality which constitutes the relation to God, good or bad. Reconciliation here is the movement through this experience to greater integration. Such self-estrangement is also self-injustice. Here is a case where love and justice go together. Only a positive self-regard will make it possible for one to deal with oneself in a just way and experience oneself as just.

The sacramental liturgy must always be a call to such reconciliation. Hopefully, it will give the experience of acting justly toward and dealing justly with oneself. The rectification of the right order of one's relationship with God is trivial and monstrous if one does not feel better about oneself, which is

---

[13]See Chapter Three: "Sexual Alienation: The Dualistic Nemesis," in *Embodiment* by James Nelson (Minneapolis: Augsburg Publishing House, 1978).

the result of personal integration, and if one cannot truly claim that justice within oneself is part of one's personal growth and being.

In other words, the justice to oneself that is celebrated in this sacrament is the humanization that takes place when there is the restoration and discovery of those self-images which are based on a proper relationship with God and which are grounded in the goodness of one's being. It is the kind of human growth or reconciliation with one's self that accepts a radical dependence on God because one need not fear to reach out. It implies an openness to community because one can securely move from one's own resources and self-under-standing.[14] It facilitates a willingness to share and to receive from others because one actually loves oneself. And this self-love is in reality the human experience of reconciliation or of justice to oneself. One is forgiven because one can forgive oneself and one can do that because one has overcome alienation from oneself through self-acceptance. Thus, one can love unconditionally because one is moving toward integration. One can accept love unconditionally because one need not fear the closeness of others. In such an experience of justice, the sacrament of reconciliation proclaims that God is found in our bringing together that which in the final analysis cannot be separated, our lives. Any experience of social justice in this sacrament presupposes this aspect of reconciliation. This flows from the basic gospel insight that one cannot love one's neighbor unless one loves oneself.

The third dimension of alienation which is resolved in the reconciliation process is alienation from society. When one thinks of liturgy and social justice, it is this area of human relationships that first comes to mind. And certainly the sacrament of reconciliation articulates the healing that is taking place between individual/community and society.[15] One cannot

---

[14]Coleman Grabert, O.S.B., "Christian Existence in a Reconciled Community," *The Rite of Penance: Commentaries, Background and Directions* (Washington, D.C. The Liturgical Conference, 1978).

[15]Christian Duquoc, "Real Reconciliation and Sacramental Reconciliation," *Sacramental Reconciliation, Concilium 61*, ed. E. Schillebeeckx (New York: Herder and Herder, 1971), p. 36.

experience full justice in the liturgy as long as one contributes to present-day social disintegration and is entrapped in the sinful structures of community, country, and the world.[16] Such structures are considered sinful when they take on an absolute character, when there are no alternatives to relativize them. In other words, when one's life is so completely determined by status, job, relationships, the expectations of others, or by the economic and political life, the very structures that support one's humanity become oppressive and so sinful. The humanization that is celebrated in this sacrament is the transcending of these various structures. To be converted in regard to them means to be able to live in between these structures. A call to such living is the challenge of the official liturgy to such societal sinfulness.[17]

One experiences this alienation from society when one finds oneself in an alienating atmosphere or possessed by an estranging world view. Such a context is what makes structures sinful.[18] One can call sinful those elements of society (such as corporations, governmental procedures, local civil agencies and political organizations) to the degree that they find their meaning in and are concrete examples of a "sinful" world view. Such a sinful perspective or orientation brings about despair, dehumanizing resignation or requires a positive support of such an estranging system.[19] Reconciliation here means the humanization that takes place when people can extricate themselves from such systems of reality. It is the church through its sacrament of reconciliation that must provide support and motivation to the worshipers so that they can effectively remove themselves from the tyranny of structures

[16]Robert M. Friday, *Adults Making Responsible Moral Decisions*: A 1979 Resource Paper of the National Conference of Diocesan Directors of Religious Education (Washington, D.C. C.C.D.) p. 20.

[17]Bernard Cooke, "The Social Aspect of the Sacrament of Penance," *Proceedings of the Catholic Theological Society of America*, 22nd Annual Convention vol. 22, p. 182.

[18]John Topel, S.J., *The Way of Peace: Liberation Through the Bible* (Maryknoll: Orbis Books, 1979), p. 133.

[19]Leonardo Boff, *Liberating Grace* (Maryknoll: Orbis Books, 1979), p. 143.

which are actually committed to discouraging the humanization process.

Often people who must constantly live in oppressive and debilitating situations experience a form of alienation which is described as the loss of one's sense of ultimacy or transcendence. In other words, there is no reality in their lives that they can name as God. These people find that their lives are meaningless; there is little that can evoke a response in them; there is almost no emotional hold on them. To use the distinctions of David Tracy,[20] their lives are not only devoid of meaningfulness, there is also no sense of meaning and truth. That means that even in terms of others and the society in which they live, there is no inner sense of significance and destiny. This is usually concretized in the experience of directionlessness and boredom. It is basically an estrangement from life itself. Only a sense of something more than oneself, of something more than the meaning that one achieves in the society of others, can restore life's significance. But a significant life is not possible for many people because not only is there no personal meaningfulness or communal cultural meaning for them; there is also no referent in their lives beyond themselves and society. There is no truth. The absence of transcendence, of God, in a person's experience is the ultimate in dehumanization. In this realm of human living, reconciliation is necessary if the sacrament is to articulate both justice to oneself as a sinner who is loved by God as well as assist one to extricate him/herself from sinful institutions. No one, no community, celebrating this sacrament can challenge society's evils if it is not reconciled to life itself.

In order to understand how the sacrament of reconciliation is a celebration and a call to justice in the church, it is necessary to grasp the fullness of the meaning of reconciliation. The

---

[20]David Tracy, *Blessed Rage for Order* (New York: The Seabury Press, 1975), p. 71: A particular experience or language is "meaningful" when it discloses an authentic dimension of our experiences as selves. It has "meaning" when its cognitive claims can be expressed conceptually with internal coherence. It is "true" when transcendental or metaphysical analysis shows its "adequacy to experience" by explicating how a particular concept (e.g. time, space, self, or God) functions as a fundamental "belief" or "condition of possibility" of all our experience.

liturgy of this sacrament celebrates the event of reconciliation not only on the level of a personal relationship with God, but also that of the sinner to him/herself, to society and to life. With this richer notion of reconciliation it is possible to reveal more of the relationship between the sacrament of penance and social justice.

We now turn to the matter of Christian repentance. In examining the meaning of reconciliation in relationship to social justice, there emerges a clearer understanding of the meaning of repentance. The repentance celebrated in this sacrament is not a mere legal or juridical reality. There is no true forgiveness of sin on God's part unless the Christian is willing to forgive his/her neighbor. Just as sin is relational, so is conversion.[21] It must manifest itself in the manifold relationships which the Christian has with others. Conversion refers to more than one's personal relationship with God. Conversion also calls for more growth, more love of others.

Conversion implies a transformation which is more than a change in oneself. The kind of new understanding that happens in the process of repentance results in changes in one's relationship with others.[22] Salvation is not a purely individual affair. Repentance is communitarian. It is an ecclesial reality. Just as when one is reconciled to the church, one is reconciled to Christ, so when one repents in the church, one finds forgiveness in Christ. Thus, the whole liturgy of reconciliation and certainly the formula of absolution should reflect the communal nature of conversion.[23] This sacrament is not primarily concerned with a Jesus-and-me spirituality. But it articulates that in one's commitment to community and in the community's communal

[21]Charles Curran, "The Sacrament of Penance Today II," *Worship* vol. 43:10, p. 590ff. See also: Jerome Murphy O'Connor, O.P., "Sin and Community in the New Testament," in *The Mystery of Sin and Forgiveness*, ed. Michael Taylor, S.J. (Staten Island: Alba House, 1971) and Paul Anciaux, O.S.B., "The Ecclesial Dimension of Penance," in the same volume.

[22]F. J. Heggen, *Confession and the Service of Penance* (Notre Dame: University of Notre Dame Press, 1968), p. 54. For a full treatment of the various levels on which conversion takes place see Donald L. Gelpi, S. J. *Experiencing God: A Theology of Human Emergence* (New York: Paulist Press, 1978). He has since added the level of social conversion.

[23]Heggen, *Confession and the Service of Penance*, p. 104.

repentance the reconciling Christ is made present. For this reason the communal penance service brings out the true nature of this sacrament more adequately than individual auricular confession. Monika Hellwig says of these communal services:

> They are in themselves community celebrations that lend themselves best to a more communitarian style of examination of conscience. This is the inspiration that has often been behind the groups practising *revision de vie*. When people come together solemnly to read scripture, meditate on it and try to put their own lives under its scrutiny it is to be expected that it is in the first place of their common life and common situations that they will be thinking.[24]

The point is that the liturgy of reconciliation does not bring about Christian conversion. It presupposes it. It ritualizes a given stage of affairs. As in the case of the other sacraments, reconciliation is a celebration of something already present. It is a ritual enactment of the fact that as members of the Christian community reconciled in Christ the worshipers are already on the way to forgiveness. They have been forgiven and now give praise and thanks for that in this rite. This is not to suggest that Christian liturgy itself is not a factor in the process of Christian conversion. It is because it advances the process by incorporating it into the visible, sacramental aspect of the church and its life in a paradigmatic way and by offering further support from the community.

But significantly, what is being thematized is the social nature of the church. The purpose of the liturgical forgiveness of sins is not simply to reveal the sinfulness of ordinary human beings. Certainly such celebrations should make one more aware of personal isolation, alienation and lack of direction. But they must also catch one up into that constant proclamation of forgiveness which is ever taking place in the church.

---

[24]Monika Hellwig, *Sign of Reconciliation and Conversion* (Wilmington : Michael Glazier, Inc. 1982), p. 143.

The liturgy is founded on reconciliation with the Christian community and so it implies a more obvious commitment to the mission of that community.

The Rite of Reconciliation: Sin, Guilt and Judgment

The social justice aspect in this part of the rite, which deals with confession, satisfaction, absolution, praise, and thanksgiving becomes transparent through a closer examination of the meaning of sin, guilt and judgment. If sin is the result of alienation on one of the several dimensions described above, then sin cannot be understood univocally.[25] The most important repercussion here is that sin can no longer be viewed as an individual phenomenon. It cannot be a question of a disruption only between God and oneself. Rather, sin shows its effects in society as a whole. Thus, one can speak of alienating institutions or sinful structures. Sin can no longer be seen primarily in terms of the model of law and obedience which presupposes that sin is a dimension of a specific external action. Rather, a more contemporary and biblically based understanding of sin uses the model of multiple relationships.[26] Immediately, this moves sin from an individualistic concern to one which is both more social and ecclesial. Sin is better interpreted in terms of a relationship which affects not only the individual's relationship with God but also with his/her neighbors. This more relational view sees sin not as a dimension or a quality of external actions but as a fundamental choice. Sin is a question of the basic orientation of a person in many relationships.

Perhaps the greatest effect that such an understanding of sin has had on the level of liturgical practice is that the rite of reconciliation presupposes this social or ecclesial understanding of sin.[27] To enter into this sacramental situation it is not enough

[25]Bernard Cooke, "The Social Aspect of the Sacrament of Penance," and Friday, *Adults Making Responsible Moral Decisions*, p. 17ff.

[26]Curran, "*The Sacrament of Penance Today I,*" p. 518. See also: James L. Empereur, S.J. "Theology of the Sacrament of Reconciliation," *Modern Liturgy* vol. 2:1 (January 1975), p. 4.

[27]Bernard Cooke, "The Social Aspect of the Sacrament of Penance," p. 174.

to experience sin as an offense against God or the trespassing of some divine precept. Rather, in order authentically to give praise to God that one has been forgiven, one must understand and experience sin as a disruption of one's relationship in society and with other people. There needs to be a grasp that personal sin is always contextualized in a larger framework, that to sin personally is to contribute to societal sin. In this sense, the experience of reconciliation is always an experience of justice.

Another area which is affected by this social understanding of reconciliation is guilt. What is the meaning of feeling guilty once one broadens the concept of sin beyond the confines of a personal relationship with God and Jesus? Often guilt which is articulated and experienced in this sacrament is too readily modeled on civil law. But guilt in this sacramental situation is not primarily the result of decisions to go against some regulations such as not going to mass on Sunday or even the result of making human mistakes such as becoming angry and injuring one's neighbor. While the latter form of guilt may well be appropriately part of the sacramental process, it is not the guilt that most clearly reveals the meaning of liturgical reconciliation and of this sacrament's relationship to justice.

The guilt that is the proper matter for this sacrament is guilt before God. It is the guilt of protesting against life which, in effect, is equivalent to rejecting God. Guilt before God, to use Karl Rahner's language,[28] is not the transgression of some law. It is not guilt that flows from any particular event. Rather this guilt is the dark side of oneself which is not one's real self. Human guilt is human inauthenticity. One is guilty when one does not open oneself up to future possibilities. One is guilty when one does not include others in the horizons that define one's existence. People are guilty when they are not communal, social persons. They are guilty when they allow themselves to be defined by the status quo and by institutional structures.

Often theologians have treated guilt in the sacrament of reconciliation as analogous to what is experienced in civil

---

[28]Karl Rahner, "Guilt and Remission: The Borderland Between Theology and Psychotherapy," *Theological Investigations, Man in the Church*, vol. 2.

society when one has committed a crime, regrets the action, and makes retribution. People can distance themselves from their sins freely according to this model of the law courts. But social guilt before God is one that cannot be cancelled by human efforts alone. One cannot reverse the sinful orientation of one's life by one's own endeavors. Forgiveness begins with God. Sinners hear this word of forgiveness spoken in the depths of their existence, surely, but as Christians it comes to them in community. There this word of forgiveness is spoken in Jesus Christ in an unconditional way and this word remains present in the church sacramentally. People are released from this guilt when they respond to this word in the church. This is social forgiveness. It is communal reconciliation in a most profound sense.

Unlike the guilt one has because of individual transgressions, this guilt is all-pervasive in human experience. It is the cause of the existential anxiety that all humans feel. Their guilt over individual actions or omissions is but an instance of this guilt before God coming to expression. It is a guilt all share in common. It is social guilt. All are bound together in this guilt. It is a communal, concrete experience of being caught up in a good but also sinful world. It is the human experience that sinfulness goes beyond people and their individual relationship with God. It is the experience of alienation in and from human society. This is the reason why an individual at any given time cannot be considered responsible for the sinfulness of structures. The sacrament of reconciliation should be the way one gets handles on this experience of alienation which is presently part of the human condition. This does not mean that one can move oneself beyond the network of sinful institutions in some angelic or spiritual way. It does not imply that the sinful fabric of human living will disappear. But it does mean that one's imaginative life can present further options and ways of living so that one is not overcome by the alienating factors. Such options should be experienced in the sacramental celebration. In this sense the sacrament can prevent alienation from taking concrete form in one's life and thus being able to produce its destructive effects in the world.

Finally, what light does the notion of social justice cast on the meaning of this sacrament as a form of judgment? In the past the acts of satisfaction (penances) and absolution were seen primarily in terms of the juridical model. The judgment of the sacrament was the way in which the priest would make an evaluation of the penitent's disposition for receiving God's forgiveness and then exacting that forgiveness in the name of the Trinity through absolution. But this pronouncement of forgiveness has been broadened to express the proclamation of reconciliation by Jesus Christ which is constant in the life of the church. Such a pronouncement is a formal liturgical action. It is an act of praise and thanksgiving. It is worship. It proclaims that God through the death and resurrection of Christ has sent the Holy Spirit for the forgiveness of sins and that sins are forgiven through the ministry of the church. This has important ramifications when looking at the aspect of social justice in the practice of this sacrament. It is no longer legitimate to ascribe to the analogy of the courtroom when describing what is going on in this sacramental process. In the past, the relationship between priest and penitent was seen as similar to that between judge and defendant. At least that was the case on the level of practice. The role of the judge-priest was to decide on the appropriateness of absolution. The analogy breaks down on several levels, even prescinding from the societal, ecclesial context in which this rite must now be situated. Even when restricting the analogy to the priest and penitent in an individualized framework, it is easy to see the limitations of the forensic model.[29] The priest is dealing more with the moral order than he is with the juridical. One hardly goes to the civil courts to receive the forgiveness of sins.[30] Unlike the civil defendant the penitent is not there to plead his/her innocence.

But even further does the analogy go awry when considering the social nature of sin. It is more difficult to make a judgment about the worthiness of the penitent when sin is more a question of orientation based upon the model of multiple

---

[29]Curran, "The Sacrament of Penance Today II," *Worship* 43:10 p. 609.

[30]Frank Nikolasch, "The Sacrament of Penance: Learning from the East," *Sacramental Reconciliation, Concilium* 61, p. 74.

relationships.[31] More is going on in in this sacrament than the verification of the state of an individual soul. To the degree that one can speak of judgment in this sacrament, it is that of God's constant proclamation in the worshiping community of God's saving word of pardon. The rite of pronouncing absolution is similar to the act of proclaiming the Eucharistic Prayer, namely, an articulation of the community's proclamation to the individual and to the community itself that reconciliation is an actuality because the community experiences itself as reconciled through this ritual activity. Thus, this more ecclesial understanding of the sacrament makes it impossible to narrow it to the act of confessing one's sins. It is more than a listing of personal transgressions upon which judgment is to be passed primarily in juridical terms.[32] One of the concluding prayers of thanksgiving in the *Rite of Penance* succinctly illustrates the connection between reconciliation and justice in the world:

> God and Father of us all,
> you have forgiven our sins
> and sent us your peace.
> Help us to forgive each other
> and to work together to establish
> peace in the world.[33]

What is important to note is that the meaning of justice gets expressed in this sacrament in a special way insofar as it involves the judgment of God. This is clear if we recall that the Hebrew words for justice entail the active process of making right, establishing right order, and above all God's making right and that this notion of justice is not so much a matter of

---

[31]Curran, "The Sacrament of Penance Today II," *Worship* 43:10, p. 610. This is not to deny that sin as orientation is still expressed to some degree in actions or that it is possible for the confessor to make a moral judgment about the penitent's orientation. To some degree the latter is necessary if the confessor is to be of any help to the penitent. This judgment is *not* the judgment of forgiveness, however.

[32]José Ramos-Regidor, "Reconciliation in the Primitive Church," *Sacramental Reconciliation, Concilium 61*, p. 85ff.

[33]#57 G.

condemnation as it is of setting right, which may, as a consequence, mean someone's being condemned. God's judgment makes us right, puts us in order, straightens us out, establishes us in justice, and as a consequence what is wrong and out of line is condemned and destroyed. This justice from God's judgment is deeper, more profound, than our ordinary standards of justice.

The Concluding Rites: Dismissal

To understand how reconciliation is a sacrament that does justice, it has been necessary to open up the various levels of the experience of reconciliation as well as to recontextualize the concepts of sin, guilt, repentance and judgment. But such clarification alone is insufficient. Since the sacrament of reconciliation is worship, as in the case of all Christian rites, it presupposes community, a community which has a mission. This is simply but eloquently brought out in one of the brief dismissal prayers:

> Go in peace,
> and proclaim to the world
> the wonderful works of God,
> who has brought you salvation.[34]

As in the other sacramental instances in the church, reconciliation cannot create a just community on the spot. There must be a justice-directed spirituality already alive in the worshipers. But when a significant number of members of a congregation live out a social justice perspective, adequate ritualization can allow these members to be more sensitive to the effects of their lives on others and can enable the community as a whole to be more discerning of how it has participated in social sin.[35]

The salient point here is that Christians find their forgiveness

---

[34]#47 E.

[35]Heggen, *Confession and the Service of Penance*, p. 92ff.

from their brothers and sisters in community. This community is their point of contact with Christ. And the sinner can enter into the Paschal Mystery through the believing church because this church is a reconciling community. The rite of reconciliation is not simply directed to the penitent. Sharing in the liturgy of reconciliation makes sense for all Christians, all people in the liturgical assembly, because in order to be a reconciling community, and so a just community, they must be engaging in continual conversion. The very presentation of sins to the church must be done in a way that moves the confession of sins to become an act of worship done in community. To acknowledge one's sinfulness is to make an act of faith in the forgiving mercy of God in Christ. But it also means that what and how one confesses is a community event. This is clearly set out in communal reconciliation services, but even what happens in individual confession must look to and follow from these more normative rites.[36]

Part of any good communal reconciliation service will be the call for the community as a whole to reflect critically upon its identification with inhumane causes or structures. Conversion to a life-style which distances the worshipers from the forces of corporate sin is the test of the authenticity of such liturgy. What happens in the community after worship is surely one criterion for discerning this authenticity, but the very

---

[36]Although several Christian churches have revised their rites of reconciliation to give greater emphasis to them as actions of the church, the actual rituals are disappointing. The *Lutheran Book of Worship* contains a rite entitled: "Corporate Confession and Forgiveness." But the view of sin presented is a very individualistic one. This is especially the case in the common prayer of confession which is still in the first person singular. The social justice dimension is present, albeit somewhat minimally, in one of the prayers which contains this sentence: "Help us forgive each other and to establish justice and concord throughout the world." See pages 193-95.

The Roman Rite has a communal reconciliation service (Form II), but because it demands individual confession and absolution as part of it, it presents an ambivalence which diminishes the liturgy's power to convey the notion of forgiveness in community. See *Rites of the Catholic Church*, p. 385ff.

The *Book of Common Prayer* contains two forms of individual reconciliation (p. 447ff.). Its Penitential Orders for Rites I and II make for quite acceptable communal reconciliation liturgies. However, the fact that they can also be used before the eucharistic rites does introduce an ambiguity regarding the Eucharist as the primary sacrament of reconciliation.

celebration of reconciliation through symbols will be an evaluation of the symbols themselves, since they can be the basis of an unjust experience in our worship. Our interpretation of the symbols can be shaped by institutional injustice and so our liturgical experience can be contaminated by such corporate sinfulness. The symbols of reconciliation must sit in judgment upon themselves. No community is free from involvement in social sin. Injustice and justice exist together in the church. And the liturgy of reconciliation can reveal the social evil that is hidden in a just community at that same time that it blesses the goodness that is found in this world.

The experience of worship should provide ritual and psychological room for the worshipers to experience themselves as just (that is, fully lovable because loved by God) in experiencing the personal forgiveness of their brothers and sisters. But this is an experience of justice that involves commitment to those harmed by society, those outside the church.[37] Such commitment takes on differing forms in different parts of the world. In Latin America, the commitment may focus on redressing the harm done by economic institutions. For Black people in the United States, it may mean commitment to avoid judging themselves and being judged by white values. And all Christians are called to be a reconciling community by reaching out to the poor and victims of prejudice.

Moreover, the liturgical celebration itself must be a paradigm of justice in the world. Here there can be no distinction of class, color, or sex. There are no superiors/inferiors in this liturgy. Manipulation and exploitation have no place at the worship in which the reconciliation of Christ is brought to the reality of sinful lives. Rather, the basic human experience of which reconciliation is paradigmatic is the experience of rupture or break from the human community followed by reintegration back into a more just humanity. It is the revelation that in human forgiveness and healing the liberation of

---

[37] A good treatment of the kinds of justice of God which are celebrated in the liturgy is found in Mark Searle, "Serving the Lord with Justice," *The Liturgy and Social Justice* (Collegeville: The Liturgical Press, 1980).

Jesus Christ and the establishment of God's kingdom of justice are found.

Finally, we need to note that the area of social justice is one where a sacrament of reconciliation becomes especially meaningful and helpful. We live with some guilt about the misery of many people in the world, yet find it difficult to pinpoint our own personal responsibility, what precisely we are contributing to the evil; or, if we can pinpoint something, we have no way of avoiding it or assessing the degree of our cooperation's gravity. So we are left confronting and immersed in "a mystery of iniquity," a "mystery of sin." How are we to deal with that? Only by recourse to a "mystery of forgiveness," a "mystery of mercy and grace"—which can be expressed and encountered only symbolically, sacramentally, through words, gestures, etc. which are inadequate to the expression of both good and evil. One of the problems with the sacrament of reconciliation is that we try too hard to make it perfectly intelligible and reasonable. It is not. It is a superrational act, if you will, to deal with a superrational mystery of evil. The value of the communal reconciliation rite is that it makes us aware of the mystery of evil, our indefinable involvement, and then directs us to the mystery of mercy.

Bibliography

Burghardt, Walter, S.J. *Towards Reconciliation,* Washington, D.C.: USCC Publications, 1974.

> This essay deals with reconciliation between God and ourselves, within ourselves, between ourselves and others and between ourselves and nature.

The Catholic Theological Society of America. *The Renewal of the Sacrament of Penance,* C.T.S.A., 1975.

The document includes a theological consideration of sin and grace, a look at the new liturgy of penance, and the history of the sacrament. The bibliography is exhaustive.

Dallen, James. *The Reconciling Community: The Rite of Penance,* New York: Pueblo Publishing Co., 1986.

This is a very competent presentation of both the history of the sacrament and the revised ritual of the Roman Catholic Church. The author pays special attention to the area of reconciliation and social action.

Gula, Richard, S. S. *To Walk Together Again: The Sacrament of Reconciliation,* New York: Paulist Press, 1984.

This is an overview of reconciliation which begins with the idea of community and hospitality. The author reviews the modern approaches to grace, the function of sacraments, and sin. There are helpful chapters on the history of the sacrament and on communal reconciliation rites.

Hellwig, Monika. *Sign of Reconciliation and Conversion,* Wilmington: Michael Glazier, Inc. 1982.

This competent treatment of the various aspects of the sacrament includes a section on its relationship to social justice.

Jeep, Elizabeth McMahon, ed. *The Rite of Penance: Commentaries: Implementing the Rite,* vol. 2. Washington D.C.: The Liturgical Conference, 1976.

This volume puts the sacrament in the perspective of the special needs in the community, such as the young and elderly.

Keifer, Ralph and McManus, Frederick, eds. *The Rite of Penance: Commentaries: Understanding the Document,* vol. 1. Washington, D.C.: The Liturgical Conference, 1975.

This is a worthwhile introduction to the new *Rite of Penance* in the Roman Catholic Church. Chapters four and six which deal with communal celebrations are especially helpful in bringing out the ecclesial dimension of forgiveness.

Mitchell, Nathan. *The Rite of Penance: Commentaries: Background and Directions,* vol. 3. Washington, D.C.: The Liturgical Conference, 1978.

The collection contains many good theological essays dealing with aspects of reconciliation both in general and in terms of the new rite. Chapter Eight: "The Rite of Penance/Reconciliation: Christian Existence in a Reconciled Humanity," by Colman Grabert, O.S.B., is especially recommended.

Schillebeeckx, O. P., Edward, ed. *Sacramental Reconciliation: Concilium 61,* New York: Herder and Herder, 1971.

This volume contains a number of articles dealing with guilt, Eucharist as reconciliation, and some specific historical problems.

Taylor, Michael, S.J., ed. *The Mystery of Sin and Forgiveness,* New York: Alba House, 1971.

This collection of essays covers most the aspects of reconciliation, confession, and original sin.

8

Justice in the Church:
Liturgies of Ministry

"Anyone who ventures to speak to people about justice," said the Second Synod of the Roman Catholic Bishops in 1971, "must first be just in their eyes. Hence we must undertake an examination of the modes of acting and of possessions and life-style found within the church herself [sic]."[1] A way into this investigation is through the liturgies of ministry.

Here we reserve the name "liturgies of ministry" for those rites which initiate Christians into some specific function in the church, whether in service to the church's members or in service to all men and women. Most obvious among these liturgies in the Anglican, Orthodox and Roman communions are the rites of ordination for deacons, presbyters (priests), and bishops—rites of the sacrament of holy orders. The Roman rites of institution of readers and acolytes can also be included, as can the rite commissioning special ministers of Holy Communion.

Some parishes provide ceremonies of prayer and blessing for people undertaking various ministries, for example, directors of religious education, parochial school teachers, catechists, church musicians, visitors of the sick and elderly, staff members of offices for justice and peace, directors of communications, etc. Though these rites of prayer and blessing are

[1]*Justice in the World,* no. 40, in Joseph Gremillion, *The Gospel of Peace and Justice* (Maryknoll, N.Y.: Orbis Books, 1976), pp. 522.

often not found in the official liturgical books of the churches, they are still truly liturgy, the worship of the local church. They are included among liturgies of ministry.

The *Roman Pontifical* contains rites for a bishop's blessing of an abbot or abbess. Certainly an abbot or abbess is assigned a special ministry in the church in becoming the leader of a monastic community. The *Prayer Book* of the Episcopal Church contains a "Celebration of a New Ministry" which can be used on various occasions of induction and installation. These rites, too, we include among liturgies of ministry.

How do these liturgies of ministry lead into a consideration of social justice in the church? In assigning members of the church to specific ministries, these liturgies introduce differentiation and organization into the church's overall manifold ministry rooted in Christian initiation. Structure appears in the church: some are designated priests, others bishops, others readers, others directors of religious education, others catechists, and so on. As these people cooperate to carry out the total ministry of the church, patterns of interaction enter into the life of the church: bishops assign deacons to particular services, and deacons are assigned; directors of religious education hire and fire, and religious education teachers are hired and fired. So the questions arise: Are the organization and behavioral patterns introduced by liturgies of ministry into the church socially just? Do they respect the rights of everyone, ensure each person's fair share of the church's religious resources, and facilitate the practice of every sort of loving justice in the Christian community?

Common elements in these liturgies of ministry enable us to break down this general question and focus on particular issues of social justice in the church. An examination of the rite of ordination to the presbyterate in the Roman Catholic Church reveals these elements.[2]

After the candidates have been called to come forward before the ordaining bishop, a designated priest announces: "Most reverend Father, holy Mother Church asks you to

---

[2] *The Rites of the Catholic Church*, vol. 2 (New York: Pueblo Publishing Company, 1980), pp. 60-69.

ordain these men, our brothers, for service as priests." The
bishop responds: "Do you judge them to be worthy?" In answer
the priest says: "After inquiry among the people of Christ and
upon recommendation of those concerned with their training,
I testify that they have been found worthy." The bishop then
declares: "We rely on the help of the Lord God and our Savior
Jesus Christ, and we choose these men, our brothers, for
priesthood in the presbyteral order." Then all present say
"Thanks be to God," or give their assent to the choice in some
other way according to local custom. In many places in the
United States the congregation applauds.

This ritual exchange supposes the community's participation
in the choice of those who are to serve as presbyters. It also
expresses concern about the candidates' worthiness. This
worthiness may be understood to refer to both competence in
ministering and the moral integrity expected of Christian
ministers.

A homily follows. The bishop speaks to the congregation
about the significance of the presbyterate, and to the candidates
about the principal responsibilities they are about to assume.
After the bishop examines the candidates' intention and
receives their pledge of obedience, the entire congregation
kneels to pray the litany of saints over the candidates prostrate
on the floor in their midst. The bishop then lays hands on the
heads of the candidates and offers the prayer of consecration,
calling on the Holy Spirit to bless the candidates for the priestly
ministry. This prayer is offered, of course, in the name of the
whole community.

The community's prayer—the litany of saints and the consecratory prayer—is both for the community and for the
candidates. The people have assembled with their bishop for
the critical task of designating ministers to serve them in their
life and mission; they will suffer from a mistaken choice. So
they pray that these candidates may indeed be made worthy
and empowered by the Spirit for their task. The people's role
in the selection of ministers comes to the surface again.

After the consecratory prayer, the newly ordained presbyters
are clothed in stole and chasuble, signs of their role in the
community; their hands are anointed with oil; and they accept
from the bishop the gifts of bread and wine which the people

have brought up to the table for the eucharistic celebration which is about to begin. A kiss of peace concludes the ordination rite. Notable in all this activity is the new presbyter's receiving the gifts for the Mass, an action symbolizing their acceptance, not of power to dominate, but of ministry for others.

We note, then, three elements in the rite of ordination to the presbyterate: (1) the community's call to ministry; (2) inquiry into ministerial competence and moral worthiness; and (3) acceptance of service to the community. These three elements are also found in the rites of ordination to the diaconate and the episcopate, which have the same pattern as the rite of presbyteral ordination.[3] In the rite of blessing for an abbot or abbess, the people's call is reflected in the opening affirmations of the abbot's or abbess's having been elected by his or her community; there is inquiry into the qualities which the abbot- or abbess-elect brings to the office; and the rite concludes with the presentation and acceptance of symbols of ministry—the monastic rule, the ring, and in the case of an abbot, miter and staff.[4] In the briefer rites of institution of readers and acolytes, the community's concern about the choice and the competence and worthiness of the candidates is implied in the assembly's prayer for them; the focus of the rites is the presentation and acceptance of symbols of service—the Bible in the case of readers, a vessel of bread or wine in the case of acolytes.[5] The rite of commissioning special ministers of Holy Communion contains explicit inquiry into the intention of the candidates to serve and to serve worthily; the people's call is implied in their prayer for the candidates; there is no symbolic gesture of acceptance of ministry, though acceptance is expressed verbally in responding to the inquiry already noted.[6]

The pattern in the Roman rites has its counterpart in other Christian rituals. For example, the *Book of Common Prayer* prescribes that representatives of the diocese, both priests and

[3]Ibid., pp. 49-59, 87-100.

[4]Ibid., pp. 115-31.

[5]Ibid., pp. 12-17.

[6]Ibid., pp. 165-67.

lay persons, present the candidate for episcopacy to the presiding bishop. After requiring certain promises from the bishop
elect, the presiding bishop asks the assembly, "Is it your will
that we ordain N. a bishop?" An examination precedes the
consecration.[7] A similar pattern is observed in the ordinations
of priests and deacons and in the celebration of a new ministry
of some kind. In the *Prayer Book*'s ordination of a deacon, the
bishop asks of the one to be ordained: "Will you look for
Christ in all others, being ready to help and serve those in
need?"[8] According to the Presbyterian *Worshipbook*, in the
ordination of ministers of the word, elders, and deacons, an
elder presents the candidate to the moderator, who examines
the candidate; the people then express their acceptance and
(noteworthy) their support of the chosen person.[9] Similar is
the pattern for the installation of commissioned church
workers, e.g., trustees, church-school teachers, etc.[10]

The Community's Advice and Consent

As we have said, each of these common elements brings to
the fore issues of social justice in the church. The first element—
the community's advice and consent in the designation of
ministers for the service of the community—is not a concession
bestowed on the community by a benevolent ruling class or
monarch, namely, the body of bishops or the pope. We may
have been able to think of it in this way for much, though not
all, of the church's history. But the lay movement in the church
and accompanying theological reflection, especially in this
century prior to Vatican Council II, led the council to affirm
the basic equality of all members in the church and coresponsibility for the life and mission of the church. Not only
the pope and bishops have a commission from Christ, but the

[7] *The Book of Common Prayer* (New York: Church Hymnal Corporation, 1979),
pp. 513-25.

[8] Ibid., pp. 526-28, 531-32; 538-40, 543-44; 559.

[9] *The Worshipbook: Services and Hymns* (Philadelphia: Westminister Press, 1972),
pp. 90-93.

[10] Ibid., p. 96.

laity also: "From the fact of their union with Christ, the head, flows the laity's right and duty to be apostles. Inserted as they are in the mystical body of Christ by baptism and strengthened by the power of the Holy Spirit in confirmation, it is by the Lord himself that they are assigned to the apostolate."[11] This truth, emphasized by the sixteenth century reformers, has at last been officially, if not fully, recognized in the Roman communion.

If the laity are to exercise coresponsibility for the mission of the church, they "should disclose to their pastors their needs and desires with that liberty and confidence which befits children of God and brothers and sisters of Christ. By reason of the knowledge, competence or pre-eminence which they have the laity are empowered—indeed sometimes obliged—to manifest their opinion on those things which pertain to the good of the church."[12] Pastors, on the other hand, "should recognize and promote the dignity and responsibility of the laity in the church. They should willingly use their prudent advice."[13]

Choice of ministers certainly concerns "the good of the church" for which the faithful have an equal though diverse kind of responsibility relative to the bishops and clergy. They have "prudent advice" to offer on this matter. The ritual call to ministry and consent to the bishop's choice, or the local pastor's ought then to be the ritualization of a real procedure carried on in the life of the church. Not to provide such a procedure deprives the faithful of a right to contribute to the shaping of the church's life and mission, a right founded on the responsibility conferred on them in baptism and confirmation.[14] Such a procedure has its precedents in history. Although the practice of community consultation died out in

---

[11]Decree on the Apostolate of the Laity, no. 3, in Austin Flannery, ed., *Vatican Council II: The Conciliar and Post Conciliar Documents* (Collegeville, Minn.: Liturgical Press, 1975) p. 768.

[12]*Constitution on the Church*, no. 37, in Flannery, p. 394.

[13]Ibid., in Flannery, p. 395.

[14]See James Provost, "Structuring the Church as Mission," *Jurist* 39 (1979): 238-42, on the basis of the rights of the faithful.

the fourth century, it was recalled at the Council of Trent by
the Dominican Pedro de Soto.[15]

To say that the community has a right to choose its ministers
does not mean that the community is the source of their
authority. To call, or to choose, ministers is not the equivalent
of ordaining them. Ordination, insertion into the college of
bishops or the presbyterium of the diocese, if that is the local
church's polity, is performed by other bishops in the college,
or by the bishop who is assisted by the presbyterium in the
ministry. The mission, empowerment, and authority which
any of these persons receives is derived from Christ through
his Spirit and those holding apostolic office in the church.[16]
But because the bestowal of these ministries pertains to the
welfare of the whole church, the whole community should
have some say in the choice of the candidates who are to be
empowered or authorized. The calling of candidates for the
ministry and the ordination of these candidates will take shape
differently in the various Christian denominations. Pluralism
here is to be expected and desired.

Something similar can be said about the other ministries
insofar as they proceed from a charism, or gift of the Spirit,
calling and empowering a Christian *from within* herself or
himself to assume a particular ministry in the church. From
this point of view, the community does not empower them.
On the other hand, for these people to act in the name of the
Christian community in the exercise of their gift in response to
their vocation, the Christian community needs to approve
them, for there is need to "make sure that everything is done
properly and in order" (1 Cor. 14:40).

How the community can have some input into the choice of
ministers of whatever kind, what sort of structure can imple-
ment the faithful's responsibility and right, is not necessarily
easy to determine. A one-person-one-vote democratic procedure is not the only way of implementing this responsibility;

[15]See Ramon Arnau, "Lay Participation in Choosing Ministers," *Theology Digest*
28 (1980) 137-41.

[16]We are aware that this presupposes a certain theological position which is
unacceptable to many Christians.

sometimes societies function through representatives. A thoroughly democratic form of election may be unwieldly, and it may not be the best way to truly test competence and worthiness. But what we wish to note here is that it is a matter of social justice to establish procedures for the faithful's input into the choice of ministers, ordained and non-ordained, in the various spheres in which they will serve, where such procedures do not now exist or where they are mere formalities.

Besides the choice of ministers, other matters pertain to "the good of the church" and affect its life and mission, for which the faithful have "prudent advice" to offer: for example, determining the needs to be served within the church and in the world; setting priorities among the services to be provided; deployment of personnel, allocation of financial resources; administering church property; determining just wages for those working for the church; protecting the rights of church members to freedom of expression and thought; providing women with their share of responsibility and participation in the life of the church; speedy and just judicial procedures.[17]

Hence, the establishment of parish councils (new Roman Code of Canon Law, canon 536), diocesan pastoral councils (canons 511-14), and priests' senates (canons 495-502) is not merely the church's supreme authority indulging the laity's and lower clergy's modern obsession with democratic processes; it is, in social justice, providing structures necessary for the faithful to exercise responsibilities and rights which they derive from their baptism and confirmation and, in the case of the priest's senate, also from their ordination. Where these bodies do not exist, or where their functioning is prevented or hampered, social justice calls for a change.

It may be objected that these bodies are only consultative; they do not make legislation which bishop or pastor must accept (canons 500, 2; 514; 536, 2). In response it must be noted that social justice is not some abstract formality, like a cookie cutter, that is imposed uniformly on every social group. Each society and its particular circumstances must be exam-

---

[17]Cf. Second Synod of Bishops, *Justice in the World*, nos. 41-46, in Gremillion, *Gospel of Peace* pp. 522-23.

ined in itself to determine what constitutes social justice for it. The social teaching of the church has moved increasingly in the direction of recognizing this truth.[18] The nature of the church is not the nature of civil society. We cannot say, a priori, that, because one or several modern societies operate as democracies in which elected legislators make the laws which leaders *must* accept, the same structure is appropriate to the church. For instance in the case of the Roman church, it is neither a democracy nor a monarchy nor an oligarchy; all power is not in the people, nor is it all in the pope, or bishop, or college of bishops with the pope. The current endeavor in this church to promote a consultative form of government may be quite adequate to realize the social justice which should characterize ecclesial life. Experience will tell.[19]

Worthiness and Competence

The second element in liturgies of ministry—namely, the test for worthiness and competence for the ministry one is about to assume—is meant to be a ritual expression culminating a testing, correcting, nurturing, and retesting that has gone on in a very real way before the liturgical action. Social justice demands this real testing. Those called and appointed to minister to the community must have moral integrity, for without it, they are too easily tempted to use ministry for personal benefit or the benefit of "friends," rather than for impartial loving service to the whole community and each of its members. They may misuse ministry and even alter it permanently, thus introducing a corrupt, unjust church order. Without competence, their blunders in fulfilling their ministry deprive many people of benefits to which they have a right. Their bungling may also result in lasting changes which cause socially unjust order to develop among Christians.

---

[18]See summary of M. D. Chenu's *La "doctrine sociale" comme idéologie* by Donald Goergen in "Current Trends: From 'Social Doctrine' Gospel Values and Signs of the Times," *Spirituality Today* 35 (1983): 155-69.

[19]See James Provost, "The Working Together of Consultative Bodies —Great Expectations?" *Jurist* 40 (1980): 257-81.

It falls within the scope of social justice, then, for the church to lay down certain requirements to be met by those who would undertake various ministries in the church. Also within the scope of social justice is the church's setting certain conditions under which ministry is to be carried out and people are to qualify for receiving approval to exercise these ministries. The Spirit is not to be smothered, but spirits are to be tested (cf. 1 Thess.5:19-22).[20]

An enemy of just social order is discrimination against individuals or groups. In regard to ministry, discrimination can occur when no provision is made for ministry to a group within the community for whom provision ought to be made but is not because of prejudice or indifference, for example, the elderly, the disabled, native Americans, or others deserving of special care. Discrimination can also occur when people are excluded from exercising a ministry because of some personal characteristic which is irrelevant to the practice of that ministry, even though these persons have the requisite moral integrity and professional competence. Such a case is the refusal to admit women as special ministers of Holy Communion or as readers in the liturgy because they are women, even though they are morally worthy and as competent as any man.

Discrimination is an especially insidious enemy of social justice in the church because it so easily insinuates itself into the church from the general social milieu. People bring to church the prejudices they encounter and absorb in society. If racism, ethnocentrism, and sexism are rampant in society, they are very likely vigorous in the church. This is one reason for recognizing that the church, though a divinely given mystery, is also a church summoned by Christ to "continual reformation of which she [sic] always has need, insofar as she is an institution of men and women here on earth."[21]

Because racism is still virulent in the United States, questions can be raised about Christian communities' openness to, and service of, Afro-Americans, Native Americans, and Asians. Ethnocentrism raises questions about the treatment of the

---

[20]Cf. *Constitution on the Church*, no. 12, in Flannery, pp. 363-64.

[21]Cf. *Decree on Ecumenism*, no. 6, in Flannery, p. 459.

Spanish-speaking. Because of an atmosphere of individualistic philosophy, a highly competitive economic system, and a penchant for comfort and convenience, we may wonder whether the United States church can really serve the poor, both in the economic sense and in the sense of society's outcasts.

A strictly inner-church problem is the lack of ways for laity to offer input into decision-making for the life and mission of the church, for which they have a responsibility from their baptism and confirmation. Mostly from the laity come the funds which make it possible for the Christian community to function, but the laity have little say about the distribution of that money.

Women are notoriously discriminated against in society and in the church. Women are still paid less than men for equal work. The burden of poverty falls more on women than men.[22] Within the church we find the embarrassing, scandalous situation where women are treated as marginal and dependent and are excluded from positions of power except of a very limited sort determined entirely by men,[23] as several episcopal pastoral letters, statements, and addresses have recognized,[24]

---

[22]M. P. Burke, *Reaching for Justice: The Women's Movement* (Washington, D.C.: Center of Concern, 1980), especially chap. 41; U. S. Commission on Civil Rights, *A Growing Crisis: Disadvantaged Women and Their Children* (Washington, D.C., 1983).

[23]See Sandra Schneiders, "The Effects of Women's Experience on Their Spirituality," *Spirituality Today* 35 (1983): 100-116.

[24]"Women in the New World," Bishop Leo Maher, San Diego, 1974 (*Origins* 4 [1 August 1974]: 113-19); "Women: Intrepid and Loving," Bishop Carroll Dozier, Memphis, 1975 *Origins* 4 [23 January 1975]: 481-85; "Reflections on Women in the Mission and Ministry of the Church," Archbishop William Borders, Baltimore, 1977 (*Origins* 7 [1 September 1977]:167-70); "The Future of Women in the Ministry," Auxiliary Bishop P. Francis Murphy, Baltimore (*Origins* 7 [13 October 1977]: 267-72); "Justice and the Role of Women" and "Contemporary Women and the Church," Bishops of Minnesota, 1979 (*Origins* 8 [26 April 1979]: 709-15, 715-18); "The Oppression of Women," Bishop Robert Lebel, Valleyfield, Canada (*Origins* 10 [23 October 1980]: 302); "Women in the Church," Archbishop Peter Gerety, Newark, 1981 (*Origins* 10 [26 February 1981]: 582-88); "Statement on Women in Ministry," Bishop John Cummins, Oakland, 1981 (*Origins* 11 [5 November 1981]: 331-33); "Male and Female He Created Them," Bishop Victor Balke, Crookston, and Bishop Raymond Lucker, New Ulm, 1981 (*Origins* 11 [5 November 1981]: 333-38; "The Fire in the Thornbush," Bishop Matthew Clark, Rochester, 1982 (*Origins* 12 [14 October 1982]: 273-86).

and as is symbolically demonstrated in every concelebrated Eucharist.

The most neuralgic point in regard to women's place in the church is the possibility of their ordination. Here we wish to make only two comments.

The *Declaration on the Question of Admission of Women to the Priesthood* by the Roman Sacred Congregation for the Doctrine of the Faith, 15 October 1976, ruled out the possibility of women's ordination on the basis of the church's constant tradition, the attitude of Christ, the practice of the apostles, the relationship of the ministerial priesthood to the mystery of Christ and to the mystery of the church.[25] The *Declaration*'s arguments are not without their weaknesses.[26]

Radical shifts, however, have occurred in the church's position in the past: for example, in regard to the supreme temporal power of the pope over all rulers of nations,[27] the morality of slavery,[28] civil religious liberty,[29] involvement in the world and marriage as means of sanctity,[30] the necessity of

[25]*AAS* 69 (1977): 98-116; English translation in *Women Priests: A Catholic Commentary on the Vatican Declaration* ed. Leonard Swidler and Arlene Swidler (New York: Paulist Press, 1977), 37-49.

[26]See the commentary mentioned in the previous note.

[27]See Archbishop Peter Kenrick's view of the intent, understanding, and history of the papal bull *Unam Sanctam* of Boniface VIII at the beginning of the fourteenth century, quoted by P. K. Hennessy, "Infallibility in the Ecclesiology of Peter Richard Kenrick," *Theological Studies* 45 (1984): 708-9.

[28]Contrast mentality behind Eph. 6:5-8 and Col. 3:22-24 and church's stance today, especially as revealed in Vatican II's *Constitution on the Church in the Modern World*.

[29]Contrast Vatican Council II, Declaration on Religious Liberty, 7 December 1965, with previous church teaching on religious liberty especially during the nineteenth century. Consult the works of John Courtney Murray, S.J., in this field and assessments of his work, in particular the radical revolution it achieved in Vatican Council II. See, e.g., entry "Murray, John Courtney," *Encyclopedic Dictionary of Religion*.

[30]Contrast the Council of Trent, session 24, canon 10 and the interpretation which this affirmation of the superiority of virginity and celibacy had in shaping a negative attitude toward lay life and marriage in terms of Christian holiness with the statement of Pope John XXIII about the value of activity in the world, *Mater et Magistra*, 15 May 1961, no. 255, in Claudia Carlen, comp., *The Papal Encyclicals* (Wilmington, N.C: McGrath Publishing Co., 1981), 5:86.

explicit submission to the pope for salvation,[31] Protestant churches as means of salvation,[32] genuine exchange or dialogue with Protestant churches rather than unconditional submission to the Roman see,[33] the moment of hominization of the human fetus,[34] the Mosaic authorship of the Pentateuch (the first five books of the Bible),[35] repudiation of the idea that Jews are a "perfidious people" (a phrase deleted by Pope John XXIII from the General Intercessions of the Good Friday liturgy) who have been abandoned by God,[36] the extent of Jesus' knowledge while he lived on earth.[37]

Not all of these matters are related to God's revelation in

---

[31]See Vatican Council II, *Constitution on the Church*, nos. 15 and 16, in Flannery, pp. 366-68. Note in no. 14 the qualifications placed on the quality of knowledge of the church as the divinely necessary means of salvation and on the refusal to enter it or to remain in it, for lack of submission to entail damnation.

[32]*Decree on Ecumenism*, no. 3, in Flannery, p. 456.

[33]Ibid., no. 4, in Flannery, p. 457.

[34]Joseph F. Donceel, "Catholic Politicians and Abortion," *America*, 2 February 1985, pp. 81-83, argues a radical change in the understanding of when hominization of the fetus occurs in relation to animation as a certain fact, and not merely as possible or probable. He reviews the teaching from Augustine through St. Alphonsus Liguori and eminent moral theologians in the first quarter, at least, of this century, as well as editions of the Catechism of the Council of Trent and a response of the Holy Office in 1783. In the last few decades "the certain fact" has been replaced by another "certain fact."

[35]On the Decrees of the Pontifical Biblical Commission issued between 1905 and 1915 and in 1933, the *Jerome Biblical Commentary* (72:85) remarks: " ... few modern Catholic scholars adhere today to the positions on authorship, the dating, and the unity of the biblical books proposed in the decrees." " ... many of those decrees now have little more than historical interest, being implicitly revoked by later decrees, by *Divine Afflante Spiritu*, and by Vatican II." Among the items covered in these decrees were the Mosaic authorship of the Pentateuch, the first five books of the Bible. Decades after the decrees had been issued, they were still being taught in seminaries with a certitude far beyond their actual worth.

[36]Vatican Council II, *Declaration on the Relation of the Church to Non-Christian Religions*, no. 4, in Flannery, p. 741.

[37]Jean Galot, a moderately conservative theologian, in his Christology, *Who Is Christ? A Theology of the Incarnation* (Chicago: Franciscan Herald Press, 1981), recognizes limitations in the knowledge of the earthly Jesus that were not common place in the usual presentation of Jesus from the Middle Ages until well into this century. Noteworthy is his handling (pp. 357-58, note 33) of a decree of the Holy Office in 1918 and two encyclicals, *Mystici Corporis* (1943) and *Haurietis Aquas* (1956), which attribute the beatific vision of the earthly Jesus—a kind of knowledge, which Galot argues persuasively, the earthly Jesus did not have (pp. 353-57).

the same way; some have to do with historical circumstances which have obviously changed; some have been theological speculations or conclusions; nor did the "teaching church" propose them with equal certitude or expect the same sort of response from the faithful with regard to each. But at one time or another the general run of Catholics and their leaders took these now abandoned positions with high degrees of certainty and would have had a difficult time arguing that they were not a part of "the church's teaching" which is irrevocable. This phenomenon suggests that we ought not to be overly hasty in concluding that some church teaching, unless formally defined doctrine or most obviously a part of the universal ordinary magisterium, is irrevocable, even though proposed most vigorously by church authorities.[38] And if it proves to be irrevocable, questions of its precise sense, or meaning, can arise and can modify the way in which such teachings are understood or implemented in practice. In a positive vein, we can hope that, in regard to the ordination of women, various church communions, in light of further study, reflection, and experience, may eventually adopt another position than the present one. Social justice seems to call for such openness in the present moment of history.

With the *Declaration* we admit that the answer to this question must be based on revelation; it is not simply a matter of human rights naturally discernible. The question remains, however, whether or not the social justice proper to the church in the light of revelation excludes the ordination of women. The *Declaration* clarifies—it does not "define"—the inherited position in a time of turmoil, in order to provide the faithful with a certain measure of security. But, for reasons mentioned above, it seems possible to hope for further understanding and a different conclusion, without being judged disloyal or a dissenter.

Our second comment is that we must not confuse the question of women's ordination with the issue of social justice

---

[38] For additional shifts in more recent church teaching made by Vatican Council II, see Avery Dulles, "Authority: The Divided Legacy," *Commonweal*, 12 July 1985, p. 401.

for women in the church. The latter is much broader than the former. If the question of women's ordination was settled tomorrow in one way or another with everyone's agreement, much would still remain to be done for women to take their rightful place in the life and mission of the church. The experience of ordained women in the Protestant and Anglican churches testifies to this sorry truth.[39] Women constitute half the membership of the church—the more faithful and zealous half—yet they have extremely little say in the governance of the church; and even their associations (religious congregations of sisters, for instance) function only with the approval of male superiors. Some may regard this situation as fulfilling a divine design. We regard it as sexism and paternalism rooted in the "old Adam" and to be exorcised from church and society as inconsistent with the new creation in Jesus Christ, like anti-Semitism, racism, ethnocentrism, and slavery. From ushers to welcome people to Sunday Eucharist, to servers, readers, and distributors of Holy Communion, and on to diocesan super-intendents of schools and chancery officials, and further to consultors in the congregations of the Roman curia serving the pope, women have yet to come to their rightful place in the Roman communion, as they have yet to come in other churches as well.

Acceptance of Ministry

The third common element in the liturgies of ministry is the candidates' acceptance of ministry expressed in the presentation and reception of symbols of that ministry—Book of the Gospels, ring, miter, and pastoral staff for bishop; bread and wine for presbyter; Book of Gospels for deacon; a vessel of bread or wine for acolyte; a Bible for reader; the rule for the abbot or abbess; and so on. Our interest, however, is not

---

[39] Arlene Swidler, "Women in Ministry: Some Ecumenical Lessons," *Spirituality Today* 30 (1978): 4-13; Elizabeth Howell Verdesi, *In But Still Out: Women in the Church* (Philadelphia: Westminister Press, 1973); Virginia Lieson Brereton and Christa Ressmeyer Klein, "American Women in Ministry," in Rosemary Ruether and Eleanor McLaughlin, eds. *Women of Spirit* (New York: Simon and Schuster, 1979), pp. 302-32.

precisely in the symbols of ministry but the fact that what is given and accepted is ministry, or service, not power or prestige. *Ministry* is the translation of the Latin word *ministerium*, which, in turn, was employed to translate the New Testament Greek *diakonia*, for which another English translation is *service*. *Diakonia* is a very prominent word in the New Testament.

Jesus said of himself that he had come "not to be served by others, but to serve and to give his own life as a ransom for the many" (Matt. 20:28). Those who were to be in authority in the community of disciples were to act in a way different from that of gentile rulers: "You know how those who exercise authority among the gentiles lord it over them; their great ones make their importance felt. It cannot be like that with you. Anyone among you who aspires to greatness must serve the rest, and whoever wants to rank first among you must serve the needs of all" (Matt. 20:25-27). Jesus instructed his disciples that they were to be servants, indeed slaves, by his dramatic action at the Last Supper—he washed their feet.

St. Paul struggled to make the members of his Corinthian church see that their gifts of the Spirit were to be exercised for the common good, not to outdo others or to win a following (1 Cor. 12-14). Paul saw himself and other apostles as "servants of Christ" (1 Cor. 4:1) and servants of the Corinthians for Jesus' sake (2 Cor. 4:5). "The gift of ministry," Paul wrote to the Romans (12:7), "should be used for service." "Put your gifts at the service of one another" is the exhortation in 1 Pet. 4:10.

Christian ministers through the centuries have striven to follow the pattern set by Christ and reaffirmed by Paul and other New Testament authors; but it must also be admitted that the human condition and historical circumstances have often obscured the New Testament understanding and practice of ministry.[40] When Christianity was accepted into the Roman empire and became an official religion, bishops were frequently

---

[40]Yves Congar, *Power and Poverty in the Church* (Baltimore: Helicon, 1964), passim; John McKenzie, *Authority in the Church* (New York: Sheed and Ward, 1966), passim.

co-opted to serve as local government officials. In the Middle Ages and into modern times in Germany, bishops were prince-bishops and elector bishops, simultaneously political and ecclesiastical figures; in France, bishops were generally drawn from the nobility rather than from the lower class. The papacy for many centuries up until the last decades of the nineteenth century was not only the center of the Roman Catholic church but the ruler of the Papal States. In circumstances such as these, it became an irresistible tendency, or even an unavoidable style, to conduct Christian ministry, not as service in the likeness of Jesus, but as domination and control in the likeness of secular rule—even though those exercising the ministry most often were personally very sincere and holy people, acting in good conscience.

Christian ministry does involve power and authority. It is not service rendered from weakness, though its possessors are weak (cf. 2 Cor. 12:5-10). Directors of religious education, for example, have knowledge and skills which many others do not; they have respectable moral character and a commission to function on behalf of the local community; they have the prayers of the church to intercede for the fulfillment of their service; they are able, therefore, to influence the actions of others—which is what power and authority do. Power and authority are to be exercised for religious purposes, of course; that is, they aim at developing people's full potential for this redeemed human life and for union with God now and for eternity; Jesus healed bodies and psyches, as well as forgave sins. Since redeemed humanity calls for a just social order, ecclesial power and authority aim at promoting, among other things, social justice in the church and in society. Ecclesial power and authority are also exercised as service by adopting a Christlike manner; they function with compassion, understanding, respect, gentleness, and patience such as Jesus manifested in his ministry. Christlike exercise of power and authority begets social justice in the church by organizing church life in a way which facilitates and develops everyone's charisms and talents for the benefit of all.

But we also must recognize that Christian ministry, though intrinsically religious, can be accompanied by power and authority which are secular in their impact. To be bishop of

Chicago, for example, the appointed leader of the local church whose members constitute half the population of the vast metropolitan area, is to be inevitably, by reason of circumstances, in a position to influence the secular life of that area and, therefore, to exercise secular power and authority. A similar situation exists for pastors in small rural communities or in urban neighborhoods. That secular power and authority ought not to be ignored or denied, but exercised in a Christlike way, as service, not domination and control, and for the welfare of secular society, in particular for social justice in society's organization and procedures.

Service to the World

This recognition of secular power and authority adhering to Christian ministry reminds us that the church is essentially a mission to the world, the herald of the coming reign of God over all creation. God's reign in the world means, of course, social justice in society. Thus the Second Synod of Roman Catholic Bishops meeting in Rome in 1971 declared: "Action on behalf of justice and participation in the transformation of the world fully appear to us a constitutive dimension of the preaching Gospel, or, in other words, of the Church's mission for the redemption of the human race and its liberation from every oppressive situation."[41]

The bishops recognize, however, that the church's call for social justice in the world will not be credible if such justice is not at least striven for in the church. Hence, their document proceeds to list areas of church life calling for concern with regard to social justice: respect for the ordinary rights of the church's members; fair wages; social security; means of promotion for those who work for the church—including clergy, religious, and lay people; increased participation of lay people's function with regard to church property and its administration;

---

[41]"Justice in the World," no. 6, in Gremillion, *Gospel of Peace*, p. 514. See Charles M. Murphy, "Action for Justice as Constitutive of the Preaching of the Gospel: What Did the 1971 Synod Mean?" *Theological Studies* 44 (1983): 288-97.

women's share of responsibility and participation in the life of the church; freedom of expression and thought and the right of everyone to be heard in a spirit of dialogue; the right of an accused person to know his or her accusers, to have proper defense, and to a speedy trial; the church's members' sharing in decision making through councils as recommended by Vatican Council II; acceptance of privileges and use of possessions consistent with the mission to preach the gospel to the poor; individuals' life-style in keeping with the church's mission and the hunger prevalent in the world.[42]

But the church, constantly scrutinizing itself to promote social justice within itself, not only proclaims social justice *to* the world but also *in* the world. It carries out this effort especially through the laity. The laity are the church, the people of God, just as much as clergy and religious are. Hence, when the laity work for social justice in the world carrying out their daily tasks, the church works there. "The apostolate of the laity is a sharing in the salvific ministry of the church ... The laity are given this special vocation: to make the church present and fruitful in those places and circumstances where it is only through them that she [sic] can become the salt of the earth."[43] This ecclesial mission in the world includes working for social justice: "Let the laity so remedy institutions and conditions of the world ... that these may conform to the norms of justice."[44]

The laity may work for justice *in* the world *against* the world, so to speak, or *through* the world. To work for justice *in* the world *but against* it means to work outside the institutions of society, challenging them and fighting them from without. This kind of social action for justice often makes the headlines. We read about demonstrations at nuclear power plants, prayer vigils at the headquarters of weapons manufacturers, picketing the mayor's office for increased police protection, sit-ins for equal rights for women.

---

[42]"Justice in the World," nos. 41-48, in Gremillion, *Gospel of Peace*, pp. 522-23.

[43]*Constitution on the Church*, no. 32, in Flannery, p. 390.

[44]Ibid., no. 36, in Flannery, p. 393-94.

Work for justice *in* the world *but through* the world means working through institutions of the world, seeing such an institution as "an engine of change," as Edward Marciniak notes.[45] By entering into the structures of society and bringing to bear on daily decisions and choices the values of the gospel, people can work toward the development of just social systems. "The Chicago Declaration of Concern" stated:

> The impression is often created that one can work for justice and peace only by stepping outside of these ordinary roles as a businessman, as a mayor, as a factory worker, as a professional in the State Department, or as an active union member and thus that one can change the system only as an "outsider" to society and the system. Such ideas clearly depart from the mainstream of Catholic social thought which regards the advance of social justice as essentially the service performed within one's professional and occupational milieu."[46]

This mission of the laity—to be the church in the world and to bring into the world the message and grace of sanctification and to renew the temporal order[47]—is part of the public claims made in the church by the rites of Christian initiation.[48] It is not simply a participation in the apostolate of the hierarchy.[49] We see, then, that we could also designate baptism-confirmation-first Eucharist as liturgies of ministry insofar as they commission every member of the church to ministry in the church in the world. The *Prayer Book* of the Episcopal Church in its rite of ordination of a priest has the bishop address the ordained with these words: "All baptized

[45]Edward Marciniak, "Being a Christian in the World of Work," *Origins* 12 (29 July 1982): 139.

[46]"The Chicago Declaration of Concern," in *Challenge to the Laity*, ed. Russell Barta (Huntington, Ind.: Our Sunday Visitor Press, 1980), p. 23.

[47]*Decree on the Apostolate of the Laity*, nos. 2, 5-8, in Flannery, pp. 767-68, 772-76.

[48]Ibid., no. 3, in Flannery, p. 768; *Constitution on the Church,* no. 33, in Flannery, p. 390.

[49]*Constitution on the Church*, no. 33 in Flannery, p. 391; *Decree on Apostolate of the Laity*, no. 20, in Flannery, pp. 787-88.

people are called to make Christ known as Savior and Lord, and to share in the renewing of his world. Now you are called to work as a pastor, priest, and teacher, ...[50]

Our main concern here, however, has not been to classify or name liturgical rites but to see the implications for social justice in a set of rites which consecrate or bless those assuming certain ministries within the church. Our analysis of these rites indicates that in their provision for the people's invitation and consent to candidates' assumption of ministry, in their test of the candidates' assumption of ministry, in their test of the candidates' worthiness and competence, and in their call to serve others rather than their conferring worldly prestige and status upon the recipients, they refer to social justice within the church. They point the way towards the church's being a credible prophet of social justice to the world and, especially through the laity, in the world.

꽃

Bibliography

Arbuckle, Gerald A. "Dress and Worship: Liturgies for the Culturally Dispossessed," Worship: 59:5 (September, 1985)

This is a case study of the Maori Catholics, a cultural minority in New Zealand. The author draws upon cultural anthropology in discussing the implications for liturgy and culturally dispossessed peoples.

Bausch, William J. *Ministry: Traditions, Tensions, Transitions,* Mystic, Conn.: Twenty-Third Publications, 1982.

This is a popular presentation of the history of ministry, the present problems, and the hopes for the future. Bausch

---

[50] *The Book of Common Prayer*, p. 531.

stresses collaboration between the ordained and the unordained ministers. The book is an invitation for priests and lay ministers to work together.

Burrows, William R. *New Ministries: The Global Context,* Maryknoll: Orbis Books, 1980.

This approach to ministry comes from the perspective of someone who has been a missionary and has worked in the third world. The author argues convincingly that the older forms of church and clerical life do not work in the third world and that for that part of the church, at least, new forms must be encouraged.

Leap, Frances M. "On Women and Worship," in *Liturgy* 7:4 (Spring 1989).

This article examines the relations of women to worship as an issue of ethics and justice. The author describes ways in which religious feminists respond to the dilemma presented to them by worship, and suggests an alternative model for action.

McCormick, S. J. Richard A. "Bishops as Teachers and Jesuits as Listeners," in *Studies in the Spirituality of Jesuits* 18:3 (May 1986) published by the American Assistancy Seminar, Fusz Memorial, St. Louis University, 3700 West Pine Blvd., St.Louis, MO 63108.

This study by a prominent moral theologian indicates the meaning of appropriate dissent from church authority by examining the doctrinal status of moral statements, the levels of authority in the church, and the proper response to episcopal teaching. Although directed to Jesuits, it contains some sound guidelines in the matter of dissent in the church.

McManus, William E. "Putting Our House in Order: Economic Justice within the Church," *America,* Vol. 153:8 (5 October 1985), pp. 190-95.

The retired bishop of Fort Wayne-South Bend, Ind., assesses the strength and weaknesses of the church's efforts to provide for social justice within itself in order to become a credible preacher of justice in the world.

O'Meara, Thomas F. *Theology of Ministry,* New York: Paulist Press, 1983.

This work explores in sweeping views the continuing historical adaption of ministry to suit cultural needs and situations, notes the changes now taking place in the church's ministry, and suggests more appropriate ways of viewing and implementing ministry in our age.

Neu, Diann. "Our Name is Church: The Experience of Catholic-Christian Feminist Liturgies," in *Concilium: Can We Always Celebrate The Eucharist?* edited by Mary Collins and David Power, New York: The Seabury Press, 1982.

This is a provocative essay that explores the question of feminist liturgies. The author suggests three phases of liturgy that would embody the shift from a patriarchal past to a feminist future, and offers theological reflection on each of these phases.

Power, David N. *Lay Ministries Established and Unestablished,* New York: Pueblo Publishing Company, 1980.

Starting with the recently established lay ministries of lector, or reader, and acolyte, the author explores the history of lay ministries in the church's history, their place in the mystery of the church, and the opportunities for the present and future.

Provost, James H. ed. *Official Ministry in a New Age,* Washington, D.C.: The Canon Law Society of America, 1981.

This series of scholarly papers takes up such issues as the public language of ministry, the basis for official ministry in the church, the fullness of orders, and a renewed canonical understanding of official ministry. It is highly recommended.

Schillebeeckx, Edward. *The Church with a Human Face: A New and Expanded Theology of Ministry,* New York: Crossroad, 1985.

This is a revision, amplification, and replacement of the author's early book, *Ministry: Leadership in the Community of Jesus Christ,* where he concluded that celibacy and ministry are separable, that there is no real objection to the ministry of women, and that new forms of ministry are developing. This book represents an expansion of this material both historically and theologically.

Spirituality Today, vol. 30, no. 1, March 1978.

This issue of the journal is devoted to examining the theme of women in ministry from various points of view— scriptural, historical, spiritual, experiential. Authors are Arlene Swidler, Thomas O'Meara, Marlene Halpin, Benedict Viviano, Thomas McGonigle, and Richard Weber.

Terwilliger, Robert E. and Holmes, Urban T., eds. *To Be A Priest: Perspective on Vocation and Ordination,* New York: The Seabury Press, 1975.

This collection of essays from Roman Catholic, Orthodox, and Anglican scholars deals with the meaning of priesthood in the bible and history, the functioning of the priest in the parish and in the world, and the challenges of the priestly vocation today.

9

Marriage:
A Liberating Relationship

James White has observed that sacraments can reinforce oppressive and unjust relationships, especially those based on inequality, subordination and subservience.[1] Some of the clearest examples of this are found in the wedding service where the bride is treated as inferior to her husband. "I now pronounce you *man* and wife." What are the implications of not saying husband and wife? It may be that marrying rites reflect a cultural context. But they also can be a powerful force in keeping society's stereotypes alive. Formerly, some rites prayed for the fidelity and chastity of the women but did not do the same for the man. Thus, sacraments can reflect many of society's unarticulated assumptions about human relationships. We have been to weddings which reinforce certain socially conditioned sex roles. The husband is to provide shelter and money and the wife is to make a good home.

Sacraments can be moments in the church when we can promote a greater consciousness of the injustices that are present in the community. In preparing for the celebration of matrimony we could ask: What does it mean for the father of the bride to give her away? Even many socially aware women opt for that form of entrance procession. We need to promote

---

[1]James F. White, *Sacraments as God's Self Giving* (Nashville: Abingdon Press, 1983), p. 95.

an awareness of what is suggested by such a practice. White points out:

> The whole wedding ceremony remains rife with actions that imply subservience rather than mutual service. Being a star for a day hardly compensates for being submerged for a lifetime. Most of the words have changed. But some of the actions still strongly imply disparity in the human value of the contracting parties or undervalue both.[2]

White's point could be illustrated many times over with the various ceremonies in the marriage rite which are taken for granted. For instance, what is theologically implied by the practice of the bride and groom lighting a single candle from two lit ones? It is theologically unacceptable to claim that they surrender their selfhood to each other. Two do not become one; they remain distinct in their union. Because of such implicit injustice, we need continually to review our sacramental practices. Sacraments can be great forces for justice in the church, as the previous chapters have hopefully demonstrated. But they are only so when they make the full human worth of others manifest in the worshiping assembly. Marriage can be an excellent example of how this can be done, since it is not only a sacrament but also a human reality. In fact, as Bernard Cooke points out, marriage is the paradigm of the fundamental sacramentality of all human experience.[3] It seems logical, then, to begin our investigation of the relationship of marriage and social justice by exploring marriage as both human and sacramental reality.

Marriage as a Human and Sacramental Reality

Any treatment of marriage from a Christian perspective must begin with it as a human reality with its own history. The

[2]Ibid., p. 102.

[3]Bernard Cooke, *Sacraments and Sacramentality* (Mystic, Conn.: Twenty-Third Publications, 1983), see chapter seven.

reality of marriage did not begin, obviously, with the recognition of its sacramental status. The connection of social justice to marriage is based on marriage as a sacrament in the church, but even more fundamentally on marriage as a phenomenon which makes sense on its own terms even prior to any specifically Christian dimension.[4] However, this is not to imply that marriage was not considered a "religious" reality by early Christians.

Marriage is a commitment to human loving in a specific bodily way. It cannot be equated with a mechanistic contract no matter how oppressive the relationship may be. Human loving in marriage is seen as a freeing of oneself and the other in order to be whole. One need not own marriage as a sacrament to recognize and support the equality of men and women in the marital relationship and to reject the notion of woman as only man's helpmate. Marriage need not be acknowledged as a symbol of the mystery of Christ to affirm that the relationship is equal if both persons' needs and desires are taken into account or to hold that the challenge of the contemporary marriage is to counter the societal notion of seeing women as sex objects or domestic maids.

Again it is not because marriage is a sacrament that we conclude that the procreative aspect must be broadened to emphasize the married couple's responsibility to *choose* children and to have the necessary resources to care for them, to recognize that the erotic, loving relationship is itself generating new freedom and wholeness in the married couple, and to acknowledge that a liberating marital relationship will culminate in the married couple's outreach of helping those in need and of caring for those less loved and loveable. We would hope for the same in marriages of Jewish and other religious traditions.

But Christian marriage is also a sacramental reality and has its own history. There have been two major images through

[4]E. Schillebeeckx has treated marriage as both a secular reality and a sacrament in his *Marriage: Human Reality and Saving Mystery* (New York: Sheed and Ward, 1965). See also: Paul Palmer, S.J., "Christian Marriage: Contract or Covenant?" *Theological Studies* 33 (1972): 617-65.

which this sacramentality has been expressed. They are (1) the relationship between Christ and the church and (2) marriage as a sign of the united oneness of Christian community.[5] Marriage as a Christological symbol was idealized in terms of the qualities that characterized Christ and the church: unity, sharing, life-giving, commitment, permanency, and devotion. Many of these same qualities describe marriage under the second sign: oneness of the Christian community. Often the quality of exclusiveness is emphasized in both.

An overly literal application of these traditional images has been the source of much injustice in marriage. The relationship between Christ and the church is understood to be perfect. How is that possible for any Christian marriage? The Christian community projects its own hoped for but unattained image of unity on to married couples. Married people are not allowed to have the failures common to the entire community. There are unrealistic expectations placed on marriage in Christian communities. It must be perfect from the beginning. Thus, when marriages break down, the only way to handle the separation legitimately is through annulment, or claiming that there never was a marriage. The most obvious and painful results of this expected image of marriage is the curtailment of community involvement on the part of the divorced and remarried to the point of exclusion from the sacraments.[6]

A more helpful image for marriage, one which builds on the model of covenant love so generally espoused by sacramental theologians today, is that of the liberating love of Jesus. This New Testament covenantal love is one which calls people to love themselves as totally as possible. It is love which is a process and this process is the experience of liberation. People who are liberated can invite other persons into personal sharing. They are open to being a part of another person's life. This makes it possible for two people united as one in search

---

[5]The Christological image is explored in Jack Dominian's *Marriage, Faith and Love: A Basic Guide to Christian Marriage* (New York: Crossroad, 1982). For marriage as a sign of community see *Partners in Service* by Elizabeth and Mulry Tetlow, (New York: University Press of America, 1983).

[6]Some helpful pastoral reflections on marital breakdown and divorce can be found in Dominian, p. 172ff.

for an authentic love to reach beyond themselves and to share this love with friends and family even in areas of unfreedom. And this same love will invite the couple to reach beyond their circle of friends to be sensitive to a world that has much injustice and lack of love. The couple will be encouraged to look at the areas of injustice in their own love. The model of the liberating love of Jesus finds its value in the life the couple gives to it.[7]

The re-imaging of marriage in a liberation perspective has a number of ramifications for a theology of marriage. Such re-imaging will flow from the several particular characteristics of marriage when it is viewed from this perspective: (1) Marriage is more than a social or religious reality, it is also political. Does the mutual binding imply bondage? Is marriage (at least in its present western form) a product of capitalism? Can one be committed to both liberating and romantic love at the same time? (2) Marriage is a statement about freedom and justice. Commitment must bring about greater freedom because of mutual respect and equality. On the other side, marriage as a commitment is more effective in helping the couple to carry out God's call to build the kingdom. (3) Marriage is an exodus experience. It has both freedom and "desert" time. (4) Marriage is a celebration of God's activity in the lives of people. God is active in bringing these two people together in a world of diversity, isolationism, and in danger of destruction. (5) Marriage is very much in the context of community. It is not just a private act between two people. It is not just a commitment to each other, but also to community. (6) Marriage is a statement against the isolationism of the world. This union is to empower people to live more fully, to connect and act together. (7) Marriage needs liberation from certain assumptions about the function of marriage. It is not just for procreation, but is for mutual joy, help, and comfort.

[7]For the biblical background for this position see chapter one of *Partners in Service.*

Marriage as Liberating Partnership

Justice in marriage is seen in terms of right relationships and the inner peace, wholeness, completion, health and fullness which are the result of this equality. Right relationships are supposed to realize the greatest human potential. And this implies that marriage is more than a love relationship. The bodily nature of the human person means that it is never possible to speak of marriage without keeping in mind that there are physical, emotional, social, cultural, and economic factors which must be acknowledged.

A liberating married couple try, in their relationship with one another, to respect the dignity and freedom of the partner. They hope to affirm one another and respect the partner's wish to make choices which lead to growth and life. But this cannot be done unless married persons put into perspective their relationships with their in-laws, their children, their neighbors, their servants, friends, and co-workers. Their in-laws or extended family households will hopefully be treated with affection, concern, and compassion. They can be welcomed for their wisdom and affirmed as important in the life of the family. Children can be cared for and affirmed as unique human persons who bring joy, enthusiasm, and their own special giftedness to the family. Physical abuse and psychological violence can have no place among parents who profess themselves to be loving and just.

Neighbors will be affirmed by the hospitality and warmth of the couple. A sharing in the joys and sorrows of others manifests a concern and a willingness to do for others as for one's partner. Many times there are employees in a household—a baby-sitter, a maintenance man or woman, a person who cleans and cooks—these persons have a right to receive a just and living wage, to be accepted, appreciated, and affirmed for their skills and talents. Tom Hart speaks of the hospitable marriage.

> Such a place is an oasis for outsiders to come to, a place of grace, a home in which one feels welcome and from which one emerges refreshed in mind and spirit and recharged for the challenge and opportunities of life. To offer this kind of

welcome and hospitality to people is surely to do Christian ministry in the best New Testament sense.[8]

A husband and wife who become burned out because of long hours at work are challenged to consider the effects of such a schedule on their relationship with their spouses, offspring, and members of the community. Disharmony is generally the result and inner peace, health, and fulfillment are lacking in the marriage.

Liberating partnership implies a life of union based on the couple's mutual love and respect for their bodies, their unique ideas and insights. The couple provide hope for the future because they themselves are responsible and caring for each other. Thus the couple can help breakdown some of the barriers to justice and the building of the kingdom. They can be a sign of unity to a world craving for reconciliation and community. Because they want continually to strive for wholeness and a freeing relationship, they can help witness to each other and the community the ability to overcome fear of the unknown.

Marriage can be a liberating partnership when marital intimacy is present in that the couple invite from each other their best characteristics. Marital intimacy, which is more than sexual experience, brings to light certain gospel values. The incarnational character of the gospel is especially found in marital intimacy.

> One may have to possess all the scars of adult wisdom—the risk of being close to another person—to understand the profundity of the gospel. In intimacy the world became flesh. Intimacy invites us to come alive to each other. It is the special milieu, the shifting ground on which two persons learn about each other. Only here do we find the operational definitions of commitment, trust and fidelity that are the blood and breath of Christian love.[9]

---

[8] *Living Happily Ever After: Toward a Theology of Christian Marriage* (New York: Paulist Press, 1979), p. 65.

[9] M. Kathleen Schaefer, "The Nurturing of Marital Life," in *Liturgy*, vol. 4:2, p. 70.

Among the several gospel values found in marital intimacy are empathy, genuineness and warmth.[10] To be empathetic means entering another person's world with understanding. This difficult task presumes relativizing one's own worldview. But it is through intimacy that we move out of isolation and self-preoccupation to experience the uniqueness of another. Such empathy between couples can become a paradigm of how larger groups such as nations need to learn how to enter each other's horizon of understanding. From this comes a basic trust which includes the feelings of the other. A just relationship must have that minimal kind of trust.

The quality of being genuine is best manifested in people who are open and honest. Such persons are not defensive and are available for relationships. They do not hide. They do not pretend. They do not project a false image. They are not difficult to know. These people are revelatory. It is obvious how such genuineness is a necessary condition for marriage, but also how such a quality is needed at the bargaining table, in international negotiations, and in dealing with governments. Differences in ideology, limitations in vision of various groups and leaders can be more readily tolerated if the individuals involved are more candid about themselves. Just as no marriage can survive without such genuineness, so it is impossible to establish just relationships without it. It is hard to see how social justice is possible without mutual faith. Such faith is the same as the openness and honesty which exists between persons.

Warmth as a quality of marital intimacy needs no proof. It is central to such intimacy. Sexuality is clearly most human when it is connected with warmth. But what has warmth to do with social justice. Warmth speaks to us of closeness to another. This is a most difficult thing to achieve because two people can never become one. Love is only possible when

---

[10]Kosnik, Anthony, ed., *Human Sexuality: New Directions in American Catholic Thought* (Garden City, New York: Doubleday and Company, Inc., 1979) speaks to these qualities and others when it describes the specific values that sexual behavior is to realize: self-liberating, other-enriching, honest, faithful, socially responsible, life-serving, and joyous. See pages 112-116.

people are separate and distinct. Union differentiates. People can only be intimate with another if they are intimate with themselves. This closeness, which is not the same as identity, is what makes the warmth of the marital experience possible. It is this non-identical closeness which characterizes situations of justice at their best. Rich are not to become poor, whites are not to become blacks, men are not to become women. But all groups need to become close, if a more just world is to be possible.[11]

The above description of marriage as a liberating partnership could in itself become a form of oppression for married couples if it is understood in an unrealistic way, a rather romantic view. In fact, as most married couples will affirm, marriage is working for these ideals day-in-day-out. They achieve them in a piecemeal way. There are failures, but the successes are found in the constant efforts to go on: learn from the failures, grow, and try again. Married people often are more conscious of failure than success in achieving the goals of marriage. They know them but they do not meet them. Any theology of marriage as well as any understanding of marriage and social justice must be accompanied by the encouragement to try again and again those ways which constitute growth and which commend the couple's efforts, fragile and imperfect though they may be.

Marriage and the Community of Justice

The entire church community has responsibilities to the couple in very specific ways. It should provide marriage preparation, inspirational models of living, and continual support and help in difficult times. And the married partners can respond to this support by becoming active participants in community life. There are many ways in which the community can manifest an attitude of justice regarding marriage. It needs to affirm the goodness and religious dimension and permanency of secular marriage. It can demonstrate openness to new understandings and nuances regarding the nature of

[11] I wish to acknowledge my debt to M. Kathleen Schaefer for these insights.

permanent commitment. One example of this would be how permanency is to be seen more in terms of the totality of the commitment now, rather than something which is a fixed and static reality based primarily on a past decision. There needs to be a greater acceptance and welcome of the divorced into church community life as well as material, spiritual, social, and emotional care for those whose spouses have died.

The local community's justice to the married is concretized in its ongoing formation for married couples. This will consist in formal programs as well as informal assistance for helping people in their early years, especially in terms of housing and child-rearing. Couples need help to learn to pray together. People need the community at those times of middle-age marriage crises. Married people can be incorporated into the community's ministry when practical help is provided for good quality child care centers for working parents. The community can become an advocate for women's rights and men's new self-understanding. Individual marriages will not easily be liberating experiences if the community does not model these several relationships of justice.

As in the case of the other sacraments, marriage is a path by which the community can move into the world. There are several ways in which marriage is a liberating force in the world. First, since faith is the foundation of the Christian's thirst for justice, it is important to have a human example or image of the experience of faith. This may occur in marriages when there is real communication between the people in love. Secondly, since marriage is always a secular reality, always of this world, the family is able to witness to the world without setting itself over against it. Thirdly, when marriage is an experience of liberating women and men from sexist structures, married people have the opportunity to prefigure in their marriages a more just society. And finally, marriage as a sacrament stands in human life as a symbol of the creator God. For us, that God is just and loving. Marriage is an image of that love and justice, both in itself and in the world.[12]

[12]For further development of these ideas see chapter four: "Marriage and Ministry," in *Partners in Service*.

There will always be a tension between the family and the community in the matter of ministry to social justice. The married person has a primary ministry within the family to spouse and children. Yet marital life is not limited to the family. The Christian family, as the church, exists to build up the kingdom of God. For the ordinary Christian this will mean concretely the way that the human community is built and strengthened. The most usual way will be through the various means that a family has for its support. The professions of the husband and wife, whatever their paid occupations may be, whether as people in business and the trades or being teachers, doctors, or lawyers, all have a ministerial dimension. These are not just jobs; they are ways of bringing to others their own commitment regarding social justice.

Most Christians who live out a justice oriented spirituality will extend themselves into the wider community through voluntary services. Sometimes this is informal and hidden in its quality of justice, such as supporting friends, giving assistance to the aged and helping those in need. Other times it will be more organized as when one participates in such programs as Bread for the World or Pax Christi. Some of these will be more church-related as when there is support for Courage as well as Dignity, both gay/lesbian organizations, or for the organization called Beginning Experience which is a structure to promote support and equality for the divorced and separated. Other times there will be little religious explicitness as in the case of protestations against the nuclear arms race or the contributions to the starving in such countries as Ethiopia. But whatever service for the larger community is involved, justice forbids any sexual stereotyping. Both spouses must have the opportunity to move into the larger community whether for pay or as a volunteer.

The more difficult part of the mutual relationship between marriage and the larger community is that of the community itself. What are the experiences of justice that the church, government, and society can provide for the married? Justice in the church will come when it practices what it preaches. All the religious rhetoric about the holiness of marriage, its reflection on the relationship between Christ and the church and its being the extension of the ministry of Christ to the world must be taken seriously. In the first instance this means that the church is challenged to find ways to affirm the value, dignity, and worth of the vocation of marriage in relation to the vocation to priesthood and religious life. All vocations are to build up the body of Christ and different people are called to do that differently. The point is that we need to appreciate and value each of them as complementary and for the common good. A quarter of a century ago Pope John XXIII spoke to this matter with beauty and conviction:

> 255. Indeed, when Christ our Lord made that solemn prayer for the unity of His Church, He asked this from the Father on behalf of His disciples: "I do not pray that Thou take them out of the world, but that Thou keep them from evil." Let no one imagine that there is any opposition between these two things so that they cannot be properly reconciled: namely, the perfection of one's own soul and the business of this life, as if one had no choice but to abandon the activities of this world in order to strive for Christian perfection, or as if one could not attend to these pursuits without endangering his own dignity as a man and as a Christian.[13]

Another instance of justice in the church for the married would be greater visibility for them in the worship of the church. Justice is not done until parents have public liturgical roles and when they can become leaders of prayer. Also, the church will be just to the married when it pays an adequate wage to its married employees. Finally, when families are struggling with sickness, lack of money or family break-up, the church should in justice be present to those situations.

The enumeration of the ways in which the government can act justly to the married would produce a lengthy list. It would include a better and more equitable tax structure and better educational opportunities for all. The government, as well as all of us, is called by justice to show a more positive attitude

[13] *Mater et Magistra* (*Christianity and Social Progress*, May 15, 1961) in *The Gospel of Peace and Justice* presented by Joseph Gremillion (Maryknoll: Orbis Books, p. 196).

toward those who decide to have children. We need to encourage people to put their families first by providing them with money and leisure and not excluding them from housing complexes. Perhaps, if families had been more enthusiastically encouraged in the past to perform the various ministries they could do, we would need less welfare, health centers, and places for the elderly and handicapped.[14]

Specific Issues of Justice and Marriage

Most of the issues considered here are dealt with in a view that sees marriage as a "free and full commitment of partners to share in the mutual task of building the future," (124)[15] and marriage as one of "mutual commitment to responsible partnership," (128) and one in which "sexual intimacy is integrated into the whole life of the married couple" both within the mutuality of their two lives, as well as in the lives of those who are affected by their relationship.(129)

The first issue is that of social justice and responsible parenthood. This statement from the Second Vatican Council gives the background for our considerations:

> This council recognizes that certain modern conditions often keep couples from arranging their married lives harmoniously, and that they find themselves in circumstances where at least temporarily size of their families should not be increased ... They will thoughtfully take into account both their own welfare and that of their children, those already born and those which may be foreseen. For this

[14]In this section, I am indebted to William P. Roberts, *Marriage: Sacrament of Hope and Challenge* (Cincinnati: St. Anthony Messenger Press, 1983), pp. 77-82.

[15]The numbers in parentheses refer to the pages of *Human Sexuality* (Doubleday). These descriptions of marriage are not idiosyncratic to *Human Sexuality*. Further development of these characteristics can be found in *Marriage, Faith and Love*, Jack Dominian; *Christian Marriage: A Journey Together* David M. Thomas (Wilmington: Michael Glazier, Inc., 1983; *Chicago Studies* 18:3 (1979) and *"Questions of Special Urgency" The Church in the Modern World: Two Decades after Vatican II* edited by Judith Dwyer, S.S.J., (Washington, D. C.: Georgetown University Press, 1986). See especially "Marriage and Family: Between Traditions and Tensions" by James Gaffney and "Marriage and Human Dignity" by William E. May.

> accounting they will reckon with both the material and
> spiritual conditions of the times as well as of their state of
> life. Finally, they will consult the interests of their family
> group, of temporal society, and of the church herself.[16]

Concretely, in justice to themselves and others, parents who
make a decision regarding responsible conception must ask
themselves about the medical, psychological, economic, and
religious implications of the method under consideration. This
questioning cannot be limited to their own well-being but
must include the larger society and the church. Avoiding
pregnancy as well as having a child has consequences for the
family and society. Will the use of the method "affect either
party's emotional response to life and society and to the
marriage relationship?" (138) "What is always to be condemned
is not the regulation of conception, but an egotistic married
life, refusing a creative opening out of the family circle, and so
refusing a truly human—and therefore truly Christian—
married love." (142). The critical question is whether the couple
is upholding the principles that make for a creative Christian
marriage where there is integral growth not only between the
couple but also in relation to society. The great challenge of
justice for any couple will be how to hold together the unitive
and procreative factors of the sexual act and keep these in
balance with the value of human growth and creativity.

Another important area in the relationship of social justice
and marriage is divorce. The fact of divorce needs no proof. It
is all around us and it affects the way we view and live the
married life. The disintegration of marriage is not something
that we can wish away. No marriage is immune against the
perils of breakdown and divorce. In that sense there is a way
in which divorce has the role of witness in the church. It is a
call to the married to enter more deeply into their lives together
and to determine to make their marriages work. In the words
of one writer on this matter:

---

[16]*Church in the Modern World*, 50 and 51.

We must decide that we *want* to make our marriages work and then utilize all the inner and outer resources available to make a success of our relationship. We must reject the notion that what happens to our marriage will be a matter of fate or external pressures. We must believe in ourselves and the power of our love so we can do all we can *now* to build together the strongest marriage possible and to satisfy each other's deepest needs and yearnings. Our best efforts will not provide a guarantee against divorce, but we nevertheless can provide the best possible foundation for a happy outcome.[17]

Individual couples and the church community are called to act justly toward the divorced.[18] Divorced people cannot remain marginal. They should receive healing support from others. They are in need of care. Since divorce is part of the tragedy of the world, but a world which has been redeemed, punitive and judgmental attitudes on the part of Christians are clearly out of place. The church needs to continue to explore humane ways of dealing with marriage cases. We need to find options for people when annulments are not possible. The question of eucharistic participation for the remarried is a thorny problem. The issue is whether the present practice of some churches is sufficiently justice-oriented.

Married couples have a responsibility toward those whose marriages ended in divorce. Justice here is the same as a compassionate and empathetic attitude where, far from assuming a condemnatory stance, there is a recognition of the trauma of the struggle and the sacrifices for personal integrity which are often involved. Married couples need to make a point of including the divorced in their social lives, of listening in a healing way, and giving assistance such as in the case of the single parent and the rearing of children.[19]

[17] *Marriage: Sacrament of Hope and Challenge*, p. 122.

[18] A helpful article dealing with the ministry to the divorced is Thomas J. Green's "Ministering to Marital Failure," *Chicago Studies* 18:3 (Fall, 1979).

[19] For an excellent article dealing with the plight of the single parent see Monika Hellwig, "Christian Spirituality for the Single Parent," *Spirituality Today* 36 (1984): 47-55.

Christian marriage can also witness to justice for the gays and lesbians in the church. Christian married life is the paradigm of how we are summoned to be just to gay/lesbians. We are obliged to respect them as persons, as we would any heterosexual person. They have a dignity as persons which commands respect. They have rights to a good reputation and to freedom from discrimination in regard to housing and jobs. We need to distinguish between homosexual orientation and homosexual activity. The efforts of those who seek to deal with their sexual orientation by living a life of embodied honesty and commitment should be lauded and supported and encouraged. And whatever practical choices individual homosexuals make regarding their sexual lives, we should help them move in the direction of values which are truly human and Christian. These are especially the goodness of sexuality and its expression and the fact that they are loved by God. If we are to be just to these often marginal people, we must keep in mind that God's love is found in ways not always apparent to us, and that God's acceptance transcends our own which is often limited and distorted by our biases.[20]

Both married couples and the local church are called upon to be just in their relationships with single people. Most fundamentally that means the public acceptance that persons can be liberators in their lives by remaining single because of career, profession, fear of divorce, or the high degree of mobility required by American economic forces. Since in the past, the church has paid so little attention to the single person, there may be the need of personal healing in many cases. Those people with whom singles relate need to be under-

---

[20]There is a great deal written about homosexuality. We suggest for a comprehensive discussion of views the following: "Letter to the Bishops of the Catholic Church on the Pastoral Care of Homosexual Persons," from the Congregation for the Doctrine of the Faith (Vatican City, 1986); James B. Nelson, *Embodiment: An Approach to Sexuality and Christian Theology* (Minneapolis: Augsburg Publishing House, 1978) chapter 9; Robert Nugent, ed. *A Challenge to Love: Gay and Lesbian Catholics in the Church* (New York: Crossroad, 1983); *A Study of Issues Concerning Homosexuality,* Report of the Advisory Committee of Issues Relating to Homosexuality Lutheran Church of America (Lutheran Church of America: Division for Mission in North America, 1986). John Fortunato, *Embracing the Exile,* (New York: Seabury Press, 1982).

standing and just in their relationships with them and at the same time challenge those who remain unmarried that this choice has not become an occasion for living solely for oneself. Among those who are single we include today the elderly, the widowed and the divorced.[21]

The single life has a specific ability to witness to the kingdom of God in that it provides a balance to marriage which, while it is needed to maintain societal existence, can be absolutized. The single life challenges the male assumption of female availability and so relativizes a societal presupposition. The single life indicates that there is another alternative to marriage besides religious life which itself can come under the power structures in society. Some consider the single life as being selfish if a personal career is pursued. This but reflects society's tendency, especially in the past, to force women either into marriage or convent life. But the single life witnesses to the value of women who follow career opportunities and challenges the accepted structure of male superiority. These comments have been about the single female. But it is true that both men and women remain single and the single life has the same meaning for both. But the single life of a woman is often more marginated than that of a man, and so lack of social justice is more obvious in the case of a single woman.

The single life style is growing more popular and is developing a critique of the institutional structures of society. The large number of single people presently in the country constitutes considerable human wealth which unfortunately is not being tapped by the institutional church. These people are sustained and nurtured by a spirituality that enhances the uniqueness and individuality of the single person. With Jesus as the prime example of the single life, a spirituality can be developed to affirm the single life vocation. But this spirituality can be threatening to church and society wherever conformity rather than uniqueness is stressed. The relative freedom of singles encourages them to be socially present in a unique,

---

[21]A brief but excellent statement on the single life is found in "Singleness and the Church," by James Nelson in his *Between Two Gardens: Reflection on Sexuality and Religious Experience* (New York: The Pilgrim Press, 1983).

self-giving and spontaneous way. But this is in opposition to our prevailing cultural group expectations and inevitable collective compulsions. Singleness challenges stereotyping or denial of a person's unique call. Single people call us to live more in tune with reality and to allow time to confront life's limits and possibilities. Singles can create a non-manipulative space around themselves where others can really feel comfortable being themselves. Instead of concentrating solely on demonstrable objectives, singles can remind the rest of us of the invisible, imponderable truths of spiritual living. It is God, not church structures which fills our hearts. Marriage and religious life place great value on public identity as being salvational. The single life places emphasis on bringing to light hidden or neglected dimensions of our relations with others and God. The deeper spiritual life is not the sole province of the clergy or religious.

The single life vocation within the church can have a prophetic quality. In church structures, the emphasis has been on stability, the receiving of answers. The single life offers a challenge to the concept of static knowing of what life is about by acknowledging in its liminal ambiguity, the struggles that are undertaken in an ongoing quest. The single life that rejects adherence to institutional emphases, can lessen the preoccupation with power, pleasure, and possessions and enable one to see beneath the surface of things to a deeper, transcendent meaning.[22]

In any discussion of life styles it is important that all forms of human living and loving be affirmed. If in the past, in the Roman tradition especially, religious life and celibacy were so exalted that marriage comes off as second class, justice demands that today we not simply reverse the claims and depreciate the celibate way of life. Today, to say something positive about marriage is not to say something negative about

---

[22]For further development of these ideas see Susan Annette Muto, *Celebrating The Single Life* (Garden City: Doubleday and Company, Inc., 1982). On single life-style, see Francine Cardman, "Singleness and Spirituality," *Spirituality Today* 35 (1983): 304-17, which touches on the unjust expectations that married and celibates have of young people, and on the needs which single people have which are not met in society and church.

religious life. The celibate way of living suffered in the past because of an inadequate theology of marriage. Today, placing celibacy in a negative light will ultimately do harm to the experience of married love in the church. One of the insights and contributions of the Roman Catholic Church has been that marriage and religious life maintain a balance in the Christian vision: each symbolizes values that both need.[23]

There is increasingly less and less cultural and community support for the celibate way of life. There is considerable division on the need for celibacy in the Roman Catholic priesthood. A case can be made that celibacy supports pastoral charity for the minister of the church. This is not to say that pastoral charity could not exist in another way or be supported through the married life. If the Roman Catholic Church abandons mandatory celibacy for its clergy, it should not be done on the basis that celibacy is no good. If celibacy is abandoned, it should be done for other reasons than the goodness or evilness of the practice. Perhaps, it will be because of a shortage of people willing to assume it, however good it may be, or can be. In the meantime, we should affirm the potentialities of the fullness of that life style. Anything else is clearly unjust.[24]

The Marriage Rite and Social Justice

The liturgy of marriage, which expresses the Christian perspective on marital spirituality, incorporates in varying degrees the elements of the social justice relationship to the sacrament already discussed in this chapter. The most significant of these is the rendering public of the love that the spouses have for each other. That social dimension is clear in the opening words of the rite of the Roman Church:

---

[23]For a forward looking and provocative discussion of the meaning of celibacy in the Christian life see Gerard Fourez, *A Light Grasp on Life* (Denville, New Jersey: Dimension Books, 1973).

[24]For a clear, stimulating, and up to date presentation of religious life see Sandra Schneiders, I.H.M., *New Wine Skins: Re-Imaging Religious Life Today* (New York: Paulist Press, 1986). Chapters 7 and 11 deal with religious celibacy.

> My dear friends, you have come together in this Church so
> that the Lord may seal and strengthen your love in the
> presence of the Church's minister and this community.
> Christ abundantly blesses this love.[25]

Several of the opening prayers reiterate this public character
when they speak of the bride and groom pledging their love or
praying that their lives bear witness to the reality of their love.
(106) Is this the case? Technically, any member of the parish
can be present for the liturgy. What usually happens is that we
have at weddings in church the same group of people we
would have were the wedding held in a private home. We need
to find ways to make weddings more obviously ecclesial.
Perhaps, greater involvement on the part of the parish staff or
other parochial representatives would raise marriage from an
overly individualized affair to one which is really celebrated
with a witnessing community.

The liturgy of marriage images the relationship of husband
and wife in terms of the new covenant. One of the prefaces
says: "This outpouring of love in the new covenant of grace is
symbolized in the marriage covenant that seals the love of
husband and wife and reflects your divine plan of love." (116)
The American *Book of Common Prayer* speaks of marriage
as covenant in several places. The celebrant in the opening
address says: "The bond and covenant of marriage was
established by God in creation"; the declaration of consent
contains "to live together in the covenant of marriage"; and in
the blessing of the marriage the celebrant prays: "O God, you
have so consecrated the covenant of marriage that in it is
represented the spiritual unity between Christ and his
Church."[26]

It is precisely this new covenant by which humanity is
restored to grace that is the basic Christian theological foundation for the pursuit of justice in the world. To bring justice

[25]Numbers in parentheses refer to the sections of the Roman Catholic *Rite of
Marriage* (1970). The Episcopal *Prayer Book* is rich in its references to the social
nature of marriage. The *Lutheran Book of Worship*, however, is disappointingly
sparse in this matter.

[26]*Book of Common Prayer*, pp. 423ff.

to contemporary society is to participate in the life of divine love. As the third Roman Catholic preface for marriage says: "Love is man's [sic] origin, love is his constant calling, love is his fulfillment in heaven." (117) Ultimately, the task of social justice is to realize the covenant of love between Christ and his church of which marriage is the primary symbol. The love that Christ brings to his relationship with the world is an unselfish one. It is this unselfish love which is to be found in marriage. It points to the fact that the building of the kingdom of God can never be founded on self-interest, even that of reformer or revolutionary.

The way in which the marriage rite deals with the procreative aspect of marital love is instructive from a justice-directed perspective. The questioning early in the Roman rite, the prayers, and nuptial blessings all speak of the willingness of the couple to accept children as the fruition of their love. Children are seen as a blessing and the family is affirmed as a place where the gospel can be lived out. But what is to be noticed is that love is not subordinated to the producing of children. It is the other way around.[27]

Rather, procreation is seen in a more significant way, one which brings marriage to bear on the furthering of the kingdom. The opening prayer of the Roman Catholic liturgy says: "Make their love fruitful so that they may be living witnesses to your divine love in the world." (109) While the rearing and educating of a family is implied in this witness of God's love, there is clearly the highlighting of the justice dimension of marital spirituality. This is also clear from the blessing at the end of mass: "May you be ready and willing to help and comfort all who come to you in need and may the blessings promised to the compassionate be yours in abundance." (37) And "May you always bear witness to the love of God in this world so that the afflicted and needy will find in you generous friends." (125) Christopher Kiesling has succinctly summarized this notion that marital spirituality is not limited to the confines of the family structure:

[27]The *Lutheran Book of Worship* makes no reference to children at all, whereas the Book of Common Prayer does in a way similar to the Roman Rite.

> It (marital spirituality) is envisioned in the liturgy of
> Christian marriage as extending beyond the couple, beyond
> their own children, to the wider circles of Church and world,
> and especially the afflicted and needy. The love of the couple
> is fully fruitful when its beneficence touches those in need
> who are not part of the family. Insofar as this care includes
> not only alleviating the suffering of the needy but also
> rectifying the causes of that suffering by establishing just
> social structures, marital spirituality includes concern for
> social justice.[28]

As in the case of all liturgy, the rite of marriage creates
nothing on the spot. Here too, liturgy presupposes community.
If there is little appreciation for the Christian perspective on
married love, the liturgy itself will be nearly dysfunctional. We
cannot leave it up to the marriage partners alone to witness to
marriage as the image of God's covenant with God's people
and Christ's love for his church. The community must call any
marriage to be open to those in need, those who exist outside
of the immediate confines of the family. It is not that an
individual family in isolation is the sacrament of a new social
order where justice and peace abound. Men and women can
only incarnate, in a fleshy and living way, what is already
present in the community. The sacrament of marriage can
either perpetuate the structures of society which lead to
oppression or be a viable sign of the reality of God's justice
and freedom in the world. Thus, part of the way this sacrament
is related to social justice is through support groups and
programs, all of which make it possible for marriage to become
an embodiment of social equality. Again, marriage as the
sacramentalizing of sexuality can bring its influence to bear on
a variety of justice issues which are sex-related. Some of these
issues are: women's rights to bodily control, prostitution,
pornography, rape and wife-beating, protection of minors,
sexual well being of people in prison, and all of those issues
which are related to equal pay, job access of women, day care

[28]"The Liturgy of Christian Marriage: Introduction to Marital Spirituality," in
Spirituality Today 34 (1982): 53-54.

facilities, and more creative ways of addressing the economic value of housework. The point is that marriage through its bringing a sacramental dimension to human sexuality can help people overcome the various forms of sexual dualism which underlie so much social violence, racism, and the way we deal with nature in our technological society.

In the liturgy of marriage, we celebrate the presence and coming of God's kingdom. Marriage has an eschatological character, for it symbolizes our human longing for oneness. It is not good for us to be alone. In marriage we prefigure the bringing together of that which is scattered, the internal and the outer, the integration we are always seeking. Christian marriage as an identifiable reality in the church is the kingdom in miniature. In the words of Kenneth Stevenson:

> Marriage rites in Christianity are a rich tapestry, woven with care and love and creativity. They speak of the things of the kingdom of God in the differing ways in which the central relationship of humanity has been, is and will continue to be experienced within the Body of Christ. It is a story of humankind restored and forgiven, lost and loved, resolute to undertake a commitment to live together, "in sickness and in health," as prophetic sign of the new creation which Christ "adorned and beautified" at Cana.[29]

❧

Bibliography

Dominian, Jack. *Marriage, Faith and Love: A Basic Guide to Christian Marriage*, New York: Crossroad, 1982.

The book is a treatment of marriage from a theological, historical, and social point of view. There is considerable

---

[29] *Nuptial Blessing: A Study of Christian Marriage Rites* (New York: Oxford University Press, 1983), p. 213.

discussion of the psychological stages married people go through in their life time. The treatment of marriage and its breakdown and how to prevent it from happening is especially relevant.

Hart, Thomas. *Living Happily Ever After,* New York: Paulist Press, 1979.

This readable presentation on the theology of marriage contains some helpful references to the relationship of marriage to social justice.

Kiesling, Christopher. "The Liturgy of Christian Marriage: Introduction to Marital Spirituality," *Spirituality Today* 34 (1982).

This article is an analysis of the marriage rite, making explicit the marital spirituality found in the liturgical texts.

Kosnik, Anthony, ed. *Human Sexuality: New Directions in American Catholic Thought,* Garden City, New York: Doubleday and Company, Inc., 1979.

This overall treatment of contemporary thinking on sexuality is helpful not only for providing background in the area of sexuality, but also for the way in which it stresses social responsibility as one of the values that should be realized in sexual behavior.

Lawler, Michael G. *Secular Marriage, Christian Sacrament,* Mystic, Conn: Twenty-Third Publications, 1985.

A popular but important presentation of the *Christian* character of the sacrament of marriage and how the indissolubility of marriage is only in proportion to the sacramentality of any given marriage.

Nelson, James B. *Embodiment: An Approach to Sexuality and Christian Theology,* Minneapolis: Augsburg Press, 1978.

The chapters which especially relate marriage and sexuality to social justice issues are 6: "The Meaning of Marriage and Fidelity," and 10: "The Church as Sexual Community."

Roberts, William P. *Marriage: Sacrament of Hope and Challenge*, Cincinnati: St. Anthony Messenger Press, 1983.

This popular presentation treats marriage from a contemporary perspective. The chapter, "Marriage as Ministry," is especially pertinent.

Silberman, Eileen Zieget. *The Savage Sacrament: A Theology of Marriage After American Feminism*, Mystic, Conn.: Twenty-Third Publications, 1983.

While the purpose of the book is to set the stage for more dialogue between Christian theologians and Christian feminists, it also provides a feminist view of marriage today. This is an attempt to present a lived theology of marriage.

Tetlow, Elizabeth and Tetlow, Mulry. *Partners in Service*, New York: University Press of America, 1983.

This biblical theology of marriage sees marriage as a community of equality and mutuality. It also treats marriage as a ministry and as a sacrament from the point of view of discipleship.

Celebrating Marriage, Liturgy. Journal of the Liturgical Conference, vol. 4:2.

This series of articles dealing with the theological and liturgical dimensions of marriage contains some which treat marriage as an inclusive symbol and as a personal witness to the kingdom.

Marriage. Chicago Studies 18:3 (Fall 1979).

The articles in this issue are focused on the topic of ministering to marriage. An especially relevant chapter is "Marriage as an Institution of Socialization."

10

Anointed For Justice

A New Context for the Sacrament of Anointing

Anointing is a recently rediscovered ritual in many of the Christian churches. The members of the Anglican communion have revised their rites and a ritual of anointing is increasingly acceptable to the Protestant churches. The rite of anointing in the Roman Catholic Church is among the most successful of its liturgical reforms in this post-Vatican Two period. The revised liturgy itself has achieved little notice, but the pastoral results have been striking and have been verified by those who minister to the sick, the elderly and the dying. This sacrament has been rescued from the obscurity of being the church's last contact with a dying person to become a ritualized call to ministry both on the part of the anointing community and the anointed Christian. No longer an extreme unction reserved to the private encounter of the priest with the patient after the medical profession can do no more, it has emerged as the communal expression of a way of being church. It raises to visibility the Body of Christ as a community of mutual healing and support. It publicly recognizes that there is a value to being "sick and elderly in the church." Anointing is now viewed as the paradigm of the salvific character of all human suffering. What is given in this sacrament is the community's care and concern as the epiphany of Christ's own love for his suffering people. What is received is the proclamation that the kingdom of God is one of wholeness and that salvation still comes in the flesh, which is touched and oiled. This coupling of healing, anointing, and coming kingdom is alluded to in the preface for the service of anointing within mass:

> In the splendor of his rising
> your Son conquered suffering and death
> and bequeathed to us his promise
> of a new and glorious world,
> where no bodily pain will afflict us
> and no anguish of spirit.
> Through your gift of the Spirit,
> you bless us, even now,
> with comfort and healing,
> strength and hope,
> forgiveness and peace.
> In this supreme sacrament of your love
> you give us the risen body of your Son:
> a pattern of what we shall become
> when he returns again at the end of time.[1]

Today the sacrament is being contextualized in a different way by theology and pastoral practice. Examining it in the light of the church's commitment to social justice moves the experience of anointing into a more comprehensive and rich human situation. It also brings out an ecclesial and social quality of the sacrament which was concealed in the former more individualized approach to the ministry to the sick, aged, and dying. Any thinking about anointing from a social justice perspective must build on this pastorally and theologically enlarged context for experiencing this sacrament. This relatively new conception can be briefly summarized in the following three points: 1) the biblical ministry of healing, 2) the sacramental ministry to the whole person, and 3) the relation of suffering to liberation.

[1] *Pastoral Care of the Sick: Rites of Anointing and Viaticum*, #145.

The Biblical Ministry of Healing

What scripture says of healing flows from the biblical view of sickness. In the Hebrew scriptures sickness is spoken of in the psalms as a motive for the sick person to turn to God in blessing:

> Bless the Lord, O my soul;
> and bless all my being, bless his holy name.
> Bless the Lord, O my soul, and forget not all his benefits.
> He pardons all your iniquities,
> he heals all your ills.
> He redeems your life from destruction,
> he crowns you with kindness and compassion. (Psalm 103)

The Wisdom literature adds that the cure of sickness also has human agents, i.e. doctors. But basically sickness is an occasion to plead that one might not go down into Sheol. Sickness is a signal of the approach of death and the possible ambiguous existence of afterlife. Healing comes from God. It represents a return from the dwelling place of the dead. Late Old Testament healing, especially after the second century B.C.E., can be seen as a preparation for the belief in the resurrection. In healing, sick persons receive the gift of God's goodness and through this gift they can depend on God to escape death.[2] For instance, Isaiah, chapter 35, contains many of these themes.

> Here is your God,
> he comes with vindication;
> With divine recompense
> he comes to save you.
> Then will the eyes of the blind be opened,
> the ears of the deaf be cleared;
> Then will the lame leap like a stag,
> then the tongue of dumb will sing.

---

[2]André Marie Dubarle, "Sickness and Death in the Old Testament," in *Temple of the Holy Spirit: Sickness and Death of the Christian in the Liturgy* (New York: Pueblo Publishing Co., 1983). See also N. Lohfink, "On the Enemies of the Sick in the Ancient Near East and in the Psalms,"*Great Themes from the Old Testament* (Edinburgh: T & T. Clark; Chicago: Franciscan Herald Press, 1981).

> Those whom the Lord has ransomed will return
> and enter Zion singing,
> crowned with everlasting joy;
> They will meet with joy and gladness,
> sorrow and mourning will flee.

The New Testament presents us with the unfolding of the ministry of Jesus Christ. That ministry manifested itself in teaching and healing. These two cannot and should not be divided. It is true that the gospels do speak of the works of Jesus primarily in terms of healing. He healed blindness; he cured the lame and deaf. But he also healed the diseases of ignorance and social oppression. Compassion, concern for the bodies of men, women, and children, sensitivity to poverty and exploitation all become part of establishing the kingdom of God. Bernard Cooke summarizes Jesus' ministry of healing by extricating some guidelines for Christian ministry. They are: 1) Healing must come from within, because God can heal only if the person or group desire healing. We think of the cure of the blind man, Bartimaeus, who when asked by Christ what he wanted, spoke out unambiguously, "I want to see." (Mark 10: 46-52) 2) Those who are in need of healing must truly want to be healed. They must have faith in God and faith in other persons. An obvious example here is the cure of the centurion's servant, when after the centurion's pleading, Jesus says: "I assure you, I have never found this much faith in Israel." (Matthew 8:5-17) 3) Healing is tied to conversion. It involves inner healing, the forgiveness of sin. For instance, the healing of the paralytic in Mark 2:1-12 where Jesus cures by telling the man that his sins are forgiven. For Jesus to heal was to give himself. It was one of his ways of self-revelation through symbolic communication. Recall the context of the healing of the man born blind. When the disciples ask Jesus whose fault it is that the man is blind, his parents or his own through sin, Jesus answers that it is neither.

> Rather, it was to let God's works show forth in him.
> We must do the deeds of him who sent me while it is day.
> The night comes on when no one can work. While I am in
> the world I am the light of the world. (John 9:1-7)

For Cooke the sacramentality of healing (and so anointing) is based on this symbolic encountering.[3]

The healing ministry of Christ is part of his larger ministry of reconciliation. The biblical view is that sin and illness are closely connected just as faith and wholeness go together. New Testament healing is reconciliation which overcomes sinful alienation. In this view, bodily healing is secondary. That healing was central to Jesus' ministry is beyond dispute, as should be clear from the previous paragraph. Examples of acts of healing abound.[4] The point is: what do they mean? Jesus himself gives the meaning. His works point to him as the awaited Messiah, as the one who brings life to the world. The healing miracles of Jesus are signs of the kingdom of God, signs looking to what is now established. For instance, in Jesus' response to the disciples of John the Baptizer as to whether he is the long-awaited Messiah, the imagery goes beyond mere physical healing. The blind can see the glory of God. The lame can walk along the paths of God. The lepers are absolved from their sins. The deaf do not just hear sounds; they hear the Good News. The dead are raised to life, but it is life in Christ. The richness of the poor is their preaching of the gospel. The sight of the man born blind points to Christ as the light of the world and the raising of Lazarus points to Jesus as the resurrection and the life.

This healing ministry has passed over into the sacraments, especially initiation and anointing. Both the gospel healings and the Christian sacraments proclaim the kingdom by calling for a converted community, and they realize it in the present through the changed lives of Christians. It is on the level of eschatological signs that gospel healing stories and the sacrament of anointing are defined in terms of justice. Charles Gusmer puts it well:

[3]Bernard Cooke, *Sacraments and Sacramentality,* (Mystic, Conn: Twenty-Third Publications, 1983) pp. 175-6.

[4]For the exact references see Charles W. Gusmer, *And You Visited Me: Sacramental Ministry to the Sick and the Dying,* (New York: Pueblo Publishing Co., 1984) pp. 149ff.

The healing works of Jesus are therefore to be understood as signs of the kingdom proclaimed in the gospel as a new reign of peace and justice in which God will put an end to the ancient enemies of the human race: sin and evil, sickness and death ... His "acts of power" foreshadow the ultimate transformation of humanity and the universe on the day of Jesus' Second Coming, an event not yet come to pass ... At the same time, the healing miracles are eschatological signs of an "already" dimension of the kingdom, which is at work in the world through the present offer of eternal life and communion with God that begins this life.[5]

The New Testament perspective on the healing of sickness and suffering is colored by the paschal mystery. As death and resurrection go together, it is not possible to take a one-sided view of healing wherein good health is sought apart from Christ's own dying and rising. If healing is to be fully achieved now, we would be co-opted by the death-denying culture in which we live. "Being sick in the church" has a purpose beyond returning to good health. It is to remind us that we are in need of redemption.

The Sacramental Ministry to the Whole Person

All people are in need of healing. Most people need physical healing sometime in their lives. Today we are more aware that healing (and conversely, sickness) cannot be seen as primarily physical. The whole person is sick. The whole person grows old. The whole person is healed. But even beyond this a greater awareness is developing that sickness and disease have a social character. Ministry to the sick through the sacrament of anointing needs to raise this up. Bernard Cooke writes on this matter:

We now know that by far the greatest cause of physical ailments are starvation and the lack of decent drinking

[5]Ibid. p. 150.

water. Technologically we are able to remedy most, if not all, of this disturbing situation. The question is whether the people in the powerful nations of the world will decide to turn their attention and energies to the physical needs of the vast bulk of humankind. Christians in the "First World" can hardly claim that they carry on Christ's own healing ministry if they do not seriously respond to this unprecedented opportunity to heal much of the world's present physical suffering.[6]

We often relate healing to justice because sin causes suffering and oppression. But justice comes into play also because often people's illnesses result from injustice to themselves, such as in the case of the excessive use of drugs or alcohol. There is, moreover, a gross kind of violation of justice in the case of child abuse and wife-beating. Ministry to oneself is as significant as the ministry of justice to the world.

Healing for the whole person demands that there be a special ministry to those with psychological illnesses. The sacrament of anointing is also for those who suffer from severe neurosis. We need the healing of our psychological disorders as well as our physical disabilities. Even for those of us who are considered well, such a sacramental ministry can be a reminder how we all must care for the extent that we are out of touch with reality. Often psychological disturbances have a connection with personal sin, although it would be wrong to establish a one for one relationship between the two. More significantly, there is a clear connection between psychological problems and the economic imbalances, the political injustices and the cultural biases found in human society. Our concern in criminal activity today sees it often rooted in social injustice. Care of ourselves and care of the earth are part of the Christian ministry of healing. And sacramental ministry must supply not only food and medicine but also love, human understanding and hope for the spirit. As Cooke puts it: "Christian healing ministry must be directed to prevent such damage to the human person."[7]

[6]Cooke, *Sacraments and Sacramentality* p. 182.
[7]Ibid, P. 186.

In the course of its tortuous history, the liturgy of anointing took on the individualistic meaning of preparation for the passage into eternal life, the forgiveness of sins which could not be confessed, and the possibility of physical recovery. But with a renewed stress on anointing in community, the purpose of the sacrament is more clearly directed to the more social areas of human suffering. The hoped for effect on the anointed is not so much the alleviation of this suffering as it is the charge to bear witness that the person of Christ is what gives meaning in these circumstances which challenge belief and faith commitment. In the words of the General Introduction to the *Pastoral Care of the Sick:*

> The role of the sick in the Church is to be a reminder to others of the essential or higher things. By their witness the sick show that our mortal life must be redeemed through the mystery of Christ's death and resurrection.[8]

And it is not only the individual's appropriation of the death and resurrection of Christ which raises up the significance of suffering. The support of the community constitutes a public act of faith. This is especially true when death is not imminent, as in the case of the anointing of the elderly. Anointing answers the question: "Why is there suffering?", not by providing an answer, but by offering a change of experience.

Anointing is addressed to the whole human person because sickness and also old age are critical situations for the suffering person. It is a disruption in the life of communication, including life in the community of the church. Sickness and old age introduce questions in our relationship with God to the point of the possibility of despair. Such ambiguity pervades everything about those who are sick and elderly. They are truly in a liminal situation. Only a wholistic understanding of the human person addresses this kind of fragmentation. A contemporary theology of anointing is based on the person as an incarnate spirit, on the psycho-somatic dimension in the person's individuation process on the way to wholeness, and

---

[8] *Pastoral Care for the Sick* #3.

on the curative power of the unconscious life when combined with the natural process of wholistic medicine. Gusmer puts it well:

> A wise physician once remarked that there is no such thing as sickness in itself, only people who are sick. That comment should serve as a safeguard against the danger of abstraction in theologizing about human illness. Sickness is a very real phenomenon that confronts the total human person.[9]

The introduction to the *Pastoral Care of the Sick* in the Roman Catholic Church establishes the sacrament's relation to suffering but also to the larger context that relates anointing to social justice.

> The sacrament of anointing effectively expresses the share that each one has in the sufferings of others. When the priest anoints the sick, he is anointing in the name and with the power of Christ himself (see Mark 6:13). On behalf of the world community, he is ministering to those members who are suffering. This message of hope and comfort is also needed by those who care for the sick, especially those who are closely bound in love to them.[10]

Anointing's connection to suffering highlights the church's ministry of justice in a unique way. The problem of evil remains unresolved. Whether we accept the mystery of Job's suffering or the New Testament's contradiction of the cross, we still must confront the tension between God's justice and the presence of evil in the world. Because sickness and old age and death, all of which involve suffering, are facts of life to which we are reluctant to assign personal culpability, we need to find a way in which these events can take on meaning. The evil of human suffering must be moved from an individualistic context to one which is social in character. Where is the justice

---

[9] Gusmer, *And You Visited Me* p. 145.
[10] *Pastoral Care of the Sick* #98.

of God found in our communal propensity to illness, our almost universal experience of aging and our inevitable death? It is found in the fact that we can be *saved* from all three. Whether any or all result from personal sin, original sin, personal growth, or societal transformation is not the point. Taken as a whole, these common human experiences have cosmic effects. In that sense, we are not sick alone, we do not grow old alone, we do not die alone. All three are ways in which we participate in the family of humankind. Whether our sufferings are the result of our participation in the sin of the world or of our being co-creators in the advance of the world, they are symbols of our belonging to this world.

The sacrament of anointing opens up human suffering as an avenue to the kingdom of God. It proclaims that suffering can be liberation. We hear this in one of the concluding prayers from the service for Visits to the Sick: "May all who suffer pain, illness, or disease realize that they have been chosen to be saints and know that they are joined to Christ in his suffering for the salvation of the world."[11] And it is not only that the ill are cured which makes healing a sign of the kingdom. It is that society which is in some way responsible for the fragmentation of the sick and elderly is called to healing. We sense this in the words of greeting of the priest in the introductory rites for Anointing Within Mass:

> Christ taught his disciples to be a community of love.
> In praying together, in sharing all things, and in
> caring for the sick, they recalled his words: 'Insofar,
> as you did this to one of these, you did it to me.'
> We gather today to witness to this teaching and to
> pray in the name of Jesus the healer that the sick
> may be restored to health. Through this eucharist
> and anointing we invoke his healing power.[12]

The liturgy of the sick celebrates not only the new faith and life of the one anointed, but the belief that all things are made

[11] Ibid. #60.
[12] Ibid. #135.

new.[13] That is why the norm of the sacrament is not the emergency hospital room situation but the sick persons surrounded by their communities, whether this be in conjunction with communal eucharistic celebrations in a church, or this be the temporary community of those who care for and pray with the sick or elderly person.

The liturgy of anointing becomes the place where the suffering confront the evil of the world. This may be the physical evil of the diseased body, or the evil of loss of courage and hope, or the evil of the failure of the community to comfort. Whatever the form of evil, Christians find themselves in a situation of weakness and challenge. What the church provides in those often perilous, or at least frightening, times is the presence of Christ through the actions of laying on of hands and anointing. Anointing is a way of facing the complex reality of evil which, while always present, brings a special trial during sickness and old age. Through anointing, these favored of God achieve liberation from the evil of the world.[14] Not only they, but also the community, is liberated. Those who are alive and well in the church can here discover their own weakness and fragmentation. This frees them from the presupposition that things will always be as good as they are—from the "It could never happen to me" attitude. It is when the vocation of the sick and elderly is recognized by the healthy, that God's justice springs forth. Then, the barrier between sick and healthy and ministering and being ministered to is torn away. Then those anointing and those anointed share mutual ministry, for there is a gift which those who are young and well can receive from the sick and elderly. Power concludes:

> The profundity and power of human relations and the true nature of Christian hope are discovered in a special way by the ill. These enable them to communicate the same discoveries to the well, if the well have the eyes to attend to

[13]For more on this point see: David N. Power, "All Things Made New," in *Liturgy Journal of the Liturgical Conference,* vol. 2:2, "Ministries to the Sick."

[14]I wish to acknowledge my dependence on David Power (previous footnote) for this section.

what is happening and the ears to listen to what may be physically a very weak voice.[15]

Justice and the Anointed

Our God of justice is present in all aspects of life but especially in the life-contexts of those who are forced to live at the edge of society. Some of these are possible candidates for anointing. Three classes are singled out here to demonstrate the relationship of justice to this sacrament: the sick, the elderly and the handicapped. The justice of God can be especially made visible in the fragmented aspects of our personalities when these are seen as more than mere indicators of an individual's lack of integration, but rather as symbols of a broken world where the incompleteness of the kingdom of God is all too obvious. These three classes of people become such symbols through their experiences of alienation, loneliness, depression, crises of faith and fear of death. The community is called to care for these individuals as a way of expressing itself as a sign of the kingdom of God, as a place where justice is embraced, and a means of bearing witness to the healing dimension of salvation.

The sick, elderly, and handicapped are victims of injustice because in some way they have been excluded from society and alienated from community. It may be that they are pushed aside and not recognized. Their societal roles have been taken from them. Their wisdom is ignored. They are deprived of their self-esteem. The sacrament of anointing specifically says to these people that no matter how others may regard them, they are integral members of the community. From this perspective, anointing is not seen simply as an opportunity for individual spiritual healing, but as a communal celebration of Christ's saving love manifested in the person being anointed. This is but an instance of that foundational sacramental principle that while it remains true that a sacrament involves the individual Christian, it is never primarily an individual celebration.

[15]Power, "All Things Made New," p. 11.

Justice and the Sick

The rites of the *Pastoral Care of the Sick* begin with the visitations to the sick. These visits to the sick can be acts of justice as when we listen to these people in their loneliness. But anointing as a sacrament of liberation is more than laying hands on persons as a gesture of healing or comforting them by praying with them. It means moving beyond these personal acts of ministration to more societal changes of attitude such as practicing wholistic health methods, educating people regarding public health, working in a public health clinic, working in and supporting a hospice.

Ministry to the sick takes on a justice perspective insofar as the sick are publicly acknowledged as being a vital part of the community. This is done when communion from the Sunday Eucharist is taken to them, when there are monthly anointing services in the church, when part of the community is present at an anointing at home, when those to be anointed are part of the public prayers in Sunday worship, and when there is attention to their special needs such as transport to doctors, preparations of meals and the like.

Anointing's relationship to social justice is most clearly evident when it is a countercultural experience. It is this when it refuses to let society (including the church) remain indifferent to the sick. It affirms the dignity of persons as they move through this stage of their lives. There is no special place for blame; there is no room for paternalism on the part of friends or family. The nursing care does not reduce them to objects—an-out-of-sight, out-of-mind mentality. And justice for them includes being sensitive to the matter of when extraordinary means in terms of life support systems are no longer consonant with human dignity.

Anointing calls into question our society's bias toward health. Everyday newspapers carry articles on health, how to improve it, what to eat, how and how not to diet. There is a health kick abroad. Joggers are everywhere. To be firm, trim and breathing well is respectable once again. And there is much that recommends this promotion of health. By and large, jogging and other forms of physical exercise, care about one's eating habits, and concern about cholesterol, smoking, and alcohol are improvements in human living. It shows respect for and an appreciation of the God-given gift of being human beings. But anointing can remind us that physical health is not an absolute. What is challenged is the implied judgmental attitude that individuals and society have about those who do not have good physical health. Perhaps they are obese, do not exercise, and smoke too much. Or perhaps they have physical illnesses which are visited upon them and over which they have little if any control. In either case, justice is due them in terms of understanding and sympathetic attitude, rather than one which is condescending and which dismisses them as unenlightened. The *Book of Common Prayer* takes this larger view of health when in the anointing rite the priest says:

> As you are outwardly anointed with this holy oil,
> so may our heavenly Father grant you the inward
> anointing of the Holy Spirit. Of his great mercy,
> may he forgive you your sins, release you from
> suffering, and restore you to wholeness and strength.
> May he deliver you from all evil, preserve you in goodness,
> and bring you to everlasting life.[16]

Society's understanding of what it means to be healthy can be broadened by a Christian understanding of sickness and health. Officially, health is defined as "a state of complete physical, mental, and social well-being and not merely the absence of disease or infirmity."[17] Insofar as it goes, this is a helpful working definition, but it is inadequate. One which tries to include justice would call for alternate forms of being healthy. The official definition sees the individual who is ill as an integral whole. This is good. But the very methods of treatment must also be integral. Often we tend to see wholistic health care more along individual lines when in fact it should and often does represent a transformation in a group's attitude,

---

[16] *Book of Common Prayer* p. 456.

[17] Quoted by David B. Smith and Arnold D. Kaluzny *The White Labyrinth: Understanding the Organization of Health Care* (Berkeley, CA: McCutchan, 1975) p. 229.

218 Anointed for Justice

a change which speaks of justice. All those who are responsible for health care need to cooperate and to avoid the professional fragmentation which only reinforces a similar fragmentation in the individual. This point about wholistic health has been noted by Dennis Krouse:

> An intention of this approach is to overcome the divisions underlying the healing professions—physicians examining the body, psychiatrists and psychologists concerned with the mind, and clergy as attendants of the soul or spirit.[18]

This integral approach is a tangible form of social justice because the basic motivation for justice is the dignity of the human person. The *Pastoral Care of the Sick* repeatedly emphasizes this human dimension. The priest is to explain that anointing is the way that the church supports the sick in their struggles against illness.[19] The priest is to inquire about the physical *and* spiritual condition of the sick person. The priest is to become acquainted with the family and others who might be present at the celebration. The sick and others are invited to help plan the liturgy. "It is especially helpful if the sick person, the priest, and the family become accustomed to praying together."[20]

Health and social justice are bound together because both are symbols of the kingdom of God. Since Christians are joined together by a common faith and baptism, what happens to one member affects all. The message of hope and comfort which this sacrament proclaims is not only for the sick. It is for those who care for them. It is for all of us. Anointing is part of the prayer of the church which is now the eschatological sign of the coming of God.

---

[18]Dennis Krouse, "Health and Healing in Traditional Catholic Expression," in *Liturgical Foundations of Social Policy in the Catholic and Jewish Traditions* edited by Daniel F. Polish and Eugene J. Fisher (Notre Dame: University of Notre Dame Press, 1983) p. 58. Krouse is quoting from Carnegie Samuel Calian, "Theological and Scientific Understandings of Health," *Hospital Progress*, 59 (Dec. 1978), p. 61.

[19]*Pastoral Care of the Sick* #98.

[20]Ibid. #100.

The laying on of hands is a human gesture which points to human bonding in community while it also transcends this relationship. Laying on of hands means communication of the Holy Spirit as the one who heals and so speaks of new life and new health. Because of its wealth of meaning, laying on of hands points to multiple relationships to the community which become the basis for hope in the future. In all of this, health is more than physical well-being. What is offered to the person anointed as well as to the community doing the anointing is "future health." This new health is an anticipation of the kingdom of God because, through personal and communal reintegration, the sick person now has an enriched and extended future. Through the anointed person and the anointing community a disrupted humanity has in a deep sense been made whole. This is what we mean by the kingdom of God. And this is implied when the disciples of John the Baptist asked Jesus if he was the messiah, the one who was to establish this kingdom. He replied in the affirmative, the answer being obvious because "The blind recover their sight, cripples walk, lepers are cured, the deaf hear, dead men are raised to life, and the poor have the good news preached to them."[21]

There is much that is similar between the laying on of hands and the action of anointing with oil. There is the obvious healing aspect. There is also the commissioning for ministry in the church. But because anointing plays a significant role in the rites of initiation, anointing in this sacrament brings out the identification with the paschal mystery in a more explicit way. And here the eschatological dimension emerges further because the community is promising to the anointed person that death is not the final word.

It is precisely in this context that anointing clarifies the church's care for those who have AIDS. These people are truly ill, but "ill in the church." And at the present time because of the state of medicine, they are sick unto death. Because there is still considerable social stigma connected with this disease, those who suffer from AIDS are truly the marginated. What anointing can bring out is that these sick are identified

[21]Luke 7:22.

with the paschal mystery in a particular way. Because they are the victims of not only society's abhorrence of sickness and death, but also of its disgust and even hatred of some of the ways in which the disease is contracted, anointing challenges in a special way the judgmental attitude and social prejudice of many in the church. Anointing not only claims that those suffering from AIDS are integral members of the Christian community, it also raises up their ministry of being dramatic signs of the kingdom of God in our time.

Justice and the Elderly[22]

The relationship of social justice to the anointing of the elderly is found in the way the sacrament celebrates in a countercultural fashion the value of growing old. This final stage of life is recognized as a time of growth rather than mere ending. Justice for the elderly is the public acceptance of the meaning of their lives, their whole lives and not merely the younger productive segment of it. This is especially important in affluent countries such as America. James Empereur has already referred to this problem:

> This refusal to accept old age as part of one's salvation history is only reinforced by the prevailing American value system which does not cherish this penultimate period of human life as such. Americans are ashamed of their elderly and treat them as something to be avoided. They pretend old people do not exist. And thus, they culturally precondition themselves for what old age will mean for them.[23]

[22]We are not implying that old people can be anointed simply because of the accumulation of years. Old age must pose some kind of threat to the person whether that be physical, psychological, social or spiritual. This is not to divide the person into different compartments. The whole person must be threatened in some say. On the one hand, we need to avoid the narrow approach which would only anoint the elderly when they are approaching their final months of life, as well as the broad approach which would invite anyone who is old to participate in a communal anointing service. Some of these latter might still be playing golf! In the final analysis, a benign interpretation of who may be anointed is called for in this country where the elderly as a group are still marginalized.

[23]James L. Empereur, S.J., *Prophetic Anointing* (Wilmington, DE: Michael Glazier, Inc., 1982), p. 166.

The old are in need of liberation. They must be free to close life well. Their success is no longer measured by their achievements. The meaning of their lives does not come from job, status, or special abilities. Liberation comes to the elderly when they find the meaning of their lives in being old, when they need not try to relive the past, and are not threatened by their former failures and weaknesses. Injustice is inflicted on the old when they are made to feel guilty about their uselessness to society. Justice here is the support and atmosphere which makes it possible to believe in the worth of one's own life. The social sin in which so many elderly are caught is the framework that contributes to their lack of self-esteem, their suppressed self-hatred, their feeling of abandonment, and their inability to affirm their complete personal histories as good. Such a life can at best be a diminished sign of the kingdom of God, for then these people find their solace in an otherworldly spirituality—the antithesis of the basic presupposition of social justice.

The elderly bear witness to the rest of the church by calling others to believe in their present life and so to believe in God. Because they no longer need to achieve or accomplish, they can relativize our compulsions for productivity. This attitude can be most helpful, especially for many who work in social justice areas. For there is the temptation to value things in terms of results because of the presence of oppression and alienating structures. And yet the Christian vision cannot be reduced to a more just world. This is very difficult to embrace for anyone committed to alleviating the suffering of others and who is passionate about a more human way of life. Nothing of that should be lessened and yet there must be something else. The elderly know what that is. The experience of justice for the elderly has been summed up by Empereur when he wrote:

> For the elderly, anointing can assure them that in their weakness they can find their strength. They can now accept each moment of their lives as a gift. They need no longer try to control the lives of others. They can be free from the expectations to fulfill certain societal roles. No longer is there any imperative to spend time and energy on plans for

a better tomorrow. They are achieving their purposes, they are fulfilling their vocation by being old and by being old in a Christian integral way. Old people have less time but more space.[24]

But the old also call the rest of the church to justice in other ways. For they witness to the fact that God is not only to be found in human acceptance but also where growth takes place through opposition. This is significant for those deeply involved in liberation movements. Old age is not simply the end, it is also a time of advancement, although in ways that are more interior. What the elderly raise up for us is that any working for liberation must be wholistic and not selective. Just as life must be evaluated as a whole and not just in terms of success in position, money, and relationships, so workers for justice cannot pick and choose what will be Christian in their ministry of liberation. The elderly also remind us that full humanity does not simply come to us if we are survivors. It is something that we must constantly be choosing. We can build up the kingdom of God when, like the elderly, we can be "more honest, more free from the demands of technological society, more self-affirming, and more willing to face the real questions of human existence."[25] Many of these themes are alluded to, albeit discreetly, in the prayer for those in advanced age in the *Pastoral Care of the Sick:*

> God of mercy,
> look kindly on your servant
> who has grown weak under the burden of years.
> In this holy anointing
> he/she asks for healing in body and soul.
> Fill him/her with the strength of your Holy Spirit
> Keep him/her firm in faith and serene in hope,
> so that he/she may give us all an example of patience
> and joyfully witness to the power of your love.[26]

[24]Ibid. p. 174.
[25]Ibid. p. 197.
[26]*Pastoral Care of the Sick*, #125D.

Justice and the Handicapped[27]

One of the bitterest ironies is that the church, which is God's sacrament of justice, has not caught up to society's recognition of the legal and human rights of the handicapped. There has been too much talk and too little action. And while anointing the handicapped will situate them ritually and visibly in the church in a new way, these celebrations need to be accompanied by the presence of ramps, braille bibles and texts, signers and interpreters for the deaf, and by our churches in general becoming more hospitable and accepting of disabled people. It is easy to understand how the concerns for justice will involve confrontations and conflicts. But what is also a matter of justice is the aspect of hospitality. The hope is that the anointing of the disabled will help make our places of worship, as well as the worshipers themselves, those kinds of environments where not only the disabled can feel at home, but where all who join Christians in the promotion of justice are welcome.

Justice for the disabled is based on four underlying principles. (1) Disabled persons are fully human. They, like anyone else, have certain sacred rights.[28] (2) Disabled persons have the right that society respect their human dignity. Society, then, must help these people find a place in it which is compatible with their capabilities, taking into consideration whatever impairment they might have. (3) The character of a society can be determined by the way it deals with its weakest members. Thus, if injustice to the disabled characterizes a nation, that nation is most probably unjust in many other areas. (4) The ways in which the disabled share justly in the life of a people

[27]Some people do not like the use of the word "handicapped", and substitute "disabled" or "other-abled." The use of "handicapped" in this chapter is not meant to make any evaluation of the moral or spiritual quality of the person. We use "handicapped" and "disabled" interchangeably, although there is a movement to distinguish the two so that "handicapped" implies some kind of crippling that inhibits full human living. In that sense an alcoholic is handicapped. "Disabled" refers to persons with a physical limitation but who lead relatively normal lives. People with disabilities, but who have learned how to transcend them would not be the subject of anointing ordinarily.

[28]For these principles I am dependent upon Rev. Dennis O. Kennedy, S.M., "Reaching the Disabled Community," *Aim: Aids in Ministry* (Summer 1982). He includes the following Bill of Rights:

will be determined by how they are integrated and treated in a normal and personal fashion. These principles imply that the community or parish makes efforts to rehabilitate the disabled as far as modern technology allows. We need to make their lives to be as normal as possible. And normalcy is not restricted to the physical. There are the areas of the psychological and spiritual, which require development of the whole person, which must be addressed. Especially in the case of physically disabled people is it true that the only things that prevent them from leading normal lives are our architecture and our attitudes. If these principles are to be concretized in church life and liturgical celebrations, we need to listen to the voices of the disabled community. The first just gesture to these marginal people is to ask what they need.

We believe that all people should enjoy certain specific rights. Because people with disabilities have consistently been denied the right to participate fully in society as free and equal members, it is important to state and affirm these rights. All people should be able to enjoy these rights, regardless of race, creed, color, sex, religion, or disabilities.

1. The right to live independent, active and full lives.

2. The right to the equipment, assistance, and support services necessary for full productivity, provided in a way that promotes dignity and independence.

3. The right to an adequate income or wage, substantial enough to provide food, clothing, shelter, and other necessities of life.

4. The right to accessible, integrated, convenient, and affordable housing.

5. The right to quality physical and mental health care.

6. The right to training and employment without prejudice or stereotyping.

7. The right to accessible transportation and freedom of movement.

8. The right to have children and a family.

9. The right to a free and appropriate public education.

10. The right to participate in and benefit from entertainment and recreation.

11. The right to communicate freely with all fellow citizens and those who provide services.

12. The right to a barrier-free environment.

13. The right to legal representation and full protection of all legal rights.

14. The right to determine one's own future and make one's own life choices.

15. The right to full access to all voting processes.

This disabled Citizen Bill of Rights was written by members of the Center for Independent Living on the occasion of Disabled People's Civil Rights Day, October 10, 1979. The Center (2539 Telegraph Avenue, Berkeley, California 94704) has served as a model for other independent living centers created throughout the nation.

As in the case of the sick and elderly, anointing points up that the disabled too carry on ministry in the church. They too have the vocation of being disabled. They contribute to the bringing about of the kingdom of justice in several ways. (1) They are witnesses to the goodness of the human body and human feelings. Because often it is necessary for them to communicate in a non-verbal way, they make use of touch. They are more direct with and about their feelings. Their faces, as well as the rest of their bodies, are transparent. They call into question our ways (at least in the northern hemisphere) of disguising our feelings and treating the other person as an abstraction. This is surely a matter of justice to ourselves and ultimately to society. (2) Many of the disabled love in a spontaneous and uncomplicated fashion. It is love without expectations. And in general their emotional responses are uninhibited or unrestricted. They confront us with the fact that we have trained ourselves to be expressive not according to the emotions, but according to the expectations of others— not a very freeing experience. (3) Disabled people are more direct and react to things as they are. Their honesty in human interaction can be disarming. For many of us it is embarrassing. We are so used to a way of doing and speaking—there is the Christian way, the adult way, the political way, the churchy way. Their method of direct communication is a model for justice among different ethnic groups, the sexes, and the generations. (4) Perhaps most significantly these disabled challenge the parish's value system. Their very presence raises questions of the meaning of life. In Berkeley, California, there is the Center for Independent Living. In Berkeley, especially on the campus of the University of California, there are many severely handicapped people who move around campus in their motorized wheel chairs leading a relatively normal life. But their presence also arouses a lot of feelings in those who watch them. Often these feelings are very ambiguous. Many have commented on how their presence has made them stop and reflect about what are the significant values in life. On this campus where, like so many others, there is an almost frenetic pursuit of that which will confer power, status, and prestige, it is disarming to discover the presence of a group who reverse those values and give top priority to human relationships.

(5) Developmentally disabled people are models for dealing with frustration and failure. They know how to let go. Not everything works for them. They cannot have the relationships they desire. They are often, no doubt, grieved over what cannot be theirs, but then they can turn their attention to other areas, convinced that there are other things to live for. There are other adventures to pursue, other relationships to hope for.

These are some of the ways in which the disabled bear witness to justice in the church community. It is not because they are holier than the rest of us. It is not because of their sufferings. We place a distance between ourselves and them when we operate out of those assumptions. And that is unjust. Often these people do not look upon themselves as sick. That is the kind of stereotypical thinking which puts them in a separating category. And that is most unjust. They are more like than unlike us. They have their joys and conflicts, their need to understand their role in society, their need to deal with the issues of family life and economics. These are all the same areas which are the concern of the rest of us. Overcoming any separation between them and ourselves is primarily a change of attitude. But we cannot ignore that there are architectural barriers which must also be overcome. Places of worship should have the proper ground entrances, ramps, restrooms, access to elevators, and safe parking. Some churches are now making use of braille scripture and liturgical texts. More and more the use of sign language is being incorporated into worship. It can be most effective in drawing in the entire congregation in what is happening. When possible, disabled people should be encouraged to exercise one of the liturgical ministries such as lectors, ushers, communion ministers, and contact people for the elderly and shut-ins. Often these people can do far more than we are willing to admit. Our greatest injustice in this matter is our reluctance to let them be like us.[29]

[29]For more on anointing and the handicapped see "Handicapped People and the Church," *The Way* 25:2 (April, 1985). See especially the article by James L. Empereur, "Anointing and the Handicapped."

Justice and the Anointing Community

The relation of social justice and anointing takes on special characteristics when viewed in the context of a liberating, prophetic and celebrating community. To anoint is a form of community proclamation with a purpose to further the kingdom of God. Anointing ensures that this eschatological community will be inclusive of the poor, elderly, and disabled. As already stressed, inclusion is more than liturgical, although the sacramental and pastoral care are clear indications of the quality of the celebrating community. Paradoxically, it may be the church's institutional involvement in the healing professions which may distinguish it as liberating. Denominational hospitals and patient care facilities can provide an alternative to civil programs which may not be concerned with the range of values that make up wholistic health care. And healing as a specific ministry is still more likely to be found among those who espouse religious values than not.

At times we easily equate the church's prophetic role in healing with charismatic expressions. Often such healings are part of the community's witness. On the other hand, it is neither helpful nor necessary to see everything as a miracle. More importantly, the prophetic quality of the community that anoints, emerges in its being the place where the sick, elderly, and disabled can witness. A fundamental Christian belief is that one achieves significance in relationship with a community of believers because there is a mutual challenge to faith among the members. The sacrament of anointing includes those anointed as on a par with any others in the church. Through this it calls the community to share in the healing mission of Jesus Christ. Ultimately, the prophetic character of this sacrament vanishes, if it is not seen as an instance of the call for justice, a call to deal with the *whole* human being, a call to oppose the impersonalism of civil society in dealing with the sick, elderly, and handicapped. A prophetic community will raise issues about national health policies, everyone's right to health care, a wholistic approach to health and healing, hospices, and medical care which promotes human dignity. And in a society which is permeated with a pursuit of the pleasurable and where the preference is that everything be under control, the community that anoints can provide a whole new view: "a people *sharing* life, its blessings and its burdens, a people who *are on the way*, and the way together."[30]

🌿

Bibliography

Bissonnier, Henri. *The Pedagogy of Resurrection*, New York: Paulist Press, 1959.

> One of the few fully developed treatments on the Christian formation of the handicapped. Aspects of social justice are implicit throughout this treatment of educational therapy and catechesis for the handicapped.

Bowman, Leonard. *The Importance of Being Sick*, Wilmington, North Carolina: Consortium Books, 1976.

> A good study of what it means to be sick. Special attention is given to aging, mental illness and the handicapped. The chapter on Christian sickness as prophecy is recommended.

Clements, William, ed. *Ministry with the Aging*, San Francisco: Harper and Row Publishers, 1981.

> A comprehensive collection of essays dealing with the biblical, historical, and cultural context for the meaning of aging. It presents challenges for the future as well as practical designs for now. Note the chapter on "Worship and Aging: Memory and Repentance."

Colston, Lowell, G. *Pastoral Care with Handicapped Persons*, Philadelphia: Fortress Press, 1978.

---

[30]Leonard Bowman, *The Importance of Being Sick*, (Wilmington, North Carolina: Consortium Books, 1976) p. 216.

The need for social justice and the handicapped is seen in terms of the various ways in which the Christian community can help them on their way to wholeness.

Dougherty, Flavian, ed. *The Deprived, the Disabled, and the Fullness of Life*, Wilmington, Del.: Michael Glazier, Inc., 1984.

This is a series of essays that deal with the "marginal life." Marginalization is discussed in terms of pain and suffering, the retarded, and rehabilitation.

Empereur, James L., S.J. *Prophetic Anointing: God's Call to the Sick, the Elderly, and the Dying,* Wilmington, DE: Michael Glazier, Inc., 1984.

This is a good treatment of the vocational aspect of being sick and elderly. The relation of social justice to the sacrament is dealt with explicitly.

Gusmer, Charles W. *And You Visited Me: Sacramental Ministry to the Sick and Dying*, New York: Pueblo Publishing Co., 1984.

This is an excellent commentary on the rite of anointing which deals with the history and pastoral practice. While it says little about social justice, it provides for a more comprehensive understanding in which anointing and justice can be seen.

Polish, Daniel and Fisher, Eugene J., eds. *Liturgical Foundations of Social Policy in the Catholic and Jewish Traditions*, Notre Dame: University of Notre Dame Press, 1983.

Health care and healing are placed in a social context in the Catholic and Jewish traditions. The whole volume deals with social justice issues from the perspective of these two traditions.

Ministries to the Sick, in *Liturgy.* vol. 2:2, Washington, D.C.: The Liturgical Conference, Inc.

> Among the several essays in this volume, the relevant ones are those that deal with the disabled and the elderly as well as those treating the sacrament of anointing in the African and Hispanic contexts.

Pastoral Care of the Sick and Dying: Study Text 2, Revised Edition, Washington D.C.: United States Catholic Conference, 1984.

> A very useful tool for bringing out the various dimensions of the sacrament which are emphasized in the ritual revisions.

11

Liturgy and Consumerism

Why do we not hear the message of social justice which is in the liturgy? From the foregoing chapters, it is clear that the liturgy refers much more to social justice than, in all probability, most of us ever suspected. Why have we not detected that meaning or been moved to concern about injustice in our society as a result of our liturgical participation?

One answer to that question is that our society conditions us, so that we do not discern the liturgy's message of social justice. Our minds and hearts, our perspectives on life, our attitudes and values, are shaped by our culture. When we come to celebrate the liturgy, we simply are not looking for the truths and values in the realm of justice which are contained there. According to the Gospel of Mark, Jesus concluded his parable of the seed with the exhortation, "Let the one who has ears to hear me, hear." We could say of the liturgy, "Let the one who has ears to hear its message of social justice, hear!" But too many of us do not have the ears to hear.

A variety of factors in our culture prevent us from hearing the liturgy's message in regard to social justice. A prominent factor is the assumption that religion and therefore worship are private affairs with nothing to say about organizing society. It is recognized, of course, that religion and liturgy can support the social order by helping citizens endure the sometimes unpleasant features of society, or it can threaten the social order by raising citizens' expectations. From our social environment, we Christians absorb this mentality of religion-is-a-private-affair. When we assemble for liturgy, therefore, we do not expect that it will have anything to say to us about our changing the structures of life in our society to bring about social justice. We do not hear any such message even when, from time to time, the liturgy speaks it more explicitly. We are surprised, perhaps even offended, when preachers challenge the public life of our city, state, or nation, the government or business or criminal justice or public education. Preachers are thought to be out of order in bringing up such subjects. This attitude has been challenged by the Roman Catholic Bishops in their pastoral on the U.S. economy.[1]

It is also assumed what worship has to say for our private welfare has nothing to do with society's structures. Worship has little to do with worldly existence other than enable us to bear its trials in view of promised happiness after this life. The liturgy is essentially about that promised happiness in another world, so we do not expect liturgy to speak about the present social order, except to encourage us to accept, in the spirit of Christ, the sufferings the social order may impose upon us.

Another reason many of us do not hear the liturgy's message of social justice is that we do not *need* to hear it for *ourselves* and so we do not hear it for others either. We are not suffering any great injustice—at least we are not conscious of such suffering. Economically we live respectably and are able to fulfill some of our desires. We complain about taxes, waste in government, high food prices, extreme costs of medical care, but we do not experience ourselves being reduced to helplessness. As members of the upper and middle classes, we are not likely to hear the social justice message in the liturgy because our particular needs do not attune us to that meaning of our worship. Only if, somehow, we can acquire a sense of solidarity with the truly unjustly deprived people of our city, state, nation, and world, will we discern the call to action for social justice in liturgical celebrations.

Or we may discover that we are indeed oppressed people suffering injustice, even though it may not be as obvious as the injustice suffered by the economically impoverished, the polit-

---

[1] *Economic Justice For All: Catholic Social Teaching And The U.S. Economy* (Washington, D.C.: USCC, June 4, 1986), sections 325 and 326.

ically disenfranchised, the socially segregated, or the culturally deprived. This possibility brings us to consider consumerism as a factor in our society which prevents us from hearing the liturgy's message of social justice.[2]

Though liturgy and consumerism are unassociated in our ordinary consciousness, our lives are lived and our liturgies celebrated in the context of a consumer society. The suspicion arises, therefore, that perhaps consumerism influences our liturgy in unconscious ways, prevents it from being authentically Christian worship, and prohibits our hearing its message of social justice.

Consumerism here refers to a complex consisting of: (1) an economic system which places an extremely high value on the incessant production and consumption of material goods and services at an ever higher level of physical convenience and comfort; (2) an accompanying mentality which assumes that such a system is the best or only one possible; and (3) a related tendency or even drive to find much, sometimes most, though rarely all, human fulfillment in providing and consuming these material goods and services. In contrast to consumerism would be, for example, an economic system and related mentality and tendency to produce goods and services to satisfy the basic human needs of an ever wider circle of human beings before increasing the level of physical convenience and comfort of a relatively small population, or a system to produce and consume material goods and services with primary concern for conserving natural resources and environment for needs of future generations.[3]

What is wrong with consumerism in the strict sense defined above? Consumerism entails incessant consumption and production of material goods and services. It calls forth activity—

---

[2]Other factors than consumerism can influence for the worse our celebration of liturgy. Robert Hovda wonderfully describes the way in which our society's manner of dealing with death and burial works against our grasping the profound meaning of the Christian funeral rites and incorporating that significance in pastoral practice. See Robert Hovda, "The Amen Corner," *Worship* 59:3 (May, 1985), p. 251ff.

[3]A classic work which develops these ideas is E.F. Schumacher's *Small is Beautiful* (New York: Harper and Row, 1973). The subtitle of this book is: *Economics as if People Mattered.*

the use of objects or services—to the exclusion of contemplation. Stores are open seven days a week not only because people wish to make money or because some people's needs are best served that way, but because people need to be doing something, to be active, consuming, seven days a week. Many people experience the need to "get away," to "slow down," to "go on retreat." They should, for the pressures of the consumerist society drive sensitive human beings to seek relief. The many North Americans who seek contemplation of some kind (enjoyment of nature, music, or religious retreat) do not belie the fact that consumerism implies incessant activity but rather bear witness to it by their efforts to escape.[4]

From the point of view of social justice, human beings have a need and a right to some contemplation in their lives—leisure time for enjoyment of nature and art, for reflection on life's events and goal. Without such time, it is impossible to be free and fully human. Significantly those who wish to gain mastery over others (police interrogators, promoters of cults, deprogrammers) do not give their subjects any time free for personal thought; they keep them busy answering questions or working, eating, sleeping—producing and consuming, in two words. A consumerist society is an assault on the rights of the entire population; but its attack is felt most, of course, by those who do not have the means to escape briefly the economic scramble and its propaganda.

Liturgy is meant to be contemplation. Guided and supported by the word of God and sacramental symbols, the worshiper is led to consider the mystery of God's redemptive love for each of us revealed in the death and resurrection of Jesus Christ. But do we come to liturgical celebration from our consumer society disposed for that purpose? Do we carry out the liturgy in a contemplative or a consumerist manner? Is there, for example, time to dwell on the word of God, or do the words of the first reading, the response psalm, the second reading,

---

[4]For a discussion of the effects of consumerism on sacramental life from the Latin American perspective see Juan Luis Segundo, S.J., *The Sacraments Today*, "The Bank-Deposit Approach to Education and Sacramental Administration," (Maryknoll: Orbis Books, 1974), p. 101.

the acclamation, the gospel, the homily, the creed, the general intercessions follow upon one another as rapidly as one commercial after another on TV or the radio? What place do we give to silence and reflection in liturgical celebrations?

If we are to appreciate God's redemption in Christ and its implications for social justice, we all need time, or "space" as is said today, to plumb that mystery in thought and love, contrast it with the world in which we are immersed, and see its healing and reconciling mission and our place in it. The celebration of the liturgy is meant to provide such time, such "space," but all too often we celebrate the liturgy in a manner appropriate to consumerism's incessant consumption rather than to Christian worship's reflective contemplation. As a result, we miss the implications for social justice of, for example, the fact that the bread partaken in the Eucharist is one though received by many, that it is given by Christ for *all* men and women, not just some, or those of this or that class, this or that nationality. The symbols of the liturgy are simple indeed—bread, wine, oil, laying on of hands—but they are extremely rich in meaning. They call for reverent handling and for time and silence to contemplate their significance. If liturgy appears ineffectual for promoting social justice, the problem is not the liturgy's inherent irrelevance but our introducing into its celebration consumerist habits preventing us from apprehending that intrinsic significance.[5]

A trait of North American consumerism is to bombard consciousness with goods and services of every conceivable sort. One feels the bombardment along a business thoroughfare in any city, but the bombardment is concentrated in the shopping mall. The shopping mall is indeed a marvelous place. It evokes wonder and admiration. We say this seriously. How can anyone wander through a shopping mall without being struck by the ingenuity which has produced an endless variety of goods in abundant numbers and gathered them from all

---

[5]For an excellent treatment of how an excessive individualism influences all aspects of American life, reducing our capacity for commitment to one another, limiting it to our circle of family and friends, see Robert Bellah and others, *Habits of the Heart,* (Berkeley: University of California Press, 1985).

over the world for us here in this one place, so that we may consume them? A shopping center is no small achievment when we think of our primitive ancestors in their caves and their daily hunting expeditions for the meagerest of life's necessities.

But how does this bombardment condition our participation in liturgical celebrations? A man once remarked that the real weekend liturgy for his family was the trip to the shopping center. We can picture the children scurrying here and there in curiosity and delight. We can imagine mother's enjoying the clothes on the racks, even though the family cannot afford them now. Father can look over the power tools he dreams of having some day. An ice cream cone at Baskin-Robbins makes the celebration complete. How can Sunday liturgy compete with the multiple appeals of the shopping mall?

It cannot, of course, but as a result of living in a consumer society, do we unconsciously expect it to compete? Do we approach liturgy expecting it to bombard us with appealing truths and insights and powerful Christian motivation? Do we treat liturgy as a "hot" medium requiring little participation to make it effective, or do we handle it as the "cool" medium it is, demanding considerable input on our part to complete its meaning?[6] If the liturgy is overloaded with banners, vestments, music, dances, symbols, endless words, we rightly experience dissatisfaction, for such liturgy, rather than giving us "space" in the midst of our consumerist culture, is only aping the culture.[7]

From the point of view of social justice, we can ask two questions about the shopping mall. Are we enjoying this gathering of goods and services for ourselves at the expense of some human beings suffering injustice? Do we use this assemblage of goods and services as Christian agents of change (graced ministers of God's redeeming action in Christ for the world), so that we work toward minimizing the injustice

[6]See "Liturgy Hot and Cool," by Thomas F. O'Meara, O.P., *Worship* 42:4 (April, 1968).

[7]See also: "The Liturgical Medium in an Electronic Age," by Charles C. McDonald, *Worship* 44:1 (January, 1970) and "Liturgy in an Electronic Age," by James L. Empereur S.J., *Modern Liturgy Handbook* (New York: Paulist Press, 1976).

involved, or do we use it oblivious to any other end than the satisfaction of our needs? We can bring the same questions to liturgy. Do we use this assembly for worship at the expense of others who may be suffering injustice? Do we use this assembly as Christian agents of change and so move toward correcting that injustice, or do we use it as passive Christians (merely recipients of God's grace) for our own eternal salvation? How we approach the shopping mall will influence how we enter into the liturgy, and how we enter into the latter will have its impact on how we come to the shopping center.

An element of North American consumerism is advertising.[8] An economy motivated by consumption must promote consumption lest production come to an end. Once necessities are provided for, conveniences and luxuries must be converted into necessities. The population must be conditioned to think and feel that they cannot live without these conveniences and luxuries. So the vast enterprise of advertising comes into existence to woo us with countless words and appealing pictures, even to manipulate us through our subconscious desires and fears. Government agencies are needed to police the claims that are made for goods and services, lest they become so extravagant as to be utterly untruthful, unjust, and harmful. Consumer-interest groups also patrol the advertising field to protect consumers from misleading claims.

The advertising succeeds: sales of goods and services demonstrate that. But in the process all of us—advertisers and public— become suspicious of words. We are dubious when the famous athlete or movie star proclaims he or she eats or drinks this food or that beverage, or when it is suggested that the burdens of family life will vanish when this detergent is used or this insurance policy is purchased. Together with the duplicity which frequently occurs in political language, the claims of advertising erode our confidence in words.

[8]For a Christian perspective on the problem of the impoverishment of the Christian faith which has been co-opted by a consumeristic society see: John Francis Kavanaugh, *Following Christ in a Consumer Society* (Maryknoll: Orbis Books, 1981). The subtitle is: *The Spirituality of Cultural Resistance*. See also, James B. Dunning, "Confronting the Demons: The Social Dimension of Conversion," *Conversion and the Catechumenate*, edited by Robert Duggan (New York: Paulist Press, 1984).

This erosion of confidence in words constitutes a serious injustice to everyone. Veracity of speech and confidence in it are at the very heart of life for any society. Men and women can live and work together only if they communicate and if that communication can be trusted. Agreements are impossible if one or the other party is suspected of being untruthful. The most disadvantaged, obviously, are the poor, handicapped, and elderly who rely on other people's words for so much because they do not have the resources to obtain needed information by themselves.

Is it possible for the liturgy to convey its message effectively if its participants are mistrustful of words? For many Christians, liturgy provides the few words they do trust amid all the words they hear and read in the course of a week. Their intentness during the readings of scripture manifests that confidence. But for many others, at least a residue of doubt remains in their minds even about the validity of the biblical word. The word of homilist or preacher is often little esteemed.

This suspicion of the words in worship derives not only from the general distrust of words generated by advertising but also from the conflict of values proclaimed. Jesus says: "Happiness is being satisfied with little in the way of material goods and being especially concerned with love and justice." But the message every other hour of the week is: "Happiness is consuming our products." Whose words are to be believed, if any of them? The choice is difficult, especially for the young who have not learned much as yet about how little consumer goods and services satisfy human hungers or help in life's most painful moments.[9]

If the words of the liturgy are not taken to heart, if they are

---

[9]Kavanaugh says it best: "Friendship, intimacy, love, pride, happiness, and joy are actually the *objects* we buy and consume, much more so than the tubes, liquor bottles, Cadillacs, and Buicks that promise them and bear their names. And since none of these deepest human hopes can be fulfilled in any product, the mere consumption of them is never enough; "more" of the product, or a "new improved" product, is the only relief offered to our human longings. Thus the seller drives us to greater purchasing with even more extravagantly concocted promises: more commodities as the solution to anxiety stimulated by media manipulation. Consumption, consequently, is not just an economic factor. It emerges as a "way of life." It is an addiction." Ibid, p. 23.

only half-heard in the first place, then any message for social justice which they contain will not be communicated and the liturgy will appear ineffective for social justice. For those dedicated to the latter, the question may be asked whether they carry into the liturgical celebration a mistrust of words— a mistrust compounded perhaps by their own critical investigations of corporate policies and government legislation in order to detect covert injustice. If they do carry such mistrust into liturgical celebrations, perhaps they do not perceive the message of justice in them and hence dismiss the liturgy as a force for social change. As for liturgists, this widespread mistrust of words begotten of a consumer economy and carried into the liturgy suggests that liturgists will make the liturgy an effective power to the extent that they do something to correct the consumer milieu in which the liturgy is celebrated. A revision of the language of the liturgical texts to improve their English is not going to improve notably the liturgy's impact on people if they continue to come to worship mistrustful of words. Liturgists' serious concern about vital liturgy must include vital concern about a just, humane society.[10]

Consumerism focuses on material goods and services. Part of its genius is its ability to "package" even what belongs to the mind. For no little price, exquisitely printed and bound copies of the classics of literature are available to fill one's bookshelves or to lie on the coffee table. Recordings of the masterpieces of music down through the centuries can be subscribed to, as well as courses in art appreciation. These and other offerings of the consumer society merit our admiration and praise. They make the best of human achievment the heritage of an ever wider circle of women and men for their personal growth as human beings. But they can also remain "things" nice to consume in ever greater quantity.

Consumerism is more at home in the fields of paperback books and popular music. Their mass production and consumption move quickly through one best seller or top hit to

---

[10]Ibid., p. 119ff. What Kavanaugh says here regarding prayer, both shared and individual, regarding anti-consumeristic spirituality might well be applied to the liturgy of the church.

another. Paperback novels and popular songs do not have the "status" of the classics of literature or music, but neither do they reach very deeply into the mind in many instances. They approach the products which are most at home in consumerism: soaps, toothpastes, patent medicines, furniture, homes, cars, coach or first-class seats on planes—quantifiable things.

In a consumer society we become conditioned to attend to externals, to objects, things, quantities. Producers obviously think in this direction: packaging is important for sales, and numerous sales mean more income to be counted. Consumers are led to think in these terms also: we certainly want the most for our money—the most durable product, or the highest on the social scale, or the one made of the most expensive materials.

Into liturgy we can carry consumerism's focus on the external, material, quantifiable. The institutional aspect of liturgy abets this deformity, for the institutional is readily quantifiable.[11] How many baptisms in 1988? How many communions? How many attending Sunday worship? How many confirmed? If the numbers are large, we can feel thrilled, even though the services may be poor celebrations and the participation poor, as the producer and consuming public exult in the novel which sells millions of copies or the film which attracts millions of viewers, even though the novel or film lacks substance.

The consumerist mentality tends to objectify the liturgy— make it an object, a consumable good. That mentality readily approaches the liturgy with the question: "What can I get out of it?" The consumer regards liturgy as a product or service to be received, rather than as an event which he or she is to create with others. It should be satisfying and even pleasing with little effort on the participants' part. If it is not, it is an inferior product or service to be set aside for something better in the marketplace.

---

[11]For an elaboration on the institutional aspect of the liturgy see James L. Empereur, S. J., "Models for a Liturgical Theology," *The Sacraments* (New York: Alba House, 1981). See also by the same author: *Models of Liturgical Theology* (Nottingham: Grove Books Limited, 1987).

The consumerist mentality can also objectify God to whom worship is directed. God is a consumable good to be obtained and possessed by appropriate technical manipulation of the means which lead to him, much as the desired $100,000 home is eventually to be owned by a series of carefully chosen purchases, sales, larger purchases, bigger sales, and so on.

The relationship between God and ourselves is subject to similar objectification or reification, that is, grace is envisioned as a "thing" to be obtained as the result of liturgical participation. Worship is more like the payment of an insurance premium than an expression of faith and love toward a Beloved who calls and responds. The consumer mentality can push the understanding of *ex opere operato*[12] to its ultimate deformity.

While consumerism provides large quantities and a great variety of goods and services for the welfare of many, it also trivializes objects, both by abundant supply and inferiority of craftsmanship and beauty. Indeed, many goods are made to be thrown away after extremely limited use. Consumerism does not cultivate reverence for things, care of them, contemplation of them. In a consumerist society, museums are necessary to preserve worthwhile goods and the opportunity to revere them, lest humanity at its best be lost altogether.

A population with a consumerist esteem for things is likely to be content to proclaim the word of God from a leaflet missal. Little concern will be demonstrated as to whether what is called bread in the liturgy really is bread, looks like bread, tastes like it, feels like it. Even if the elements used in worship— bread, wine, oil, water (or gestures like laying on of hands)— possess their proper integrity and are used amply enough to be recognized, their extraordinarily rich symbolism will be missed by members of consumerist culture because they are not accustomed to treating such simple basics of life with reverence and wonder. What is the model in the minds of the participants

---

[12]Literally, "from the work having been done." This technical phrase indicates that God is unfailingly faithful to God's promise to meet the Christian in sacramental activity. In a distorted sense, it gives the impression that sacraments act upon the worshiper in such a way that very little active response is required on the part of the person receiving the sacrament.

in the Lord's Supper—a carefully prepared holiday family dinner or driving up to the window at McDonald's for hamburger, fries and a coke?

Consumers presuppose producers. The consumerist mind infests the liturgy by seeing there also producers and consumers. The producers are the clergy, laity the consumers. The laity are admitted to the role of producer now, but generally in strict subordination to clergy. Sometimes they are required to dress like the clergy to be sure they are distinct from the consumers. The laity, for the most part, accept the role of consumer. They expect the liturgy to be prepared for them by the clergy or by a parish committee or by both. Expectation that a parish committee prepare the liturgy can be reasonable: preparation is necessary and an entire large congregation can do it only by choosing suitable representatives. But if that choice is only a formality half-heartedly made, then it can scarcely be said that the congregation through representatives is preparing its own celebration. The fact is that the congregation is consuming a celebration produced for them by a committee.[13] Like other products in the marketplace, they may or may not like it.

If the congregation is regarded simply as consumers of worship prepared by the producers, then the producers naturally turn to other producers to provide the materials needed for worship. Vestments, candles, altar cloths, bread for the celebration are purchased out of catalogues, not made by members of the congregation. How many Christian women who skillfully make their own and their children's clothes have ever made a liturgical vestment? How many men have ever made a piece of furniture for the sanctuary in their well-equipped and skillfully used basement workshops?

Such questions present practical difficulties. Perhaps the work turned out would be truly inferior or in poor taste. Some

---

[13]Several years ago J. G. Davis pointed out the implications for social justice that are intrinsic to this consumeristic attitude on the part of the congregation. "A laity which is passive in relation to liturgical revision and passive in the forms of worship in which they are expected to engage will inevitably remain passive in the world. Whatever they fail to be in worship, they will fail to be in mission because of the unity of the two." *Worship and Mission* (London: SCM Press, LTD, 1966), p. 148.

means of avoiding embarrassing situations would have to be devised. But consumerism leads us away from the complications of seeking a solution which would enable the members of the congregation to contribute more of their creative talent to the liturgy. Consumerism seeks efficiency:[14] produce and consume the most possible in the most convenient way in the shortest time with the least waste of money—all consonant with sufficient pleasure to placate desire but without totally satisfying it forever. In the name of efficiency, then, let the clergy and some other interested parishioners tend to the liturgy. Order the materials for worship from the catalogue. Do not call upon the members of the congregation to take time to bake bread for Sunday Eucharist or to make candles for the altar.

Clergy may think that this course of action is not merely expediency but necessity. The people as a whole do not show interest in being more involved. Of course, a few parishoners are always ready to contribute, but employing them is merely token lay participation. Significant in this assessment of the situation is the fact that the people are coming to worship with a mentality and attitude carried over from the economic system and culture in which they live twenty-four hours a day.

In many ways, then, our cultural milieu influences our celebration of the liturgy and deforms that celebration. As a consequence, the liturgy is prevented from conveying its message and grace in their authenticity and plentitude, in particular its message and grace for social justice. So those who are concerned about improving liturgical celebrations cannot rest content with making changes in the liturgy. They must also work for a more just social order in church and society, a necessary precondition for authentic worship. An adequate liturgical renewal implies a social renewal.

Those who, on the other hand, are already critical about the structures of our society, may have absorbed in their very struggle against the present social order its own limited horizon. For example, in battling injustice, they seek to win. They become competitive—the forces of justice against those

---

[14]See Bellah, *Habits of the Heart* for a discussion of this point, especially p. 46.

of injustice. They take on the very same mentality which tends
to create an unjust social order. They may, then, dismiss liturgy
as a significant force for social justice because they, too, have
assimilated the attitudes, values, and vision of the milieu in the
process of struggling against it. So they fail to appreciate liturgy
as a force for social change. Indeed, liturgy's broader horizon
is necessary to keep the struggle for social justice alive.[15] An
adequate social renewal implies a liturgical renewal, as we
shall argue in the following chapter.

☙

Bibliography

Bellah, Robert N.; Madsen, Richard N.; Sullivan, William
    M.; Swindler, Ann; and Tipton, Steven M. *Habits of
    the Heart: Individualism and Commitment in Ameri-
    can Life,* Berkeley: University of California Press,
    1985.

> This book provides an excellent analysis of how Americans
> see themselves. It shows their ambivalence regarding indi-
> vidualism and commitment. It provides an understanding
> of the public and private lives of the American worshiper.

Davies, J. G. *Worship and Mission,* New York: Association
    Press, 1967.

> An older book dealing with the relationship of liturgy and
> life, especially in terms of the mission of the church. Its
> argument for the necessity of the Christian engagement in
> the world is still urgent and contemporary.

Fritsch, Albert J. *The Contrasumers,* Praeger, 1974.

> This volume contains a great deal of information for those

---

[15]Kavanaugh has developed this point in regard to the seven sacraments. See
Following Christ in a Consumer Society , p. 123ff.

who are looking for ways to respond to conservation and economic simplicity. Its practicality makes it valuable.

Kavanaugh, John Francis. *Following Christ in a Consumer Society: The Spirituality of Cultural Resistance*, Maryknoll: Orbis Press, 1981.

This book is indispensable for anyone wishing to understand the consumeristic mentality which so affects the church's liturgical experiences. It goes beyond smashing the idols of capitalism and commodity to offer a positive Christian solution.

McGinnis, James. *Bread and Justice,* New York: Paulist Press, 1980.

This book, which deals with the problem of food distribution, economics and faith with a sense of compassion, is recommended for its helpful suggestions and references.

Mische, Gerald and Patricia. *Toward a Human World Order: Beyond the National Security Straightjacket*, New York: Paulist Press, 1977.

The authors are known for their optimistic approach to world problems of shortages of resources. Religious faith is central to their approach to a more human world order.

Schumacher, E. F. *Small is Beautiful*, New York: Harper and Row, 1974.

The author is a British economist who from a religious perspective suggests ways of living in a technological world. A good background book for understanding the consumeristic mentality.

Segundo, S. J., Juan Luis. *The Sacraments Today*, Maryknoll: Orbis Books, 1974.

This liberation approach to the sacraments is a good resource because of the section in each chapter entitled, "Clarifications," where Segundo shows the interrelationships of political, social, and economic understanding of life and the way people misunderstand the liturgy of the sacraments and celebrate them inauthentically.

Sojourners. This is a magazine dedicated to the alternate Christian lifestyle. Typically, issues contain articles on spirituality, racism, disarmament and topics from the Third World.

United States Catholic Conference of Bishops. *Economic Justice For All: Catholic Social Teaching and the U.S. Economy,* Third Draft, Washington D.C.: USCC, June 4, 1986.

This well publicized statement of the American Roman Catholic Bishops provides a Christian vision of the economic life which in turn serves as the background around which such issues as employment, poverty, food and agriculture, and the world economy can be understood.

Warren, Michael. "The Worshiping Assembly: Possible Zone of Cultural Contestation," *Worship* 63:1 (January 1989).

In this essay the author examines the transformative power of liturgy and the relationship of ritual and life structure of the worshiping community. The essay treats the intentionality of worshipers and challenges consumerism. The author argues for a religious vision that takes as its basic stance solidarity with the poor.

12

Social Justice's Need for Liturgy

A very socially minded woman, once associated with the Berrigans in their attacks on weapons plants and draft boards in the 1960's, told of a Baptist woman with whom she had become friends in Baltimore. Though elderly, the woman was intensely active in securing a decent life for the poor and unfortunate. She was doing more than good deeds here and there. She read about and studied the social and economic situation of the country and the world. Indeed, her whole life focused on caring for the needy. Her motivation was Christian, but prayer and worship occupied a miniscule amount of her time and energy. Her "philosophy" of life was that the heart of Christian life is to love actively one's neighbor for God's sake. Early in life she had determined that every day she would assist somebody in need. Doing just that has been her life—though eventually she was serving more than one person in need every day; whole days were spent serving one person after another. She said her prayer was simple: a brief acknowledgement of God each morning upon rising and a request for aid in the task of the day—helping people in need. Then she got down to business.

This account suggests that the social justice ministry does not need liturgy for its genuineness. Here is a woman who has been a steady and faithful servant of the poor for many years, giving very concrete help to countless people in real need touching upon the preservation of a decent human life and even upon survival itself. Liturgy has played practically no role in her life, and even formal prayer has been meager. While others were worshiping or praying, she was out in the neighborhood helping people in distress.

The real liturgy, after all, is what Karl Rahner calls "the liturgy of the world":

> The world and its history are the terrible and sublime liturgy, breathing of death and sacrifice, which God celebrates and causes to be celebrated in and through human history and its freedom .... In the entire length and breadth of this immense history of birth and death, complete superficiality, folly, inadequacy and hatred (all of which 'crucify') on the one hand, and silent submission, responsible even to death in dying and in joyfulness, in attaining the heights and plumbing the depths, on the other, the true liturgy of the world is present ....[1]

It is this "liturgy of the world" which the elderly Baptist woman has celebrated over the years. And the message of this book has been the necessity of engaging in this liturgy of the world if the liturgy of church worship is going to be authentically Christian, more than pious gesturing, individualistic consolation, social-class practice, or escapism.

Christian social action certainly needs living faith in Jesus Christ, the Father/Mother, and the Holy Spirit if it is to be distinctively Christian ministry and not merely secular humanism. The elderly Baptist lady was not a mere philanthropist; she was a Christian doing a Christian deed for a Christian motive. It is Christian faith which provides social justice activity with Christian motive, goal, objectives, means, and standard. For it is faith in God's infinite love revealed in Jesus Christ which prompts our actively loving others and so seeking a just society in which they might live. The goal we have in mind in social justice ministry is the coming of God's reign which Jesus announced and then commanded his dis-

---

[1]"Considerations on the Active Role of the Person in the Sacramental Event," in *Theological Investigations*, vol. 14 (New York: Seabury, 1976). p. 169.

ciples to preach, and which he himself initiated in his person. The objectives of the social justice ministry are the components of a social order which would actualize the *shalom*, that peace (personal and collective life filled with truth, justice, tranquillity, love, and freedom) which the risen Jesus wished for his disciples when he appeared to them on Easter eve (John 20:21). The radical means—those deeper than social legislation and organization—to achieve these objectives were laid out by Jesus in his preaching; they are summarized by Matthew in the Sermon on the Mount, especially in the Beatitudes (Matt. 5-7). The standard in using these means and striving for these objectives is the example of Jesus, his radical obedience to his God (Luke 22:42) and his compassion for the people (Matt. 9:36). So the social justice ministry can stand on its own two feet by means of Christian faith; it has no need of liturgy.

In fact, liturgy stands in the way of achieving the objectives of social justice ministry. Liturgy tends to confirm the affluent in their condition. They worship in well-kept churches on full stomachs in tidy suburbs and hear the message of God's forgiveness for their personal peccadillos. If they hear forceful words from the pulpit on the social implications of their faith, they tell the pastor to stick to the "spiritual" matters. On the other side of the tracks, the liturgy confirms the poor in their situation. They hear a message of Christlike courage and love of enemies in the face of difficulties.

The liturgy, then, is not a help toward social justice, but a part of the social injustice which needs to be corrected. Action for social justice does not need liturgy in order to be authentically Christian and effective. The elderly Baptist woman had it straight.

The argument we have been reviewing in the preceding paragraphs has a basis in facts which historians and sociologists could document for us, or which we have personally witnessed. The argument merits our attention. But there are still other facts that deserve to be taken into account before dismissing the liturgy as of little or no value for Christian social justice ministry.

The first of these facts is the association of liturgical renewal and efforts for social justice in the past and present. We noted instances of this pairing in the opening chapter: the movement in England in the nineteenth century and the movement begun in this country in the 1920's by Dom Virgil Michel. We would argue that this coupling is not accidental. It comes about because these two concerns—for genuine Christian liturgy and authentic Christian social ministry—intrinsically call for one another. That liturgical authenticity requires social justice ministry as the presupposition and consummation of liturgical celebration has been the theme of this book. That social justice ministry for its own genuineness calls for renewed liturgical worship is the thesis proposed in this chapter.

Jim Wallis of the Sojourners community in Washington, D.C., testifies to the validity of this thesis in his book, *The Call to Conversion*:

> Worship has become the center of the life we share at Sojourners. In worship we are refreshed and renewed, our vision is rekindled, and we remember again who we are and what we are about. People who know some of our history as a community are often surprised by our emphasis on worship. They suppose us to be solely concerned about the political meaning of the gospel, not about renewal of worship ... All this could be surprising; none of it should be surprising.[2]

By means of true worship, Wallis recalls, the Sojourners freed themselves from the idolatries of the consumer society around them. But as they were busy at the front door, as Wallis puts it, some other idols sneaked in the back door. Except for true worship, or liturgy, recalling their roots in Jesus Christ, they would have simply become captive to the idols standing in opposition to the society's current ones. The Sojourners were tempted to make idols of their own simple life style, their principle of non-violence, their prophetic vocation, even of themselves as truly "radical Christians."[3] It

---

[2]James Wallis, *The Call to Conversion* (San Francisco: Harper and Row, 1981), pp. 141-42.

[3]Ibid., p. 145.

was worship—it is worship—which constantly saves them from these idols.[4]

Wallis acknowledges the variety of reactions which the words "Praise the Lord" raise in people, including those in the Sojourners community. They can be voiced by the well-to-do praising God for their wealth they have accumulated by exploitation of the poor. But such false praise should not blind us to the value of authentic praise, so well described by Wallis. Involved as we are in a world of injustice filled with pain and suffering, praise of God prevents us from being overwhelmed; it lifts us out of our weary selves and refreshes us; it frees us and generates trust and identity. "The authority of every other god melts away in the worship of the Lord."[5]

Jim Wallis' analysis of the role of worship in *The Call to Conversion* is much more detailed and eloquent than these few paragraphs indicate. What is especially important here is that his statement about the importance of liturgy in the social justice ministry is grounded in experience. The Sojourners have found worship to be the means which brings them into touch with their roots; the mystery of God revealed in Jesus Christ and the gift of the Spirit, whence they draw inspiration, enlightenment, and constant correction for their ministry of social justice.

The real liturgy is, as Rahner says, the liturgy of the world and its history. But, also according to Rahner, that liturgy of the world includes the working of God's grace at the very heart of the world. "This liturgy," he writes, "therefore must, if the individual is really to share in the celebration of it in all its freedom and self-commitment even to death, be interpreted, 'reflected upon' in its ultimate depths in the celebration of that which we are accustomed to call liturgy in the more usual sense."[6] To put it in another way, "Christian sacraments are tiny testaments to that larger liturgy of the world where men and women experience God's presence in the birth of a child, the death of a parent, the meeting of friends, the anxious trip

[4]Ibid., pp. 146-47.

[5]Ibid., p. 152.

[6]Rahner, "Considerations on the Role of the Person," p. 170.

to the hospital."[7] The sacraments direct the Christian people
"to the whole of creation, human life, and human communion
as their trysting place with God the Father, Son, and Holy
Spirit."[8] The liturgy of Christian worship, then, enables us to
discern the real liturgy of the world and its history and to enter
into it by seeking social justice.

We often think that some of the most cherished values in
our modern world have come, not from the Christian faith or
the church, but from the world which has repudiated them
and even rejected religion altogether. These values include the
dignity of the individual person, human rights, freedom,
participatory government. We may regard them as gifts of
eighteenth century Enlightenment, or nineteenth century discovery of the social contruction of reality, or twentieth century
secular humanism. But what has really happened is that—to
borrow words from Robert Hovda —"at long last, the consciousness of the human race has caught up with the symbols
of faith."[9] Francis Schüssler Fiorenza has pointed out the
religious roots of, for example, the contemporary view of the
dignity of the human person.[10]

The symbols of faith referred to by Hovda—biblical word
and ecclesial sacrament—constitute the liturgy which the
church has celebrated for twenty centuries. The manner of
celebration has often obscured perception of their full meaning
for individual and social life; people's preoccupation with their
own daily concerns has distracted them from discerning the
full significance of these symbols for their lives; and frequently

[7]Nathan Mitchell, "The Spirituality of Christian Worship," *Spirituality Today* 34
(1982): 10.

[8]Christopher Kiesling, "Paradigms of Sacramentality," *Worship* 44 (1970): 432. See
also Philip Murnion, "A Sacramental Church in the Modern World," *Origins,* 21
June 1984, p. 87: " ... when we consider the fundamental faults of our present way of
life and then look at the features of a new way of life that would better respect the
dignity and community of all life, we find that the basic qualities of our sacramental
tradition offer a belief and perspective, a way of thinking and acting that are
desperately needed today. There lies in the heart of the church the capacities not only
to build the community of the church, but also to help form the human family."

[9]Robert Hovda, "The Amen Corner," *Worship* 58 (1984): 252.

[10]Francis Schüssler Fiorenza, "The Church's Religious Identity and its Social
Political Mission," *Theological Studies* 43 (1982): pp. 216-17.

sin has willfully ignored the most obvious meanings of these symbols. Sometimes the Spirit of God has brought the import of these symbols to the notice of the Christian people through the insights of nonbelievers and even the enemies of religion. The point is that we ought not to underestimate the wealth of wisdom, even for the social order, latent in the liturgy. Some of it has already been mined, but much more surely remains yet to be discovered. Only by immersing ourselves in the liturgy, however, can we hope to make that discovery.

If action for social justice is united with liturgical celebration, there is all the more reason to expect that our eyes will be opened to social justice implications of liturgy that we had not noticed before. As liberation theologians urge the reading of scripture in the light of experience to find new significance for daily life, especially social life, so we suggest that the "reading" of liturgy in the light of everyday experience will reveal new import in biblical word and liturgical symbol for social life and justice in the world.

The motive, goal, objectives, means, and standard of social justice ministry are indeed derived from living faith, as we noted above. But faith, both as a body of doctrinal beliefs and as the act of believing in trust and love, depends upon a community and especially the community's worship. Our personal faith is not implanted in our minds or hearts immediately by God but through the mediation of the Christian community, especially its liturgy, where that faith is professed and where newcomers and established members absorb the faith expressed in the biblical word and ecclesial sacrament. Books, pamphlets, lectures, academic and popular theology, sermons, and pronouncements from Roman congregations or denominational boards set forth and explain Christian faith, but they are secondary expressions of faith, reflecting upon the fundamental testimony of faith which is the church's worship of word and sacrament.

The elderly Baptist woman is indeed a remarkable woman. She is unusual. She shows us that poorly celebrated liturgy, or even none at all, is no excuse for not living for God, loving neighbor, working for social justice. Most of us, however, need more support for our own Christian living and ministry than she appears to have had. She is, of course, living off the

254 Social Justice's Need for Liturgy

communal heritage of the Christian church's worship, though she, or we, may not think of herself in that way. But she knows about God, she has a Bible, she has her "philosophy of life," and much more besides, from God through the Christian community that links her with the first disciples of Jesus. Since that community has actualized itself over the centuries principally through worship, she really is dependent on the liturgy for her Christian faith and social justice ministry. Perhaps now she rarely participates in the liturgy, but she has been nourished by it nevertheless, and she could be fed and refreshed and inspired by it even more if she were to participate in it often and regularly.

The elderly Baptist woman may respond that she cannot tolerate the liturgy, for it is part of the problem she works daily to overcome. Far from nourishing her social justice concern for ministry, the liturgy would gradually blunt her sensitivity and zeal and make her complacent; or else its blindness, hypocrisy, and ineffectiveness in relation to the social injustices of the day would so infuriate her that she could not worthily worship God.

We may very well have to agree with her. Perhaps in her vicinity there is no Christian liturgy which would enrich her life and ministry. It is noteworthy, however, that Jim Wallis in *The Call to Conversion* speaks about "true and genuine worship" and about "renewal of worship"; he acknowledges that " we live in a time when worship seems to lack power."[11] We recognize that also. When we refer to the need of the social justice ministry for liturgy, we are referring to a liturgy being renewed. We are not saying that any celebration of the liturgy keeps everyone's social justice ministry in touch with its roots in Jesus Christ and nourishes the faith which guides that ministry. But we are saying that both experience and theory indicate the necessity of good liturgy to sustain authentically Christian social ministry, and that those committed to the social justice ministry would want to be interested in, and work for, the best of liturgical renewal.

Those working out of a Christian context for social justice

[11]Wallis, *Call to Conversion*, pp. 140-41.

would also surely maintain that the just social order they seek to establish includes religious vision and values and therefore includes renewed forms of worship for all religious groups. The renewal of the Christian liturgy is, therefore, part of the solution being sought in the social justice ministry. Those engaged in that ministry reasonably would be concerned and knowledgeable about authentic liturgical renewal as an integral part of the goal they seek. But if one were to collect all the social justice newsletters in the United States published by Christians, would we find evidence that liturgy is a part of a just social order? John A. Coleman has argued that religion is, at least potentially, the really saving institution in the political life of this country.[12] But religion expresses itself fundamentally in liturgy. Is there enough attention given to religion and to its expression in liturgy by those in pursuit of social justice and in their description of the social order which constitutes the goal of that pursuit?

Those devoted to social justice generally endeavor to embody in their personal lives the values they seek to realize in society, as the members of the Sojourners community do. We would expect of such people conscientious celebration of the liturgy in the best possible manner. They would not be content with lackluster celebration on the one hand, nor, on the other would they manipulate the liturgy at whim, as if its shape had no intrinsic integrity and as if there were no norms of "good taste" as well as canonical legislation to guide its celebration. They may have to consult those with expertise in the field of liturgy to learn what liturgy ought to be. Perhaps those dedicated to social justice ought to be learning about liturgy from members of the North American Academy of Liturgy, or the National Federation of Diocesan Liturgical Commissions, or the National Association of Pastoral Musicians, even as members of these organizations need to be informed about social justice issues by those with expertise in analyzing situations of injustice and seeking remedies. Or, before we go to the national level, we may ask what sort of dialogue is going

[12]John A. Coleman, "The Christian as Citizen," *Commonweal* 9 September 1983, pp. 457-62.

on within dioceses between members of the offices for peace and justice, or human rights, and the offices for liturgy, or worship. Or, still closer to home, what sort of exchange and cooperation goes on at the parish level between committees for liturgy and for justice?

One reason the liturgy does not contribute to social justice lies not in the liturgy but in us. We do not participate in it because it does not meet our expectations, "move" us, provide some sort of "peak" experience. Or we do participate but fail to invest ourselves in it. If we have made up our minds beforehand that liturgy says little or nothing about social justice, we are not going to notice what it does say, nor search to find how very much it says. If we have already made all our decisions about what and how we are going to serve social justice, we are not open to be challenged or corrected or pushed further by the social justice message of the liturgy.

Regis Duffy points out how important subjective, personal, "intentional" investment in liturgy is for its fruitfulness.[13] He even argues that this factor of liturgical worship is more important than the rites or the explicit liturgical piety of the age. Down through the centuries, he notes, saints have nourished their Christian lives through liturgy, though rarely did they have at their disposal liturgical rites or sacramental theologies to match the depth and breadth of their particular spiritualities—including, we might add, their concern for the oppressed and a better world for them. St. Francis of Assisi nourished his Christian discipleship with thirteenth-century liturgy and St. Therese of Lisieux fed her spiritual life with nineteenth-century worship, neither of which liturgies and their cultural understanding would today appeal to us or meet liturgical scholars' criteria for "good" liturgy and "sound" piety. So if liturgy is to be fuel for the ministry of social justice, liturgical worship's meaning relative to justice must be actively probed and its challenge actively appropriated by the worshipers. Certainly, objectively more gripping liturgical worship is needed; but part of the problem is our catching up with the

---

[13]Regis Duffy, "Formative Experience and Intentional Liturgy," *Studies in Formative Spirituality* 3 (1982): 351-61.

symbols of faith. As Bernard Lonergan explains, we have many kinds of bias which prevent us from perceiving truth and choosing values.[14] To recognize and choose social justice, we need intellectual, affective, moral, and religious conversion, besides better designed and celebrated liturgical rites.

Even the prosaic liturgies celebrated day after day in many places convey some powerful messages of social justice, if we are not blind and deaf to them. They are gathering places for all kinds of people from all sorts of backgrounds—rich and poor, healthy and sick, fit and disabled, young and old, every racial strain and nationality. One need only think of churches or chapels buried amid the skyscrapers of major U.S. cities where hundreds of people every hour come for worship. In many ways these people hardly constitute a community, and yet their very diversity is a reminder of the university and quality of all God's people who are, after all, a very diverse lot.

The readings those people hear from the scriptures and the prayers offered hold up to them a vision of life and a set of values they do not hear on the evening news, the commercials which punctuate TV programs, or the ads which make magazines and newspapers thick. Those few minutes of reading and of prayers and perhaps a second-rate homily are not much to counteract the barrage of the secular media, the propaganda of government, or the hard sell of industry. They are indeed a voice crying out in the wilderness—but they are there, and they are crying out; and, however imperfectly, they infiltrate into some people's minds and hearts. Where else are people being comparably nourished with vision and values that make for human dignity? The arts, one might answer. The arts do indeed raise the ultimate human questions, but how often do they offer God's word, especially God's Word incarnate, in answer?

Recently the notion of ministry to others has spread—ministry not merely as acts of kindness but as service out of love in justice to others in need: shut-ins, disabled, alienated, oppressed, imprisoned. This sense of ministry has rippled out in ever widening circles from the center which has been

[14]Bernard Lonergan, *Insight* (New York: Longmans, 1957), pp. 218-26.

extraordinary ministers of Holy Communion and ministers of the word at Sunday Eucharists. Then ushers were regarded as ministers of hospitality. But if we serve people in the church building, we rightly serve them outside in the neighborhood. And so additional ministries grow up, including explicitly social justice ministries, though all ministries have their particular social justice aspect. So we arrive from a liturgical core to a whole parish structured into multiple ministries—of liturgy, of Christian education, to youth, to shut-ins, to sick and elderly, to disabled, to unwed mothers, to those needing food, clothing, shelter, to bread for the world, to peacemaking. On November 23, 1986 the parish of St. Francis de Sales, the cathedral church of the Roman Catholic diocese of Oakland, California, celebrated its centennial. The main point made by the homilist on the occasion was that because of the centrality of liturgy in the cathedral's life, it was possible for it to develop a variety of ministries and move beyond its parish boundaries to become a service to the wider church. In fact, this cathedral has achieved a national reputation as a center for good liturgical worship.

This development means that liturgical ministries have facilitated people's seeing their acts of kindness in a new light, as something to which they have a mission, something which is ecclesial and not merely private, something which is organized and which tends eventually to seek a permanent solution to needs, that is, to restructure society—in the parish, neighborhood, city, state, nation, world. Liturgical renewal and reform have contributed more to the social justice movement than many of us have recognized.

Mark Searle argues that social justice is, for the most part and practically speaking, a matter of legal justice, what the law determines to be fair and equitable. But there is a justice more profound than that, toward which legal justice strives in an imperfect and sinful world—the justice of God.[15] The justice of God is nothing less than God herself, and then the conformity of all things to God's wisdom and will. This justice of

---

[15]Mark Searle, "Serving the Lord with Justice," in *Liturgy and Social Justice*, ed. Mark Searle (Collegeville: Liturgical Press, 1981), p. 15-17.

God ultimately supports, motivates, and judges the social justice we strive to achieve. To be constantly in touch with the justice of God is critical for social justice ministry. The liturgy is the celebration of God's justice, God's reign, God's kingdom. The liturgy is, therefore, crucial for social justice ministry. It is there that we encounter the Just and Risen One, Jesus Christ, by whose Spirit we are inspired and encouraged to work toward the coming of God's kingdom, God's justice, among all men and women.

Pope John Paul II in his encyclical letter *Dives in Misericordia* (*Rich in Mercy*) reflects on how frequently the pursuit of justice in our world becomes distorted.[16] Spite, hatred, and cruelty infect it. The oppressing neighbor becomes the oppressed neighbor, denied basic human rights, tortured, even killed (no.12). Action for social justice must be rooted in, and aim at, mercy, or kindly love (no. 14); it must be seen as an aspect of mercy, as God's justice came to be understood in the Old Testament (no. 4), or as an aspect of *agape*, the form mercy takes in the New Testament (no. 6). If action for justice is not seen in this way, it easily becomes distorted, ceases to be authentic justice. True mercy is, so to speak, the most profound source of justice.

> If justice is in itself suitable for "arbitration" between people concerning the reciprocal distribution of objective goods in an equitable manner, love and only love (including that kindly love we call "mercy") is capable of restoring humanity to itself... Society can become "ever more human only when we introduce into the many-sided setting of inter-personal and social relationships not merely justice but also that merciful love which constitutes the messianic message of the gospel". (no. 14)

But that mercy of God is revealed and communicated above all by Christ in his paschal mystery (nos. 7-8). In the liturgy, however, we encounter most explicitly Christ in the mystery of his death and resurrection. In the liturgy, therefore, the social

16 Pope John Paul II, *Dives in Misericordia* (*Rich in Mercy*) 30 November, 1980.

justice ministry finds most clearly its deepest roots in the mercy of God which alone guarantees that ministry's ultimate integrity.

In the liturgy God speaks to us of love, mercy, and justice. The ultimate disaster, says Amos the prophet, is "not a famine of bread, nor a thirst for water, but of not hearing the words of the Lord" (8:11).[17]

꙳

Bibliography

Gutierrez, Gustavo. *A Theology of Liberation,* Maryknoll: Orbis Books, 1973.

> This still serves as an indispensable introduction to the many liberation themes which have been further developed theologically and which must be part of any treatment of liturgy and social justice.

Hughes, Kathleen, R.S.C.J. "The Voice of the Church at Prayer: A Liturgical Appraisal of *The Challenge of Peace: God's Promise and Our Response*" in *Biblical and Theological Reflections on The Challenge of Peace,* edited by John T. Pawlikowski, O.S.M., and Donald Senior, C. P. Wilmington: Michael Glazier, Inc., 1984.

> A critique of the Roman Catholic bishops' letter on peace from a liturgical perspective. The author argues that in the letter, the liturgy is a neglected source and an underestimated means.

---

[17]Lesson for Friday, Thirteenth Week of the Year, Year II.

Koenke, Theresa F., I.H.M. "Sacraments: For the Peace and Salvation of All the World," *Called to Prayer: Liturgical Spirituality Today*, (Collegeville: The Liturgical Press, 1986).

> This popular presentation of implications of liturgy for peace and justice and the necessary relation between liturgy and justice is helpful for someone who is beginning to think about these matters.

Laeyendecker, Leo and Thung, Mady A. "Liturgy in a Politically Engaged Church," C.I.S.R., "Acts 14" of the International Conference on Sociology of Religion. Lille, France: Secretariat C.I.S.R., 39, rue de la Monnaie, 1977.

> This article questions the feasibility of traditional liturgical rites in a church committed to social action. The authors suggest that other rituals are needed. A variety of rituals would respond to the variety of actions done by the political church. The Eucharist would be but one of these rituals.

Metz, Johann Baptist. *Faith in History and Society,* New York: Crossroad Books, The Seabury Press, 1980.

> Metz's treatment of the dangerous memory of the freedom of Jesus Christ is extremely important for understanding the relationship of social justice and the liturgy, especially in terms of the latter's anamnetic quality.

Newman, David. *Worship as Praise and Empowerment,* New York: The Pilgrim Press, 1988.

> At the present time this is the most thorough development of a liturgical theology along the lines of liberation theology. The author points out the importance of worship for the movements of liberation today.

Searle, Mark. "Pedagogical Function of Liturgy," *Worship* 55:4 (July 1981).

This paper uses the pedagogical model developed by Paulo Freire to analyze how the liturgy can be an exercise of power by one group over another and how the liturgy can exercise a role in the larger goals and work of the church.

Schmidt, Herman and Power, David, eds. *Politics and Liturgy, Concilium* 92, New York: Herder and Herder, 1974.

The many articles speak of the social significance of worship and the revelance of political action to liturgy. An article by Joseph Gelineau on celebrating paschal liberation is recommended.